# A HISTORY OF POLITICAL THOUGHT

# A History of Political Thought

Property, Labor, and Commerce
from Plato to Piketty

JEFFREY BERCUSON

UNIVERSITY OF TORONTO PRESS
Toronto Buffalo London

© University of Toronto Press 2020
Toronto Buffalo London
utorontopress.com
Printed in Canada

ISBN 978-1-4875-0851-7 (cloth)    ISBN 978-1-4875-3841-5 (EPUB)
ISBN 978-1-4875-2590-3 (paper)    ISBN 978-1-4875-3840-8 (PDF)



**Library and Archives Canada Cataloguing in Publication**

Title: A history of political thought: Property, labor, and commerce from Plato to Piketty / Jeffrey Bercuson.
Names: Bercuson, Jeffrey, 1982– author.
Identifiers: Canadiana (print) 20200278703 | Canadiana (ebook) 20200278819 | ISBN 9781487525903 (softcover) | ISBN 9781487508517 (hardcover) | ISBN 9781487538415 (EPUB) | ISBN 9781487538408 (PDF)
Subjects: LCSH: Political science – Philosophy – History. | LCSH: Economics – Philosophy – History. | LCSH: Property – Philosophy – History. | LCSH: Capitalism – Philosophy – History.
Classification: LCC JA71.B47 2020 | DDC 320.01–dc23

We welcome comments and suggestions regarding any aspect of our publications – please feel free to contact us at news@utorontopress.com or visit us at utorontopress .com.

University of Toronto Press acknowledges the financial assistance to its publishing program of the Canada Council for the Arts and the Ontario Arts Council, an agency of the Government of Ontario.

“... relentless industry from early till late ...”

# Contents

A reading list for this book is available on its University of Toronto Press webpage: https://utorontopress.com/us/a-history-of-political-thought-2.

# Abbreviations

| Abbreviation | Title | Author |
| --- | --- | --- |
| *AC* | *The Antichrist* | Friedrich Nietzsche |
| *AEM* | *Letters on the Aesthetic Education of Man* | Friedrich Schiller |
| *AS* | *The Acquisitive Society* | R.H. Tawney |
| *BGE* | *Beyond Good and Evil* | Friedrich Nietzsche |
| *C* | *Capital in the Twenty-First Century* | Thomas Piketty |
| *CEP* | *Collectivist Economic Planning* | Friedrich Hayek |
| *CL* | *The Constitution of Liberty* | Friedrich Hayek |
| *CPB* | *Common Place Book* | R.H. Tawney |
| *CSD* | *Capitalism Socialism Democracy* | Joseph Schumpeter |
| *Con* | *Confessions* | Jean-Jacques Rousseau |
| *D* | *The Dawn* | Friedrich Nietzsche |
| *E* | *Equality* | R.H. Tawney |
| *EH* | *Ecce Homo* | Friedrich Nietzsche |
| *EHCS* | *Essay on the History of Civil Society* | Adam Ferguson |
| *GM* | *On the Genealogy of Morals* | Friedrich Nietzsche |
| *GS* | *The Gay Science* | Friedrich Nietzsche |
| *HC* | *Homer's Contest* | Friedrich Nietzsche |
| *IUH* | *Idea for a Universal History with a Cosmopolitan Purpose* | Immanuel Kant |
| *Lev* | *Leviathan* | Thomas Hobbes |
| *LJ* | *Lectures on Jurisprudence* | Adam Smith |

| Abbreviation | Title | Author |
| --- | --- | --- |
| *LLL* | *Law, Legislation and Liberty* | Friedrich Hayek |
| *LP* | *The Law of Peoples* | John Rawls |
| *MM* | *Metaphysics of Morals* | Immanuel Kant |
| *NAC* | *Why I, Too, Am Not A Conservative* | James Buchanan |
| *NE* | *Nicomachean Ethics* | Aristotle |
| *P* | *Politics* | Aristotle |
| *PE* | *Discourse on Political Economy* | Jean-Jacques Rousseau |
| *PL* | *Political Liberalism* | John Rawls |
| *PP* | *Perpetual Peace: A Philosophical Sketch* | Immanuel Kant |
| *PR* | *Philosophy of Right* | Georg Wilhelm Friedrich Hegel |
| *R* | *Justice as Fairness: A Restatement* | John Rawls |
| *RRC* | *Religion and the Rise of Capitalism* | R.H. Tawney |
| *RRF* | *Reflections on the Revolution in France* | Edmund Burke |
| *RS* | *The Road to Serfdom* | Friedrich Hayek |
| *SC* | *On the Social Contract* | Jean-Jacques Rousseau |
| *SD* | *Second Discourse* | Jean-Jacques Rousseau |
| *ST* | *Summa Theologica* | Thomas Aquinas |
| *TI* | *Twilight of the Idols* | Friedrich Nietzsche |
| *TJ* | *A Theory of Justice* | John Rawls |
| *TMS* | *Theory of Moral Sentiments* | |
| *TP* | *On the Common Saying: This May Be True In Theory, But It Does Not Apply In Practice* | Immanuel Kant |
| *UKS* | *Uses of Knowledge in Society* | Friedrich Hayek |
| *UM* | *Untimely Meditations* | Friedrich Nietzsche |
| *WN* | *On the Nature and Causes of the Wealth of Nations* | Adam Smith |
| *WP* | *The Will to Power* | Friedrich Nietzsche |
| *Z* | *Thus Spoke Zarathustra* | Friedrich Nietzsche |

# Introduction

Wealth and speed are the things the world admires and for which all men strive.
— Johan Wolfgang Goethe

What follows is a series of yeas and nays to Goethe's view: *are* wealth and speed worthy of our admiration? Are *they* the goals toward which we should strive? To answer these (and related) questions – to collect those yeas and nays, however qualified each may be – this book canvasses the history of political thought. But we approach that familiar history from a new angle, by centering ideas and concepts often treated as peripheral: trade and accumulation, property and prosperity, work and leisure.

As it turns out, using the market as our master key retains our access to the core themes in political philosophy – human nature, social life, the state. These are the central themes that run throughout this book too and give it whatever unity it possesses. In each chapter, then, we are searching for answers to the following sets of questions:

- What does it mean to live *well*? What does a flourishing human life *look like*? And what role does economic activity play in that flourishing life? Is it a central and indispensable role? Are our talents and capacities developed to the fullest extent when we engage in economic activity? Or is the drive to accumulate antithetical to human well-being? Does prosperity pull us away from the things that *really* matter in human life?

- Is the market the appropriate locus for community? Is it the only reasonable way to structure cooperation and competition among (free and equal) individuals? Or do the constitutive relations of market life – producer and consumer, employer and employee – negate the possibility of salutary, mutually beneficial social relations? Is economic inequality compatible with a stable, solidaristic milieu?

- What role should the state play in the economic life of the community it governs? Should that role be limited to the preservation of law and order, the protection of private property, and the enforcement of the contracts that individuals undertake? Or must the state *do more?* And if it must, what does *more* require, exactly? An economic minimum below which no citizen rightly falls? A more demanding ideal of economic equality and, by extension, a more aggressive scheme of economic redistribution? Or, most ambitiously of all, the total ownership of the means of production and exclusive control over their use?

Of course, these sets of questions do not exist – and so cannot be treated – in isolation from each other; they intersect and overlap. How, for instance, can we speak of individual self-development without paying attention to (the enabling or stultifying effects of) the social setting in which it takes place? Similarly, how can we speak of social stability (and solidarity, even) without paying attention to politics? But we can (and should) build our account from the ground up: in order to understand why the economic status quo is a tragedy or the cause for celebration, we need to understand (its impact on) the individuals living under it; in other words, we must *start* with an account of human nature. As we shall see, this is a point of agreement throughout: every thinker covered in this book *begins* with an account of the human good, even though agreement on what that good actually *is* is rare and fleeting; and each *then* turns to the economic side of life to see whether it draws us away from, or toward, that good. Rightly so: philosophy *is* the study of ends.[1] What *is it*, if it is not *that?* Our interest, here, is whether these ends, whatever they may be, are thwarted or facilitated by involvement with the market. And if they *are* thwarted – as many (if not most) in these pages claim – what should *we* do about it? What should *the state* do about it?

# 1

Really, this is a book about capitalism; it is *not* a *history* of capitalism, though.[2] Neither does it have any interest in explicating the technical workings of capitalist markets or the quantitative models that economists use to make sense of them.[3] Rather, it's a book about how some profound minds have grappled with the moral, social, and political consequences of capitalism since its emergence (in the Italian Renaissance), consolidation (in post–Glorious Revolution England), and full-fledged triumph (in the postwar United States). In other words, this book is (to be more precise) *a history of philosophical attitudes about capitalism*, from ancient Greece to the present day – from Plato to Piketty.

Of course, it makes little sense to speak of ancient Greece (or Renaissance Europe) as *capitalist*; the term *capitalism* does not even come into existence until the early decades of the twentieth century! We need some leeway here. To get it, this book also (often) employs the term *market society*, which is to say, a society in which the central mechanism of social coordination – the site of cooperation and competition between legally free and equal individuals (and the firms they create) – is the market directed by price signals, by the laws of supply and demand. Consider, as a contrast, a feudal society, which is held together by a very different set of ideas: God-given relations of mastery and servitude, the political priority of security and stability over prosperity and innovation, a deep well of religious and cultural disdain for the economic side of life and for economic motives (profit chief among them).[4] *These* are the ideas invoked to solve society's economic problems; they determine the allocation of society's productive resources: the lord, for example, has a natural right to the labor of the serf (whom he protects but does not pay). And these ideas also determine the distribution of the social surplus generated by that labor, which, unsurprisingly, belongs to those same political elites whose ascendant position is legitimated by religious elites.[5]

In a market society, by contrast, economic activity occupies its own separate sphere: resource allocation and surplus distribution "break free" from these (feudal-religious) background ideas, which are best characterized by their hostility to commerce and to moneymaking. Now, *everything*, including labor, is commodified; *everything* is monetized and salable, made subject to the laws of supply and demand – which is to say, detached from prescribed social and religious duties. Of course, a market society (like *any* society) requires its own ideational and institutional infrastructure: a new economic attitude that celebrates the appetite for economic gain, a high level of comfort with dynamism and innovation, a mobile army of wage labor, the free flow of cash, rapid urbanization – the list goes on and on.[6] Again, it is not our purpose to document this history – the rise (and triumph) of market society from feudal ashes. Instead, this book is an examination of the ethical, social, and political consequences of this historically novel mode of organization – salutary and destructive – through the eyes of its most perceptive critics and champions.

Our history *of ideas* begins with the ancient and medieval background, when *all* forms of economic activity were automatically the object of moral, philosophical, and religious suspicion. The exemplars of this tradition are Plato, Aristotle, and Thomas Aquinas, all of whom, despite their differences, are deeply hostile to commerce and moneymaking, given the obvious threat they posed to civic virtue and to salvation (chapter 1). Modern political philosophy, which begins with Machiavelli and Hobbes, is characterized by its aim to slough off these ethical and divine constraints on the market (chapter 2). The first task in this endeavor is to challenge the authority of the ancient philosophers and medieval theologians – a task that both Machiavelli and Hobbes undertake with gusto. In the new, modern view of things, the market is no longer the object of suspicion; it is, in fact, the only stable foundation for social life! It follows that those who participate in it do not deserve our derision; their needs and interests must instead be recognized, and protected, by the state.

This brings us to John Locke, of course, according to whom the purpose of the state is to preserve our property through the force of law and, by doing so, facilitate commerce and the accumulation of wealth (chapter 3). Locke's project (of defending market society) is then taken up by Adam Smith and Immanuel Kant, both of whom try to demonstrate the salutary effects of self-interest and, by extension, commerce; such benefits include a generous increase in society's general level of well-being, good government, and even lasting peace between states (chapter 4). Indeed, it is in the pages of Smith and Kant that something like recognizably modern capitalism comes into view, and in those same pages that that system receives its first important, spirited, persuasive philosophical defense. This is Hegel's project too: to reconcile us to market society, to help us see its (hidden) virtues (chapter 6). And, in his mind, there *are* powerful reasons to be reconciled to it: when casual observers look at the workings of civil society, they see chaotic, uncoordinated, socially unproductive, self-seeking behavior; when philosophers look – especially when under the influence of Smith and Kant – they see something wholly different: a secret harmony that advances the interests of both individuals and the community at large.

Of course, these defenses are not persuasive to Jean-Jacques Rousseau (chapter 5), Karl Marx (chapter 7), Vladimir Lenin (chapter 8), R.H. Tawney (chapter 9), or Friedrich Nietzsche (chapter 10), all of whom believe (at bottom) that commercial society destroys the possibility of genuine, lasting happiness. Together, then, these chapters constitute an unrelenting, thorough, and extremely powerful criticism of market society: the way it makes us dissatisfied and alienated (from ourselves, from our work, from our compatriots); the way it rends society into classes of politically powerful owners and politically disenfranchised workers; the way it corrupts our moral and aesthetic sensibilities. In these chapters, we also encounter various proposals – some more radical than others – for the amelioration of these pressing problems: the abolition of private property (violently if necessary), the socialization of the means of production and (total) economic planning by the state; trade unionism and the democratization of the firm; the cultural reorientation (back) toward (aristocratic) ideals of beauty and self-realization.

From there, we turn to J.M. Keynes (chapter 11), Friedrich Hayek (chapter 12), John Rawls (chapter 13), and Thomas Piketty (chapter 14). In some ways, this section of the book tries to find a middle ground between elation with and hatred for market society, though that balance is never found precisely in that middle position. On the one hand, all four thinkers in this group agree that market society has real, undeniable virtues – unimaginable prosperity, a sizable sphere of liberty, the flourishing of a valuable diversity of ways of life. But none, not even Hayek, think that system is perfect. In some cases, the proposed modifications lurk at the margin: a more expansive role for the state, a more generous scheme of income redistribution, a keener attention to the intergenerational transmission of wealth. In other cases – and this is, somewhat surprisingly, most true of Rawls – these modifications are quite demanding and may in fact require the abandonment of (welfare state) capitalism altogether.

## 2

Why *these* thinkers? As always, such choices are rooted in the contingency of biography: this book covers two groups of philosophers, one with whom I was already very familiar, and one with whom I wanted desperately to *become* familiar, given my own philosophical interest in the market. The former group includes Plato, Aristotle, Machiavelli, Hobbes, Locke, Kant, Rousseau, Hegel, Marx, Nietzsche, and Rawls. No survey of the history of political thought can rightly leave these canonical thinkers out, though *we* will be looking at these familiar faces in a new light. The latter group includes Smith, Lenin, Tawney, Keynes, Hayek, and Piketty. No survey of the history of political thought *about markets* can rightly leave these thinkers out. My hope is that this group creates maximum coverage across time, across philosophical style and methodology, and, more importantly, across the political philosophical (and political institutional) spectrum; and that, as a result, this book is characterized by an open, inclusive, diverse, and productive dialogue about the successes and failures of market society.

This list (like *any* list) will not satisfy everyone, *not even me*. Edmund Burke certainly deserves a chapter (not a mere mention), and Max Weber and Michel Foucault do too. Worse, the book is exclusively Western and male, which is obviously deeply regrettable. In the end, though, my main goal was for this book to be both maximally appealing and manageable: hence the necessary inclusion of the first (aforementioned) group, and the necessary limits on membership in the second (aforementioned) group. While a (small) part of me wishes this book was longer, that part is (heavily) outweighed by a more fundamental aim: to provide *students* with an accessible and useful book. Experts may find these chapters wanting – they are indeed *short*. But that was a conscious decision of mine: I was always thinking about – and always writing for – those encountering the history of political thought for the first time. My hope is that these chapters provide *them* with a worthwhile introduction to the history of political thought and with an entry point into that history that resonates with contemporary issues and contemporary debates.

Capitalism is here to stay; one doesn't have to go far out on a limb to say *that*. But for many – including the conspicuous majority of the philosophers discussed in this book, and its author too – this fact is the source of despair: in its twenty-first-century incarnation especially, capitalist society is plagued by such a depressing litany of flaws – staggering economic inequality,[7] plutocracy,[8] the dissolution of the bonds of community,[9] and a deep-seated spiritual and cultural malaise[10] – that it seems beyond repair. As I hope to show, these are *not* new worries: they have been seen, and unpacked, by the deepest, most perceptive minds. In fact, as this book argues, grappling with market society is a permanent (though underappreciated) feature of the Western philosophical tradition since Greece. For me, that is a source of hope and energy: we are *not* powerless to change the status quo, and in these pages we have a deep well of profound ideas – ideas that help us to understand why market society is so threatening to happiness, to community, and to justice, and what can be done to make it more humane.

# 1

## "The Less They Value Virtue": Plato, Aristotle, and Aquinas on the Corrupting Influence of Moneymaking – Personal and Political

Plato's *Republic* is an anxious book, written during a time of Athenian decay: the anxiety of its author – over his city's loss of foreign influence and, even more acutely, the instability of its domestic institutions[1] – is reflected in the revolutionary overhaul of the status quo proposed in its pages. The *Republic* is indeed a radical text, radical in the sense that its political proposals are not limited by facts: Socrates gives us his account of justice, and if, along the way, it emerges that this ideal is incompatible with the world – with the interests, values, and desires of involved parties, with the likely course of events that characterizes human community – then so much the worse for the world. Justice is justice, and its feasibility – the world's potential obduracy to it – has no bearing on its nature or practical demands.

Why, according to Socrates, the protagonist of the *Republic*, is justice so ephemeral and the just city so unstable? Our focus, in this chapter, and indeed throughout this book, is on the gradual rise of commerce: we shall see that, in Socrates's mind, a city's success depends on the moderation of its citizens and that the ascendance of wealth in the city's system of values leads to widespread immoderation; the inevitable result is civic dissolution. To make and keep a city just, its powerful citizens must be insulated from commercial impulses through a variety of educational and legal measures. And so, in many ways, Socrates gives us the challenge that animates this book: unleashing the forces of commerce and moneymaking, he says, negates the possibility of lasting justice. Here, and in the chapters that follow, we examine the legacy and inheritors of this view – those who agree with Socrates's charge against our commercial impulses and those who attempt to answer it.

# 1

In the *Republic*, Socrates and his students discuss the city: What does a just city look like, they ask. What does a moderate, well-governed, productive, and cohesive city look like, they ask. And once we have articulated the institutions and culture of that city, how can we then bring that city into being? In the course of the discussion, the answers become clear: the just city – the moderate, well-governed, productive, and cohesive city – is the city in which political power is handed over to the lovers of truth and bearers of wisdom – the philosophers – and the possibility of that city coming into being depends on both the willingness of the people to be ruled by the philosophers and the willingness of the philosophers to rule the people (473c). Unfortunately, Socrates often speaks of how the people regard the philosophers as idle daydreamers, and how the philosophers regard the people as selfish, narrow-minded bigots (488b, 541a). Neither the philosophers nor the people are likely to derive lasting satisfaction from their association; and so even if this unlikely city came to be, its existence would be fleeting: the just city is unlikely to be and incapable of lasting (546a).

This raises an obvious question: Why is justice so remote, so unlikely to last? To answer it, this chapter focuses on the less than fully just cities that Socrates discusses in the later books of the *Republic*: the city ruled by its military caste, the city ruled by its richest citizens, the city ruled by the people, and, finally, the city ruled by the power-mad tyrant. Despite their differences, these inferior cities all have one thing in common: money lust, in either its sublimated or fully conscious form. In these inferior cities, powerful citizens "pull the constitution towards money-making and the acquisition of land, houses, gold, and silver" (547b); this shift in priorities, according to Socrates, is the quintessential expression of civic decay and the first step on the road to tyranny.

This political history begins with the city devoted to war, which emerges out of the collapse of the rule of philosophy, as resentment for the burdensomeness of the philosophic life grows and respect for education wanes (546d). In some respects, this city suits Socrates's tastes. What is the appeal of the martial city for Socrates? Its professed, public disdain for moneymaking: rulers here recognize the necessity of *some* commerce, and *some* private property – if only to appease the less virtuous and less daring citizens among them – but overwhelmingly prefer the pursuit of honor and glory, which can be won only through war-waging (548a). In this city, much political energy is spent in the attempt to insulate the military caste from the economy by, for example, legal prohibitions against soldiers owning, cultivating, and thus profiting from the land (547d).

But, of course, such measures are futile: war-waging, the primary activity of this regime and the main source of satisfaction for its rulers, is, at bottom, a means to the accumulation of territory *and resources*. The conquering class therefore must care – and *does* come to care – about the accumulation and protection of wealth. But they are still well-bred and well-educated: this concern with money is, for them, a source of shame, a sickness to be hidden (548a). And so too must the fruits of their conquests be hidden: soldiers do not permit the lavish indulgence of their desires, as it is made possible by their victories; no, these soldiers are stingy with their cash, storing it away in secret hiding places, and they are discreet with their pleasure, indulging desire stealthily, in their "private nests," under the cover of night (548a).

But this sense of restraint dissipates over time: indulgence facilitated by wealth will always see the light of day (550d). Eventually, the city's rulers abandon the pursuit of honor and glory through war and instead turn their attention to the accumulation of wealth. Those genuinely committed to the old system of values are persecuted, exiled, and, in some cases, put to death (553b). It is in the course of this discussion – on the abandonment of martial virtue and its replacement with accumulation and indulgence – that Socrates speaks of wealth and virtue as diametrically opposed: rulers, he says, "proceed further into money-making, and the more they value it, the less they value virtue. Or aren't virtue and wealth so opposed that if they were set on a scales, they'd always incline in opposite directions" (550e)?

Power thus comes to be distributed not on the basis of one's martial skill but rather on the basis of one's bank account: the temptations of that hidden wealth prevail, and a new class is born and comes to rule, a class equally covetous but less ashamed of its wealth; a class less compelled to mask its love of wealth as a love of war, victory, honor, glory (551a–b); a class more openly willing to manipulate the instruments of political power – and to limit access to those instruments – explicitly in the service of accumulation (550d). But the new ruling oligarchs are not dissolute: though they are consciously motivated by accumulation, not honor, they are, like the soldiers they displace, mild when it comes to the indulgence of their appetites (554a–d). Why such restraint? Because the oligarchs recognize that their wealth makes them detestable to the people – the majority – who are always poor; in fact, the wealth of the oligarchs is directly a by-product of their exploitation of the people as laborers, tenants, and debtors (555c–e). And yet, the rich need the people to defend them against foreign invaders, for they are well versed in the banking arts, not the martial arts; hence, their strategic restraint (555a).

Unfortunately for the oligarchs, the incompatibility of their interests with the interests of the poor – the fact that this "isn't one city but two" (551d), and that the flourishing of one of the city's parts depends on the immiseration of the other (552a) – cannot be long hidden: this class antagonism eventually comes to light; rather, it is actively brought to light by the persuasive, ambitious members of the *demos* (565a). And so, the people usurp the instruments of political power, just as the oligarchs usurped the power of the military class. And the fat, idle oligarchs are tempting targets for the lean, resentful poor (556b–c).

In many ways, though, the transition from oligarchy to democracy is an inside job: Socrates describes rich kids' resentment of their parents' abstemiousness, the way their parents' fear of the people manifests itself as disdain for indulgence (560a–b, 572c). Why *not* indulge, they ask? Why *not* make use of the considerable means at our disposal? But the parents are just as much to blame: their single-minded pursuit of wealth – the characteristic mark of this class (562b) – has made the oligarchs indifferent to the importance of education (554b); and, as a result, their children do not have a meaningful sense of what is important or worthwhile, nor do they have the ability to master or restrain their typically extravagant, and therefore unnecessary, desires. This combination of parental indifference and youthful resentment is fertile soil for democracy, says Socrates, because the unleashing, and gradual legitimation, of unnecessary desire leads to the desire for limitless freedom (561d–e). And democracy is the regime committed to the total freedom of its citizens: "Freedom: surely you'd hear a democratic city say that this is the finest thing it has" (562b–c). Democracy is the regime where citizens are free to indulge their every whim, and this freedom surely appeals to the impetuous children of mean and sober oligarchs (561c–d).

Once democratic institutions have been installed, citizens jealously guard their freedom: they are always on the lookout for subtle encroachments on that freedom and quick to accuse their leaders (562d). Obedience is soon conflated with slavishness, disdain for authority is celebrated as virtue, and all forms of hierarchy, even fitting ones, like the relationship between parent and child and student and teacher, are abandoned (563b). In Socrates's eyes, democracy eventually leads to anarchy: "In the end," he says, citizens "take no notice of the laws, whether written or unwritten, in order to avoid having any master at all" (563d–e).

Finally, we arrive at tyranny, "the most severe and cruel slavery from the utmost freedom" (564a). How does tyranny emerge, exactly? Its main cause, according to Socrates, is class conflict: the people – the poor *demos*, who now possess meaningful political power – want a larger share of their community's wealth; and, in order to obtain that wealth from the rich, they recognize the need for a spokesman – a "special champion" (565c) – to act on their behalf. As Socrates tells it, this populist champion knows how to manipulate – how to stir up – the people's resentment and jealousy: he persecutes the rich, expropriates their wealth under the guise of the judiciously applied rule of law, and he promises the cancelation of all private debt and the redistribution of all private property (565e). Law is no longer the source of order and justice; it is a malleable instrument for pursuing the aims of the rabble.

But, over time, such a man becomes hateful to both the rich and the poor alike: constantly in need of new sources of legitimacy and appeal, the emergent tyrant embarks on foreign adventures financed by burdensome war taxes (566e), and when revenue cannot be generated through taxation, irresponsible borrowing (573e). And eventually the political facade fades away: the purpose of the regime, first and foremost, is to fulfill the tyrant's every whim, for "feasts, revelries, luxuries, girlfriends, and that sort of thing" (573d). The regime's expropriating impulse thus turns against the people, and plots to kill the tyrant inevitably develop; what began as a populist campaign to improve the lot of the many turns into a cloistered, paranoid, rapacious regime, armed to the teeth and wholly divorced from its democratic roots (566b). In many ways, Socrates's image of tyranny – and his psychologically detailed portrait of the tyrant himself – is the heart of the *Republic* and the culmination of its central political argument: as the tyrant turns further and further inward – as he becomes more and more dedicated to self-satisfaction, at the expense of the safety and prosperity of those he governs – the desirability of the rule of philosophy becomes more and more apparent (580a).

## 2

What other lessons should we take away from the political history – the history of decay and eventual disintegration – of books 8 and 9? The first important lesson is that the accumulation of wealth plays no part in a well-lived, virtuous human life. Of course, the ideal here is the philosopher, wholly absorbed in the pursuit of wisdom, and therefore wholly indifferent to the pursuit of wealth (485d). This is the very heart of Socrates's worldview: that for the "high-minded and graceful" (487a), the "pleasures of the soul" always trump the pleasures of the body (485d); that the essential source of satisfaction has nothing to do with anything that money can buy; that genuine, lasting happiness comes only with the contemplation of life's essential questions about truth, beauty, and justice (479b), and with the knowledge that such questions defy precise, definitive answers (480a).

As we have already seen, this is also the basis of Socrates's political argument in the *Republic*: the philosophers must rule, he says, because only *they* can be trusted with the instruments of political power; only *they* will use those instruments to advance the community's ends – justice, moderation, well-orderedness – rather than their own, as the tyrant is driven to do by his reckless, insatiable desires (580b–c). But an equally important dimension of the political argument is its ultimate infeasibility: the people are too narrow-minded and selfish to recognize the desirability of the rule of philosophy, as well as the dangers associated with nonphilosophical regimes (541a); and the philosopher is too consumed with life's difficult questions to expend energy in the hopes of persuading the people to let him or her rule (496d).

This relates to the second important lesson of the *Republic*: in Socrates's eyes, human beings naturally tend toward the private; self-interest is our strongest guiding impulse. Some are driven by wisdom, some are driven by glory and honor, some are driven by money, and some are driven by the pursuit of their appetites; but human beings, even the wisest and most virtuous among us, are driven, first and foremost, by an imperative of self-satisfaction, and this imperative pulls them away from the sacrifices necessary for good citizenship. Perhaps this is why selfishness is also a source of shame: think, here, of the soldiers who guiltily hide away their war booty, knowing it will inflame the disappointment of their fellows and the resentment of their inferiors, or the oligarchs whose sense of self is defined by their mean, sober spirit. At times, Socrates treats this impulse as potentially eradicable: throughout the *Republic*, he describes the sorts of pedagogical practices and coercive legal institutions that would root out self-love and replace it with a widespread ethos of self-sacrifice (414d–20b). But he never takes these suggestions seriously: self-love is a deeply rooted and thus ineradicable part of our nature (548a). And *this* is why, in the end, the *Republic* must be read as a tragedy: justice requires a virtue too burdensome for creatures like us.

The final important lesson of the *Republic* is that class conflict is antithetical to good and stable government. When society is divided into rich and poor, both classes regard politics as a form of exclusion: the rich are always trying to raise the wealth qualifications for participation (551a), while simultaneously impoverishing the people through burdensome, irresponsible lending practices (556a); and the poor are always trying to transform the law into an instrument of wealth expropriation and redistribution (565a). Under such circumstances, a common good fails to exist – the two classes do not even see each other (555e), except as the source of shame and resentment, and eventually as targets – and the exercise of political power is thought of by all involved as a constantly fluctuating zero-sum game, with one class now ascendant, now the other (556e).

For Socrates, the city is characterized by this permanent instability: the inevitability of dissent and decay is the iron law of political life (546a). And the essential source of that decay is money. Indeed, the essential lesson of the *Republic* – for our purposes, here, at least – is that money has a corrosive effect on community: that virtue and justice, on the one hand, and commerce and wealth, on the other, tend in opposite directions. As the city turns toward the pursuit of wealth – as the primary aim of its laws and institutions is the accumulation of wealth for the politically dominant class of the day – the possibility of lasting goodness evaporates. And so the drive to accumulate wealth is something to be despised, not begrudgingly tolerated, for such naive toleration leads to the eventual but certain destruction of the city.

## 3

In many respects, Aristotle, Plato's most important student, agrees: the city dedicated, first and foremost, to the accumulation of wealth for its most powerful citizens is a tragic place, populated by those who "occupy themselves wholly in the making of money" (*P* 1257b50), and who, as a result, neglect life's truly meaningful, rewarding activities. But, unlike his teacher, Aristotle does not dismiss – or lament – the commercial impulses altogether; instead, he tries to understand the role and proper place of property and commerce in the well-governed city.[2] In the end, Aristotle concedes that the commercial impulse is a salutary one, necessary for the sustenance and well-being of the city, and therefore rightly encouraged by legislators (*P* 1259a31). Indeed, one of the fundamental principles of Aristotle's *Politics* is the acceptance of "self-love" (*P* 1263a43) – albeit to a limited degree – and he emphasizes this point precisely in the context of a thoroughgoing critique of the *Republic*: in response to Socrates's proposal regarding the collectivization of property as an antidote to social atomization and civic decay, Aristotle says, to the contrary, that private property is the source of "pleasure" (*P* 1263b41) and that without it "no man can show himself generous" (*P* 1263b12).

This difference from Plato is present from the very start of Aristotle's *Politics*. In the *Republic*, Socrates begins with, and stays wholly focused on, the soul, and he believes that the needs and desires of the body are an imposition on the soul, pulling it away from its true calling in philosophical contemplation and civic sacrifice. Aristotle, by contrast, *begins* with the body: in book 1, he discusses the prerational human instincts associated with the city's genesis (*P* 1252a28), and he also emphasizes the fact – obvious, to be sure, but overlooked by his teacher – that physical sustenance is the essential basic precondition of happiness and well-being (*P* 1253b23). "Property is part of the household," he says, "and the art of acquiring property is part of household management, for it is impossible to live well, or indeed at all, unless the necessary preconditions are present" (*P* 1252b23–6).

What are the "necessary preconditions" that Aristotle refers to here? Namely, all those resources necessary for a household to achieve "sufficiency" (*P* 1257a36): Aristotle includes slaves in this category (*P* 1254a13) – though he does recognize that not all who *are* slaves *ought* to be (*P* 1255b15) – along with land for cultivation (*P* 1256a38), the "inanimate" tools needed for the household's various productive activities (*P* 1253b29), as well as space to store food and other domestic necessities (*P* 1256b30). On occasion, the household will need to exchange with other households in order to secure what it cannot produce for itself – "wine, for instance is given, or taken, in return for wheat, and other similar commodities are similarly bartered for one another" (*P* 1257a29) – but it is clear that Aristotle has a significant degree of individual household autarky in mind. This is what he means when he speaks of "true wealth": the ability of each household to produce – and on rare occasion obtain from elsewhere – the amount of property that "suffices for a good life" (*P* 1256b32), *and no more.*

This is the heart of Aristotle's view about property, wealth, and commerce: our economic needs, he says, are "fixed" (*P* 1256b32); they are "not unlimited" (*P* 1256b34), and this limit, given to us by nature (*P* 1256b37), is the need for comfortable, not extravagant, living. What matters more than anything – and certainly more than the economic imperative of limitless accumulation – is the household's moral mission: the cultivation of good character (*NE* 1103a17), sound judgment (*NE* 1112b9), and a sense of civic purpose (*NE* 1172a11) among its members. "It is clear," says Aristotle, "that the business of household management is ... concerned more with the good condition of human beings than with a good condition of property" (*P* 1259a21).

In order to achieve its moral mission – its ultimate "end" – household management must aim at the creation of leisure: the free time necessary to pursue life's truly meaningful activities, "politics or philosophy" (*P* 1255b33). This helps us to understand the sense in which the limits to accumulation are *natural*: for Aristotle, the human being is, by nature, a "political animal" (*P* 1253a7), which is to say, a linguistic and therefore social being, the kind of creature for whom the best things in life – justice, virtue, beauty, truth – come to light only in conversation (*P* 1253a12). "Nature makes nothing purposeless or in vain" (*P* 1256b22), after all, and so if human beings communicate through language, this indicates – it is indicated to us by nature – what "living well" (*P* 1257b45) looks like: the immersion, along with like-minded fellows, in philosophical contemplation and political argumentation, both of which are premised on the leisure made possible by effective household management (*P* 1253a32).

But Aristotle concedes that we are easily led astray – that effective household management, strictly governed by natural limits, often transcends those limits and becomes "not natural" (1256b48). The source of this threat is the inevitability, and eventual ubiquity, of exchange: as we have already seen, households are not fully self-sufficient and therefore must resort to barter on occasion (*P* 1257a29); in such cases, exchange "simply serves to satisfy the natural requirements of self-sufficiency" (*P* 1257a34): it is undertaken in order to provide the household with those goods it needs but cannot produce for itself and is therefore "not contrary to nature" (*P* 1257a32). But barter, without currency, is associated primarily with the "barbarian tribes" (*P* 1257a26): "inevitably" (*P* 1257a29), as cities and households become more developed and productive, goods are produced in "superabundance" (*P* 1257a28), and the only practical medium of exchange is "money currency" (*P* 1257a36).

According to Aristotle, this is an extremely dangerous moment in the life of the household and the wider community of which it is a part: when exchange extends beyond the bounds of self-sufficiency it becomes something other than household management – it is transformed into the "art of acquisition" (*P* 1256b42). The contrast between household management and the "art of acquisition" is a prominent theme of book 1 of the *Politics*: the former is "natural" (*P* 1256b47) – in the sense already described, which is to say, it facilitates the pursuit of our natural ends as "political" animals by creating the free time necessary to learn, and practice, politics and philosophy (*P* 1253a7) – while the latter is "not natural, but is rather the product of a certain sort of experience and skill" (*P* 1256b48). Why, exactly, is the "art of acquisition" unnatural, in the Aristotelian sense? Precisely because it has no end: "There is no limit to the end it seeks; and the end it seeks is ... wealth in currency, or increase it indefinitely" (*P* 1257b43).

At first, goods were obtained solely for use; but with the introduction and growth in the use of currency, goods come to be produced, and acquired, primarily with an eye to "the greatest profit" (*P* 1257a48). But profit, by its nature, is fundamentally limitless: "All who are engaged in acquisition increase their fund of currency without limit or pause" (*P* 1257b32). According to Aristotle, this is both contradictory and perverse: the purpose of human life is to live "*well*" (*P* 1257b45) – to become a good person, trustworthy friend, and engaged citizen (*P* 1280a34), and to cultivate these qualities in concert with fellow citizens (*P* 1281b35) – not to ceaselessly strive, above all, for "iron, silver, and other metals" (*P* 1257a36). Again, Aristotle recognizes that that good life is built on a foundation of reasonable comfort (*P* 1280b31); but the accumulation of wealth and property is a *means* to that good life, and nothing is so unfortunate as when a means usurps a proper end. And yet, when it comes to commerce, neither is anything so common: "Even those who do aim at well-being seek the means of obtaining physical enjoyments; and, as what they seek appears to depend on the activity of acquisition, they are thus led to occupy themselves wholly in the making of money" (*P* 1257b47).

In the end, there are two important lessons to take away from Aristotle's treatment of commerce and property in book 1 of the *Politics*: first, that commercial activity is *both* the necessary foundation of true human flourishing *and* the greatest danger to it, always threatening to pull us away from a morally worthwhile life, and from productive cooperation with our fellows toward the pursuit of profit alone and without end. The second and perhaps more striking lesson is this: immodest economic gain is a detestable idea to Aristotle and does not figure *at all* into his idea of well-lived human life, of a life lived according to nature's purposeful design for its most exalted species. In many ways, then, Aristotle's worldview resembles that of his teacher, with its dread of commerce, its disdain for the profit motive, and its lamentation for the intractability of self-interest.

## 4

Clearly, Aristotle is deeply influenced by the *Republic*: throughout his *Politics* – and especially in book 5 – he documents this tendency of commerce to destroy both the city and the moral life of its inhabitants; he describes various cities, from the Greek world of his day, dedicated, first and foremost, to "profit-making" (*P* 1302b6), in which the rich rule and employ the law in the service of increasing their own wealth. At Rhodes, for example, oligarchs "were moved to conspire against the people" (*P* 1302b19), because they were alarmed at the gradual erosion of their monopoly of power; and at Naxos, Massilia, Istros, and Heraclea the ruling oligarchs became so detestable to the people that they generated a coup (1305b2). All these cities share a common trait: oligarchs operate under the mistaken assumption that their superiority in wealth indicates that "they are superior in all" (*P* 1280a22) and therefore the rightful possessors of a monopoly of political power; such a city is sure to be "vexed by faction" (*P* 1302a7).

Indeed, this is fertile ground for revolution: the concentration of wealth – and the concomitant concentration of political power – is sure to provoke the envy and resentment of the poor, whose "minds are filled by a passion for equality" (*P* 1302a25). And, like Socrates, Aristotle describes the emergence of a populist demagogue who encourages the people to usurp the instruments of political power and use them to gain access to, and redistribute, the wealth of the few (*P* 1304b21). This is precisely what happened at Cos, Heraclea, Megara, and Cyme (*P* 1304b27). But Aristotle is equally dubious of this populist impulse: he describes these acts of expropriation as "the extreme of injustice" (*P* 1281a20); after all, secure private property is the essential foundation of living well: destroy the institution of private property, and the conditions for the development of virtue disappear with it.

To prevent this descent into class factionalism and eventual civil war, Aristotle emphasizes the role of education – "*the* means of making ... a community and giving it unity" (*P* 1263b38); it is "by the method of social customs [and] of mental culture," he says, "that money-making and commerce stay within its proper bounds" (*P* 1263b45). And education – what Aristotle refers to as the cultivation of "moral goodness" (*P* 1260a19) – starts in the household (*P* 1295b15). But Aristotle also recognizes the importance of law as an essential force of morals-shaping: he recommends the use of coercive legislation – the institution of a "system of common meals," as in Sparta, for instance (*P* 1263b48) – in order to cultivate strong, widespread sentiments of fellow feeling and generosity. And, in a more demanding vein, Aristotle says that the law – the city's constitutional arrangements – should aim at the growth of the middle class through the proper distribution of political power and, when necessary, the redistribution of property: "A middle condition will be the best," he says. "Those who are in this condition are the most ready to listen to reason" (*P* 1295b1). After all, the middle class is characterized precisely by its moderation: it has no interest in the limitless accumulation of wealth, as do the rich, for its needs are adequately and securely satisfied; neither does it resent the wealthy – for the very same reason – and accordingly dream of the expropriation of their property under the disingenuous cover of law (*P* 1295b27). "Where the middle class is large," adds Aristotle, "there is less likelihood of faction and dissension" (*P* 1296a8), and therefore less likelihood of political instability and, worse, revolution.

## 5

Europe's rediscovery of Aristotle in the twelfth-century[3] – thanks to the translation of his works from Arabic into Latin by an international partnership of Christian and Muslim scholars – led to a major burst of philosophical energy. The most important person in this movement was the Italian philosopher and theologian Thomas Aquinas: in Aristotle's thought, Aquinas found a kind of pagan mirror for his own views.[4] Indeed, the influence of Aristotle pervades Aquinas's most important work, the *Summa Theologica*, and this is especially true in the sections that discuss commerce. Like Aristotle – and, of course, like Plato too, though the *Republic* was not available in Latin translation until the fifteenth century – Aquinas is deeply suspicious of exchange: in section 77 of the *Summa*, he addresses questions of buying and selling, and his first impulse is to question whether these actions are sinful, which is to say, contrary to the cultivation and practice of virtue. And Aquinas's answer is, yes, typically they are: it is sinful, he says, citing Matthew (7:12), to "sell a thing to another man for more than its worth" (*ST* 2.2.77.1). In other words, Aquinas here repudiates the essential heart of all commercial activity – profit without limit – warning his readers of the threat it poses to the cohesion of the community. Instead, the purpose of commerce is to advance the "common advantage of both parties, one of whom requires that which belongs to the other, and vice versa" (*ST* 2.2.77.1; cf. *P* 1257a29). Aquinas therefore counsels the virtuous to avoid "double-dealing" – selling faulty or damaged goods, for example, or failing to disclose important information about the goods in question – and, more importantly, to sell their wares at "the just price," which is to say, at a price that reflects the seller's costs, not the urgency of the buyer's needs; to do otherwise is to "deceive one's neighbour so as to injure him" (*ST* 2.2.77.1).

In the very next section, Aquinas discusses lending at interest, which, like selling above the just price, is a sin. Here, Aquinas cites Exodus (22:25), but the Aristotelian echoes are also clear: Aquinas rejects usury, "because this is to sell what does not exist, and this evidently leads to inequality which is contrary to justice" (*ST* 2.2.78.1), while Aristotle describes lending at interest as a "trade hated with most reason: it makes a profit from currency itself.... [This is] most unnatural" (*P* 1258b46). It is here – perhaps more than anywhere else – that the ancient and medieval attitude toward commerce emerges in its clearest light. Of course, from an economic point of view, the moral prohibition against lending at interest makes no sense: who, after all, would lend without the incentive furnished by interest? And how could promising, worthwhile enterprises take off, and survive, without reliable access to credit? But Aquinas's perspective – like that of Plato and Aristotle before him – is not an economic one: he cares, first and foremost, about virtue, not accumulation; and the fundamental aim of his economic teaching is to show that the value of accumulation lies exclusively in making a virtuous life possible by effectively satisfying the comparatively modest needs of the body.

## 6

This worldview persists until the end of the seventeenth century. In 1697, the French theologian Louis Thomassin publishes his *Treaty on Trade and Usury*:

> Those who accumulate possessions without end and without meas-
> ure; those who are constantly adding new fields and new houses
> to their heritage; those who hoard huge quantities of wheat in
> order to sell at what to them is the opportune moment; those who
> lend at interest to poor and rich alike, think they are doing noth-
> ing against reason, against equity, and finally against divine law,

because, as they imagine, they do not harm anyone and indeed benefit those who would otherwise fall into great necessity.... [Yet] if no one acquired or possessed more than he needed for his maintenance and that of his family, there would be no destitute in the world at all. It is thus this urge to acquire more and more which brings so many poor people to penury.[5]

And two years later Charles Davenant, an English economist, publishes his "Essay upon the Probable Methods of Making a People Gainers in the Balance of Trade": "Trade, without doubt, is in its nature a pernicious thing; it brings in that wealth which introduces luxury; it gives rise to fraud and avarice, and extinguishes virtue and simplicity of manners; it depraves a people, and makes way for that corruption which never fails to end in slavery, foreign or domestic. Lycurgus, in the most perfect model of government that was ever framed, did banish it from his commonwealth."[6]

Indeed, such sentiments would hardly have been out of place in the Spartan or Athenian assemblies. But, in many ways, Thomassin and Davenant give expression to a conservative, reactionary view: an intellectual sea change has already taken place by the time their tracts are published. And so the remaining chapters of this book describe the rapid, decisive sloughing off of the ancient and medieval worldview described in this chapter: next, we will begin to examine the coming into being of a radically different approach to commerce and private property. Indeed, starting in chapter 2, we start to move away from the politics of virtue toward the business of prosperity.

# 2

## "The Felicity of This Life": Machiavelli and Hobbes on the Possibility of Delightful Living

In many ways, Aquinas typifies medieval European scholarship: its practices, values, and standards of success. His views, once formulated in the light of intense biblical and Christian theological scholarship, are then mapped onto those of "the Philosopher," Aristotle, to ensure their compatibility. Both *Exodus* and the *Politics* warn against the dangers of usury, so Aquinas too describes the threat to community posed by lending at interest; both *Matthew* and the *Politics* urge us to treat those with whom we engage in trade as we ourselves would like to be treated, so Aquinas too emphasizes the "just price" as the only reasonable, virtuous point of exchange. What Aquinas's body of work demonstrates, in other words, is the authoritative status of Aristotle's thought in the intellectual life of medieval Europe – the way that contemporary philosophical views about virtue, justice, and community were accepted by virtue of their reconcilability with the teachings of the ancient Greeks.

This chapter describes the fundamental intellectual shift that takes place beginning in the sixteenth century, away from the medieval worldview. The two chief protagonists in this endeavor are Niccoló Machiavelli and Thomas Hobbes, who, together, are responsible for laying the intellectual foundation of the modern world. And the first step in this endeavor is to challenge the authority of the ancients.

Machiavelli and Hobbes both undertake this task with gusto: in *The Prince*, Machiavelli accuses Plato and Aristotle of constructing "imaginary republics" (Wootton trans., 48) that can never be realized in the world and are therefore idle chatter; in *Leviathan*, Hobbes dismisses the Platonic and Aristotelian texts as riddled with "insignificant speech" (*Lev* 1.1.4). And both Machiavelli and Hobbes recognize, and lament, the influence of the ancient Greeks on the political thought of their Christian contemporaries: while the Greeks and Christians have different conceptions of virtue, they are united in belief that the purpose of politics is to lead citizens to it. Machiavelli and Hobbes, by contrast, believe that virtue has no place in political life: both substitute a comfortable and even delightful life in place of the good life, and with this substitution inaugurate modernity.

## 1

In chapter 15 of *The Prince*, Machiavelli states his present aim: "My hope," he says, "is to write a book [for rulers, present and aspiring] that will be *useful*" (48; italics added).[1] What, exactly, is Machiavelli's standard for usefulness? He continues: "Many authors have constructed imaginary republics and principalities that have never existed in practice and never could; for the gap between how people actually behave and how they ought to behave is so great that anyone who ignores everyday reality in order to live up to an ideal will soon discover he has been taught how to destroy himself, not how to preserve himself" (48). Here, Machiavelli counsels rulers to avoid the realm of the imaginary: "We do not live in an ideal world" (48), he says, and so rulers must be steadfast in their commitment to seeing the world as it really is, and subjects as they really are. Unfortunately, though, the temptations to "ignore everyday reality" are great – a testament to the intellectual and political influence of all those "many authors" who have "constructed imaginary republics and principalities" (48). Clearly, this is an indictment of Plato, Aristotle, and Aquinas, who all speak, first and foremost, of moral virtue, civic sacrifice, mutually advantageous friendship, and economic restraint. Of course, these authors recognize the existence – and in some cases even the inevitability – of moral wickedness, political decay, social atomization, and economic polarization;

but in Machiavelli's mind, their emphasis on, and pursuit of, the ideal renders these philosophers politically useless.

This is particularly true of the Christian writers: in Machiavelli's eyes, their counsel has made rulers weak and, as a result, the world a less safe, more violent place. For instance, in chapter 3, Machiavelli contrasts the ancient Romans, at the height of their power, with Louis XII of France, invader of Italy, and this turns out to be a very unfavorable comparison for Louis.[2] Indeed, the Romans did everything right – "They settled colonies; were friendly towards the weaker rulers, without building up their strength; broke the powerful; and did not allow foreign powers to build up support" (10) – while Louis did everything wrong: he propped up Pope Alexander and the Venetians, and, in doing so "weakened himself, [and alienated] his friends" (12). According to Machiavelli, these mistakes are attributable to Louis's faith: he was charitable to his enemies (12) and merciful to those that betrayed him (25), and both these errors – rooted in Louis's conventional Christian morality, and his aspiration to be a good Christian – eventually forced him into impetuous, irresponsible, unwinnable wars. The Romans, by contrast, knew nothing of charity or mercy: they valued courage, fortitude in adversity, discipline, and self-assertion (11). And they also knew to never build up the strength of an enemy in the vain hope that they would return this kindness (17). In other words, the Romans saw others as they really are – possessing a short-term memory, vicious in the pursuit of their own interests – and created a lasting, glorious empire; Louis saw others as he wanted them to be – penitent, desirous of reciprocating the goodness shown to them by others – and was ejected from Italy, by former allies, a mere twelve years after conquering it (14).

## 2

What *is* the world really *like?* What *do* citizens really *want?* Throughout *The Prince,* Machiavelli stresses two intractable forces present in every city: conservatism and self-interest.[3] More than anything, he says, ordinary citizens desire the preservation of the status quo, and so he frequently advises rulers to "preserve the structures established by one's forebears,... for every change in government creates grievances" (7). And if a new government does emerge – as a result of either civil war or foreign conquest – it is essential that newly installed rulers "respect established traditions" (8) and "do not alter [the] old laws or impose new taxes" (9).[4] Indeed, while Machiavelli describes typical citizens as "ungrateful, fickle, deceptive and deceiving" (52), he also emphasizes that they are steady and unwavering in the pursuit of one thing: their own interests, which is to say, the accumulation and protection of their private property. "Keep your hands off other people's property," advises Machiavelli, "for men are quicker to forget the death of their father than the loss of their inheritance" (52).

A shocking, scandalous statement, to be sure – unimaginable in a Christian tract on politics – but Machiavelli is convinced of its truth: the more secure subjects' property, he says, the less likely they are to rebel against the political status quo. And that is precisely why Machiavelli suggests that the path to political stability goes through the people, not the nobility: "Anyone who becomes a ruler with the support of the populace ought to ensure he keeps their support; which will not be difficult, *for all they ask is not to be oppressed*" (32; italics added); and, later, he adds that "[keeping] up the morale" of the people will be "easy" if the ruler "protects their interests ... through courage and [sound] policies" (32–3), and if he is vigilant in fighting the temptation to "find excuse[s] for seizing other people's possessions" (52). In contrast to the nobility – anxious to retain the honor, glory, and secure access to the political power befitting their station – "the objectives of the populace are less immoral" (32): the people "are preoccupied with their immediate concerns" (54) and simply want peace, order, and, perhaps most importantly of all, secure private property and the legal conditions conducive to commerce. After all, "the vast majority of men, so long as their goods ... are not taken from them, will live contentedly" (56).

History, adds Machiavelli, is littered with examples of this: Cesare Borgia introduced peace, unity, and "good government" to the Romagna, making himself "loved" (27) by all who lived there; and he did so by replacing all those "weak nobles, who had rather exploited than governed their subjects," and who had permitted the Romagna to fill up with "robbers, bandits, and every other type of criminal" (24), with good laws, conducive to security and prosperity, and with "a civil court in the center of the province [headed up by] an excellent judge" (24). Machiavelli also praises the rulers of the northern German cities, who, in anticipation of future sieges, "keep in stock enough supplies to keep their subjects occupied ... in those crafts that are the basis of the city's prosperity and provide employment to the bulk of the people" (35), as well as Pope Julius II, whose modest, responsible spending helped him to avoid the imposition of "crushing taxes on the people" (49). When, to the contrary, rulers engage in lavish, irresponsible spending, they "always end up wasting all [their] resources ... and will be obliged in the end ... to pursue every possible source of income, and to be preoccupied with maximizing revenues" (49). Such a ruler is sure to become deeply hateful to the people, for nothing provokes citizens' ire like the arbitrary and unpredictable expropriation of their wealth.

Machiavelli is not squeamish about what the provision of law, order, and prosperity requires, especially in those places where lawlessness and criminality typically reign: Borgia, for one, was "thought of as cruel" – and he was indeed responsible for disturbing, violent actions (24–5) – but "this supposed cruelty of his restored order to the Romagna, united it, rendered it peaceful and law-abiding" (51). And this points to a more general lesson that runs throughout *The Prince*: be like the ancient Romans! The Romans, after all, were always vigilant and occasionally cruel, whenever necessary, recognizing that "it is much safer to be feared than loved" (51), for fear is something you can control – by making others afraid, of course! – whereas love is unpredictable and fleeting (52). But there is an important distinction between fear and hate: Hannibal, for instance, was "harsh and cruel," but his soldiers also regarded him with deep "admiration" (53). Agathocles, by contrast, possessed an "inhuman cruelty and brutality" – he massacred his fellow citizens, betrayed his friends, broke his word, was "without mercy and without religion" (28) – and this led to both the fear *and* hatred of his subjects (29). Hence Machiavelli's eventual condemnation of Agathocles, despite some unsettling early praise: although Agathocles's reign was characterized by "bold achievements" (28), he was, in the end, a most hated tyrant; he had power, certainly, but not glory, for Agathocles is surely not "*celebrated* among the most excellent men" (29; italics added).

And that is precisely the reward for those who can tread this line between fear and hate: *glory* – the ultimate prize in Machiavelli's world. And how does a prince obtain lasting glory, exactly? By ensuring "you are not despised or hated, and the people are satisfied with your rule" (57); by refusing to "prey on the possessions ... of subjects" (56), and by eliminating those "rapacious" (60) nobles who give in to that temptation; by creating, and sustaining, the "peace and quiet" (59) that the people so desperately crave; and, perhaps most decisively, by securing property rights, facilitating commerce, and promoting prosperity. To gain a glorious "reputation" (67), says Machiavelli, the prince must "encourage his citizens by making it possible for them to pursue their occupations peacefully, whether they are businessmen, farmers, or are engaged in any other activity, making sure they do not hesitate to improve what they own for fear it may be confiscated from them, and that they are not discouraged from investing in business for fear of losing their profits in taxes; instead, he ensures that those who improve and invest are rewarded" (70).

## 3

With Machiavelli, a new constellation of interests comes into view: not wisdom, virtue, or beatitude, as Plato, Aristotle, and Aquinas had taught, respectively, but rather much less ambitious ones – security, peace, and prosperity. Indeed, in *The Prince*, Machiavelli gives us a purely selfish foundation for political cooperation: we do not associate with others to realize our and their nature as the *zoon politikon*; no, our main motivation to live in the city is to live under law – to know that our property is safe and that the conditions conducive to the growth of that property are securely in place. The ruler who recognizes this will enjoy a long, glorious reign.[5] This is also Hobbes's aim in *Leviathan*: to show his readers that the basis of their obedience to the state is self-interest – that the stable existence of the state is the essential precondition of the satisfaction of their own interest in living safely and prosperously. Of course, the urgency of broadcasting this message was all too apparent to Hobbes, who lived through, and was eventually forced to flee, an intense, violent civil war.[6] Too many of his contemporaries, Hobbes thought, were under the impression that their interests were better satisfied through political disobedience and, worse, revolution, and the purpose of *Leviathan* is to disabuse of them of this deeply mistaken notion.

To make his case, Hobbes's first task is to show his readers what their true interests are, and this begins, in chapter 1, with a direct attack on "certain Texts of Aristotle," and on the "Philosophy-schooles, through all the Universities of Christendome," devoted to their careful study (1.1.4).

The problems with "Aristotelity" (4.46.370) – that "*Vain Philosophy*" (4.46.376) – are thoroughgoing and foundational: Aristotle and his medieval Christian followers misunderstand the fundamental structure of reality, attributing to all material objects some obscure metaphysical essence, one that fully reveals itself to human sense; somehow, these obscurantists teach, the immaterial "*species*" (1.1.4) of things directly communicate with our senses, producing sights, sounds, tastes, and so on.

Hobbes devotes the opening chapters of *Leviathan* to a vicious critique of the metaphysics of the Aristotelians and in his vehement disagreement shows himself to be on the vanguard of the scientific revolution of the seventeenth century. In place of incorporeal "*apparitions*," Hobbes substitutes the imperceptible and yet still corporeal "motion of externall things upon our Eyes, Eares, and other organs": we do not have direct, unmediated access to the objects that we perceive, Hobbes teaches; rather, those objects produce "divers motions," these motions then "presseth the organ proper to each Sense," and those senses in turn communicate, via the "Nerves, and other strings, and membranes of the body," with the "Brain, and Heart" (1.1.3). Hobbes's language is obscure to us – the vocabulary of modern science is not yet available to him, after all – but his worldview is thoroughly familiar: Hobbes describes the existence of various natural processes – pulses of light, the transfer of energy, waves of pressure, the compounding of chemicals – and the way that these processes interact with the mechanical, chemical, and electrical systems that make up the human body to produce sense experience.

At times, Hobbes's extended discussion of the natural world and sense perception seems out of place in a treatise on politics: why, exactly, does the nature of the material and sensual world matter when it comes to questions of political organization and obligation? In fact, Hobbes's scientific aim is importantly connected to his political aim. What he gives us, after all, is a world that is wholly mechanical and therefore wholly disenchanted: all there is, he says, is "so many several motions of the matter," within and without (1.1.3); and so, by extension, all those "fearfull apparitions," "visions," "spirits," "Fayries, Ghosts, Goblins and Witches," about which the masses speak so frequently, simply do not exist: they are merely the inventions of "crafty," "ambitious," "Ghostly men," designed to manipulate the "simple people," to nurse their "superstitious fear" and to lead them into disobedience (1.2.7–8).[7]

This is a stunning, dangerous indictment of religion in general and the "Christian faith" (1.2.7) in particular, with all its talk of "Exorcisme, of Crosses, of holy Water" (1.2.7). Hobbes here warns us against the multitudes of "evill men" (1.2.7) who use these metaphysical, mystical, and supernatural illusions to consolidate their own power, with the ultimate hope of undermining, and eventually usurping, the power of the state (1.2.8).[8] And he is equally disdainful of "the Schooles" (1.2.8) that "nourish," rather than alleviate, the people's willingness to believe that "unnatural Apparitions" (1.2.7) haunt them at every turn. But the people too are eager to believe: for Hobbes, the religious impulse is rooted in fear and anxiety – "perpetuall feare of death, poverty, or [some] other calamity," and anxiety over "the time to come" (1.12.52) – both of which are permanent, ever-present features of human life. Little wonder, then, that the "Common-people," longing for salvation and a spiritual regimen to attain it, are "like clean paper, fit to receive whatsoever by Publique Authority shall be imprinted in them" (2.30.176). And it is even less surprising that the power-hungry and ambitious manipulate, and exacerbate, these fears and anxieties in the hopes of accumulating power. This is precisely why Hobbes draws a direct connection between religion and civil conflict: we disagree about the nature and demands of these "Invisible Agents," and then we fight and kill over our disagreements (1.12.53–4).

More than anything, the opening chapters of *Leviathan* are Hobbes's attempt to show his readers that there is actually nothing out there, and so neither is there anything worth fighting about. All there is, he says, is matter in motion: all the images of our senses – our dreams (1.2.6) and our imagination (1.2.5), too – are merely the by-product of the random movement of tiny particles. Even our desires fit into this framework: "To *go*, to *speak*, to *move* any of our limbes ... is Motion in the organs and interiour parts of mans body, caused by the action of the things we See, Heare, &c" (1.6.23). And because life itself is constant motion – within and without – Hobbes speaks of our desires as "perpetuall and restless" (1.11.47): "There is no such thing as a perptuall Tranquility of mind, while we live here," he says, "because Life it selfe is but Motion, and can never be without Desire, nor without Feare, no more than without sense" (1.6.29–30; see also 1.6.24).

Here, again, Hobbes puts the ancients and their Christian followers directly in his crosshairs: all who came before spoke of the proper *ends* of human life – wisdom, virtue, beatitude – and of how the achievement of those ends puts our desires to rest. Aristotle, for example, speaks of placid moderation as the essential mark of virtue (*NE* 1119a13). And Aquinas says much the same thing regarding happiness and the contemplation of God (*ST* 2.1.1–5). But, for Hobbes, such a notion of a final end is unintelligible, unless we are speaking about death: "The Felicity of this life, consisteth not in the repose of a mind satisfied. For there is no such *Finis ultimus* (utmost ayme), nor *Summum Bonum* (Greatest Good), as is spoken of on the Books of the old Morall Philosophers" (1.11.47). This is precisely why Hobbes believes that human nature itself is best characterized by an innate impulse to *keep going*, to *strive*, to *endeavor*.

In many ways, this is the key to the entire Hobbesian enterprise: to show that there is no essential, final, complete good to orient our actions and decisions. Instead, life is nothing more than "a continuall progresse of desire, from one object to another" (1.6.47) – a reflection of the ordering of the natural world and the composition of the human body. The political implications of this are crucial: if the ancient notion of "the good life" – what Hobbes calls the *Finis ultimus*, what Aristotle calls *eudaimonia*, what Hobbes's Christian opponents call *beatitude* – is abandoned, all that remains is "the Felicity of *this* life" (1.6.29–30; italics added). For Hobbes, this is addition by subtraction: as long as *beatitudo* is a concern of political institutions – as long as those institutions try to coerce citizens into salvation on the basis of a specific image of "the good life" – civil war is inevitable, for we tend to disagree about the proper content of these ends, as well as the path to achieve them. But if we abandon the illusions of those "old Morall Philosophers," we can develop a clearer sense of our true interests and then put our laws and political institutions to good use in advancing those real interests. All of this explains why the natural philosophy is the essential foundation of the moral and political philosophy: it is only once we have made the decisive turn away from heaven, toward the earth, says Hobbes, we can finally live, and prosper, together in peace.


4


What are our *true* interests? Of course, Hobbes begins by turning away from the divine and from the idea of heavenly salvation: for a thoroughgoing materialist, talk of "Invisible Powers" and of life after death goes "against naturall reason" (1.12.58). And so Hobbes proposes a reorientation: we cannot, by definition, have any direct experience or knowledge of God, his will, or how to attain his grace; we do, by contrast, have direct and immediate access to our own inner life. And if we look at ourselves clearly – without the obfuscating force of superstition – it is obvious what makes us happy: "Felicity [or] prospering," says Hobbes, comes from "continuall successe [in] obtaining those things which a man from time to time desireth" (1.6.29–30). Here Hobbes gives us his recipe for lasting happiness: simply, the ability to satisfy our desires! Of course, these desires are constantly changing, as they emerge and wane in response to external stimuli; but, regardless of the actual content of those desires, we can be sure that as long as we are living, sensing beings, we will have and so want to satisfy them. There is, in other words, a sort of hedonism at the heart of the Hobbesian enterprise: Hobbes wants his readers to acknowledge that "felicity" is synonymous with the pleasurable experience of satisfying one's desires, with a contented life, with what Hobbes often refers to as "commodious living" (1.13.63). And so those in search of happiness must secure the conditions necessary for the satisfaction of desire, now and in future; such persons must accumulate power: "The Power of a Man," says Hobbes, "is his present means to obtain some future apparent Good" (1.5.41).

Hobbes has a multifaceted conception of power; he recognizes that power has many different sources: from the gifts acquired from nature – "the eminence of the Faculties of Body, or Mind" – to those acquired through hard work, diligence, and, at times, good luck – "Riches, Reputation, Friends, [and] Fame" – to the knowledge acquired through careful study (1.10.41). But the amount of power that is actually derived from each of these – from strength, intelligence, wealth, education, and so on – is ultimately contingent:

> The *Value*, or Worth of a man, is as of all other things, his Price; that is to say, so much as would be given for the use of his Power: and therefore is not absolute; but a thing dependent on the need and judgment of another. An able conductor of Souldiers, is of great Price in time of War present, or imminent; but in Peace not so. A learned and incorrupt Judge, is much Worth in time of Peace; but not so much in war. And as in other things, so in men, not the seller, but the buyer determines the Price. For let a man (as most

> men do) rate themselves at the highest Value they can; yet their
> value is no more than it is esteemed by others. (1.10.42)

In other words, the amount of power that people possess depends on the social matrix to which they belong; and the guiding values of that matrix receive their clearest, most important expression via the laws of supply and demand – on the open market.[9]

This is a crucial insight: what Hobbes is telling us here is that, at bottom, a stable, well-functioning market is the essential precondition of lasting happiness. Felicity, as we have already seen, depends on the ability to satisfy our desires, and this possibility of living a life of ongoing pleasure in turn depends on the possession of power. And power, Hobbes teaches, is a property of our relations with others – it is realized in our dealings with others through market activity; hence, "the publique worth of a man ... is the Value set on him by [his fellows]" (1.10.42). According to Hobbes, then, the worth of a man – his social power – is not determined by his wisdom, virtue, or piety, as the ancients taught, and the Christians continue to teach (1.15.75). Instead, the value of a man is simply the price he can fetch on the market, which has thus become the most important mechanism of social coordination – the adhesive that makes peaceful, productive living together possible. Our modern world is coming into clearer view.

# 5

Chapter 13 is the most famous chapter of *Leviathan*; it is where Hobbes discusses the abstraction for which he is surely best known: the state of nature, a state without laws or a stable political authority to enforce even a modicum of order. In such a state, we are exposed to the violence of others, fear is ubiquitous, and our lives are "solitary, poore, nasty, brutish, and short" (1.13.62). But the permanent threat of violence is not the only disadvantage of which Hobbes speaks: in the state of nature, our property, however meager, is fundamentally insecure – "no *Mine* and *Thine* distinct" (1.13.63) – and neither would there be any "place [for] Industry; because the fruit thereof is uncertain: and consequently no Culture of the Earth; no Navigation, nor use of the commodities that may be imported by Sea; no commodious Building;

no Instruments of moving, and removing such things as require much force; no Knowledge of the face of the Earth; no account of Time; no Arts; no Letters; no Society" (1.13.62).

In short, no commerce, no wealth, and thus no felicity! It is easy to see why this is the case: more than anything, commerce depends on the institution of contract. In fact, contracts are so important to Hobbes that he speaks of justice as fidelity to contracts: "Justice," he says, is "Keeping of Covenant" (1.15.73). But in the state of nature, covenants are of no effect: without law or law enforcement, no one can trust anyone else to keep them. After all, if any are so foolish as to complete their end of a bargain first – by, say, delivering a stock of goods or supplying a needed service – nonperformance is the most rational course of action for the second party, as long as they are confident that they can evade the private vengeance of the wronged first party. Indeed, in the absence of law, Hobbes speaks of first performance as a form of self-betrayal: "He which performeth first, does but betray himselfe to his enemy" (1.14.68). *This* is why the state of nature itself is such an unproductive and therefore miserable place: you can't have commerce and the accumulation of wealth without enforceable contracts.

The state is the antidote to the mutual, paralyzing "diffidence" (1.13.61) and concomitant poverty that characterizes the state of nature: it changes the "background conditions"[10] and, by extension, what constitutes rational behavior. When the state exists – when the legal, judicial, and punitive infrastructure of the state is effectively in place, and it is accepted by the coerced as legitimate – nonperformance is no longer rational, given the looming and constant threat of punishment by a powerful authority with the legitimacy to act. In fact, the state exists, first and foremost, as a deterrent against such nonperformance: "Covenants, without the Sword, are but Words, and of no strength to secure a man at all" (2.17.85). This emphasis on the "Sword" is crucial: Hobbes recognizes that the state must provoke the fear and "awe" (1.13.62) of the people in order to effectively perform its peace- and commerce-promoting function. In fact, Hobbes is trying to show his readers that they all have good reason to *want* this fearful looming threat, given their basic, fundamental interest in "commodious" living.

This should be obvious to any rational, clear-sighted person: that a decent, prosperous life is achieved more easily in civil society under law than in civil war; hence, the first law of nature, "found out by Reason," is "*to seek Peace, and follow it*" (1.14.64). What does it mean to seek and follow peace, exactly? To transfer one's right to punish nonperformers to the state *in perpetuity*: "When a man hath ... granted away his Right; then is he said to be Obliged or Bound, not to hinder those, to whom such Right is granted, or abandoned, from the benefit of it: and that he Ought and it is his Duty, not to make voyd that voluntary act of his own" (1.14.65). What Hobbes is describing here is the emergence of the modern *sovereign* state – the antidote to the havoc wreaked by the widespread recourse to private vengeance. Only the state, he says, legitimately judges the validity of all those contracts related to "buying, selling, exchanging, borrowing, lending, letting, and taking to hire" (2.24.129). Here, Hobbes pleads with those who have rebelled against the state by (illegitimately) using its authority – thus initiating civil war – and he also warns those currently living in civil society to refrain from taking up the state's rights, lest they end up back in the state of nature.

## 6

Like Machiavelli, and unlike the thinkers covered in chapter 1, Hobbes thinks of the purpose of the state in narrow terms: to maintain peace, law, and order, and also to protect private property, enforce contracts, and facilitate commerce and the accumulation of wealth. Indeed, when Hobbes speaks of the "safety of the people," he is careful to emphasize that he has in mind something more than bare self-preservation: the state must also provide "all other Contentments of life, which every man by lawfull industry, without danger, or hurt to the Commonwealth, shall acquire to himself" (2.30.175).[11] Throughout *Leviathan*, Hobbes spends much time and energy contemplating the sorts of "good Lawes" (2.30.175) conducive to such prosperity: the regime of taxation, for instance, must strike the appropriate balance between investment, on the one hand, and thrift and saving, on the other (2.30.181). And, in chapter 24, "Of the Nutrition, and Procreation of a Commonwealth," Hobbes discusses in further detail how to effectively secure the "*Plenty*" of the political community: he again discourages the state from expropriating private property through arbitrary taxation – despite its right to do so, for the provision of peace and security is surely expensive, and emergencies are difficult to predict – and he also endorses the prevailing mercantilist views of the day, suggesting that, in order to stimulate domestic industry, the state should employ tariffs designed to insulate producers at home from foreign competition (2.24.129).

What about citizens' souls? Is it the state's responsibility to ensure that those subject to its power gain entry to heaven? "All that is Necessary to Salvation, is contained in two Vertues," says Hobbes: "*Faith in Christ,* and *Obedience to Laws*" (3.43.322). What Hobbes gives us here is the least demanding Christian theology imaginable; he is purposefully silent on the religious controversies of the day: the attributes of God, the nature of the Trinity, the meaning of the Eucharist, and so on. Hobbes's silence is hardly surprising: he had direct, vivid experience of the violence and disorder caused by disagreements over these issues. And so he is adamant that the state, if it wishes to be stable, ought not have an ideological ax to grind – a set of values, a worldview, a plan of life to force upon citizens, potentially against their will. The only dogma of the Hobbesian state is a civil one: the need to secure citizens' survival and commodious living. It is precisely in this context that Hobbes emphasizes that the sovereign should not care what people think privately, as long as they keep it to themselves and do not act antisocially. In chapter 31, for example, he distinguishes between public and private worship and insists that the latter is "in secret Free" (2.31.189). And earlier, in a discussion of freedom, Hobbes says that, "[in] cases where the Soveraign has prescribed no rule, there the Subject hath the liberty to do, or forbeare, according to his own discretion" (2.21.113). In other words, Hobbes creates the civil space for the emergence, and flourishing, of potentially quite radical religious pluralism. Unlike the true believer, whose goal is to save souls, the Hobbesian sovereign looks only to temporal ends – law and order, peace and prosperity – and therefore leaves spiritual matters to citizens' discretion.

But there are limits to this freedom, to be sure. While we ought not ignore Hobbes's confident belief that the benefits of stable, productive cooperation will immunize citizens from religiously motivated disobedience, he also says that the state must always carefully monitor, and at times censor, public debate: "It is annexed to the Soveraignty, to be Judge of what Opinions and Doctrines are averse, and what conducing to Peace; and consequently, on what occasions, how farre, and what, men are to be trusted withall, in speaking to multitudes of people; and who shall examine the Doctrines of all bookes before they are published. For the Actions of Men proceed from their Opinions; and in the wel governing of opinions, consisteth the well governing of mens Actions, in order for their Peace and Concord" (2.18.91).

Here, we confront the authoritarian logic – the inexorable end point and defining feature – of Hobbes's political philosophy: the state, he says, must possess the final say on all religious and intellectual matters; and it must vigorously root out all those opinions that imperil the "Peace and Concord" of the political community by encouraging civil disobedience.[12] Indeed, Hobbes vehemently believes that, in order to effectively serve the people, the power of the state must be unlimited and absolute: the power of the sovereign "cannot be transferred to another: He cannot Forfeit it: He cannot be accused by any of his subjects, of Injury: He cannot be Punished by them" (2.20.102; see also 2.18.88–90).[13] He insists, for example, on the necessary fusion of that state's legislative, executive, and judicial branches: the power of the sword – the power to *punish* – and the legislative power must be in the same hands, because citizens will not obey those commands that they have no reason to fear (2.18.91). The right to make war and peace, which includes the right to levy taxes and to compel citizens to take up arms for the country's defense, is also annexed to the sovereign, along with the right to choose government officials and citizens worthy of political honor.

Over and over, and especially in chapter 18, Hobbes emphasizes citizens' powerlessness vis-à-vis the state (2.18.90). To the objection that he has reduced subjects to a "very miserable … Condition" – vulnerable to the absolute, awe-inspiring power of the state – Hobbes replies that "the estate of Man can never be without some incommodity," and that the incommodities of political absolutism are less damaging when compared to the "miseries, and horrible calamities, that accompany a Civill Warre"; after all, Hobbes expects *Leviathan* to be required reading of all future sovereigns, and so those in possession of political power will soon come to understand that they ought not "damage, or [weaken] … their Subjects, in whose vigor, consisteth their own strength and glory" (2.18.94). Hobbes, in the end, forces us to choose between absolutism and anarchy: in his mind, there is no middle ground. Unfortunately, for Hobbes, his argument did not convince his contemporaries.

# 3

# "The Desire of Having More": Locke on Labor and the Right to Accumulate without Limit

Throughout *Leviathan*, Hobbes emphasizes the proper, conscientiously narrow role of the state: to secure peace, order, and (what he calls) "commodious" living. The state, he says, ought not have an ideological ax to grind – an image of virtue, a path to salvation. Instead, the state should commit itself to enhancing the prosperity of those living under it. In some cases, this will require active intervention, such as burdensome taxes on the importation of certain foreign-produced goods (2.24.129). But, more often than not, prosperity demands nonintervention – the free operation of the market, within and (in most cases) across borders. Indeed, in Hobbes's mind, the market is what makes it possible for us to live together, peacefully, productively, even happily: it is, he says, "by the labour of trading from one place to another," and "by selling Manifactures," that individuals and communities are able to "encrease their Power" and thus secure lasting felicity (2.24.127).

Of course, the desirability and efficacy of the market as the main mechanism of social coordination depends on a variety of background assumptions and institutions: the widespread belief that nature – "consisting in [the] Animals, Vegetals, and Minerals, God hath freely layd before us, in or neer the face of the Earth" – is rightly appropriated as private property by individuals; that the state's essential purpose is to protect individuals' right to exclude others from the property they have accumulated (2.24.127); that the human "industry" necessary to maximize the earth's productivity is widely available through the institution of wage labor (2.24.127); and, perhaps most important of all, that individuals are driven, first and foremost, by self-interest – by the desire to create a safe, comfortable, affluent life for themselves and close loved ones (2.30.175). All of these assumptions are operating in – *directing* – Hobbes's thought: market society comes into sharper relief in the pages of *Leviathan*; it is an essential early document in the history of market society.

And yet, during his lifetime and well after, Hobbes's advocacy for the absolute power of the state made him the enemy of England's nascent bourgeoisie.[1] This is hardly surprising. After all, Hobbes believes that, in order to fulfill its commerce- and prosperity-promoting purpose, the state's powers must be indivisible and absolute: it alone must possess the right to levy taxes, though it *ought* to do so in a predictable and responsible manner; it alone must possess the right to produce and value the currency, though it *ought* to do so in a way that respects the present and future interests of those engaged in commerce, domestic and international; it must even possess the right to expropriate private property, though it *ought* to do so only under grave political circumstances and in the pursuit of the public interest (2.24.129). These *oughts* are moral not institutional, advisory not legal: the state's survival depends on the responsible exercise of its powers, to be sure; but, in Hobbes's vision of political life, there are no formal channels for subjects to articulate what the responsible exercise of governmental power actually looks like, what the public interest actually demands. To the propertied classes of Hobbes's day – to those with the most to lose from the arbitrary, irresponsible exercise of state power – this lack of an institutionalized voice was deeply worrying: they therefore rejected the Hobbesian proposition – absolutism or anarchy – and found a new, convincing champion for their rights and interests: John Locke.[2]

## 1

Like Hobbes, Locke is animated by the belief that human beings were put on this earth to thrive, not merely to survive (*Lev* 2.30.175). Though both begin with bare self-preservation – the indisputable right of all persons (§§6 and 16), and the source of our desire for stable political order (§§13 and 21) – their emphasis inexorably shifts to living *well* – not just safely, but comfortably, *prosperously*. Indeed, for Hobbes, self-preservation and commodious living are typically spoken of in the same breath: "Of things held in propriety, those that are dearest to a man are his own life, & limbs; and in the next degree ... riches and means of living" (*Lev* 2.30.179). Chapter 5 of the *Second Treatise* is also typical in this respect: in its opening paragraph, Locke invokes Adam, Noah, and David, and God's revelatory promise to each of them that "men, being once born, have a right to their preservation" (§25); but by the final paragraph of this chapter, Locke has defended much more than that: he ultimately justifies the right to the *unlimited* accumulation of private property and, by extension, potentially quite radical economic inequality. How does Locke get from point A to point B despite the apparent gulf between them?

The foundational premise of Locke's argument is the transformative power of labor: "the spontaneous hand of nature" (§26), without human effort, is basically worthless; the earth is a *potential* plenty, but it must be *actualized* by the industry and hard work of individuals. "The extent of *ground* is of so little value," says Locke, "*without labour*" (§36); elsewhere, Locke speaks of the initial "penury" (§32) of the human condition, and of "neglected, and consequently waste land" (§36), "for the provisions serving to the support of human life, produced by one acre of inclosed and cultivated land, are ... ten times more than those which are yielded by an acre of land of an equal richness lying waste in common" (§37; see also §40). This is a prominent, recurring theme throughout the *Second Treatise*: when the land is held in "common" it tends to be left "uncultivated" and is therefore unproductive (§34); simply put, it is "of no use" (§28; see also §34).[3] But this is an affront to God's will; after all, he did not make anything to spoil or go unused (§§31, 37, and 46). By contrast, when the land is appropriated as private property it is inevitably improved – transformed into something productive and valuable.

The *Second Treatise* is littered with examples of this: "The extent of ground is of so little value, without labour, that I have heard it affirmed, that in Spain itself a man may be permitted to plough, sow, and reap, without being disturbed, upon land he has no other title to, but only his making use of it. But, on the contrary, the inhabitants think themselves beholden to him, who, by his industry on neglected, and consequently waste land, has increased the stock of corn, which they wanted" (§36; see also §40). And later, a counter-example: "[The] several nations of the *Americans* are ... rich in land, and poor in all the comforts of life.... [They possess] a fruitful soil, apt to produce in abundance, what might serve for food, raiment, and delight; yet for *want of improving it by labour,* [they] have not one hundredth part of the conveniences we enjoy: the king of a large and fruitful territory [in America] is clad worse than a day-labourer in England" (§41).

All of this explains why Locke often speaks of the institution of private property as built into the moral fabric of creation: God wants his children to flourish, and that flourishing depends on plenty, which, in turn, depends on the incentives furnished by private property (§35). This also explains why all those "industrious and rational" (§34) persons who appropriate and cultivate the land – those ambitious, hardworking individuals who make the land productive, and produce a plenty for themselves and for others – are the celebrated heroes of the *Second Treatise*, without them, the possibility of "delight" – what Hobbes calls "commodious living" – is not possible: no "bread, wine [or] cloth" (§42).

Of course, the claim that labor is the essential source of value – and that land without labor is essentially worthless – is obvious, platitudinous even. But Locke goes further, and it is the next step of his argument that is the revolutionary one. Labor, he says, is both the source of value *and fully private property*: "Every man has a *property* in his own *person*: this no body has a right to but himself. The *labour* of his body, and the *work* of his hands, we may say, are properly his" (§27).[4] As we have already seen, Locke believes that labor transforms the commons into something private: once individuals have "subdued, tilled and sowed" (§32) the land, they obtain the right to exclude others from it; by extension, and perhaps more importantly, they also obtain the right to exclude others from the fruits of the earth corralled through labor (§§26–32). This is precisely what makes it rational to work hard: labor generates the exclusive entitlement to produce and consume the fruits of the earth – in order to survive (§32) – and to eventually sell whatever cannot be consumed before spoilage – in order to get rich (§48). What about those without land, which, by virtue of the earth's finiteness, will inevitably become scarce? They too fully own their own labor, and so, despite being landless, can still obtain what they need to survive by selling their creative energy for wages: "The turfs my servant has cut ... become my property" (§28).

For Locke, this ideal of self-ownership – the fully private, and therefore salable, possession of the productive energy of the human body – is the outgrowth of a more basic moral fact: in the opening paragraph of the *Second Treatise*, he asserts that "all men are naturally in ... a state of perfect freedom" – that no one is dependent "upon the will of any other man," and neither should anyone be kept in a condition of permanent "subordination or subjection" (§4). Such independent persons are therefore free, as equals, "to order their actions, and dispose of their possessions and persons, as they think fit" (§4). Indeed, Locke typically fleshes out that foundational freedom in conspicuously commercial terms: liberty, for him, means the freedom to live wherever we like (§38), make whatever is most needed (§43), and in the process accumulate as much property and wealth as we can (§46).

The familiarity of the Lockean worldview to us ought not obscure the fact that its central assumptions run fundamentally counter to a thousand years of European economic and political history. Indeed, in many ways, the *Second Treatise* represents the termination – the decisive sloughing off – of the feudal world: the liberties elucidated there are fully incompatible with the defining institutions and values of European economic life since the fall of Rome.[5] Nowhere is this clearer than in Locke's attitude toward labor, which stands as a complete repudiation of the institution of serfdom. Serfs, after all, were not free in any meaningful sense – free to rove in search of the highest wages or to shift their energy toward more profitable areas of enterprise in the hopes of accumulating wealth; no, they were indentured to land-owning lords, and thus obligated to live and work on a particular manor, in exchange for security, food, and access to capital-intensive equipment, not wages.[6] And Locke is equally dismissive of the guiding values of the feudal milieu: he substitutes its deep suspicion of market behavior – and the concomitant view, endorsed by Aquinas, that the profit motive was antithetical to salvation[7] – with an uncritical celebration of the ambitious hard workers, who advance the possibility of genuine prosperity through trade, as per God's plan for us.

Locke is clear-eyed about the inevitable outcome of these liberties, and the concomitant emergence of the market – in land, goods, and labor – as the main coordinating mechanism of society: because individuals possess "different degrees of industry," they are "apt" to accumulate "possessions in different proportion" (§48). Some are able to build up impressive stocks of "gold, silver and diamonds" (§46), while the majority – the less "industrious and rational" (§34) – must sell their labor to the highest bidder. And, in Locke's eyes, there is nothing morally objectionable about this: "the largeness of [an individual's] possession" is, to him, morally neutral; what matters, from the moral point of view, is that "nothing [perishes] uselessly" (§46). And in market society, with hard currency, nothing will: "Find something that hath the *use and value of money* amongst his neighbours, you shall see the same man will begin presently to enlarge his possessions" (§49; see also §37). Notice an important psychological assumption at work here: like Hobbes before him, Locke tacitly assumes that all persons are motivated, first and foremost, by the "desire of having more" – to accumulate as much property and wealth as possible (§37; *Lev* 1.6.47 and 2.30.175).

Chapter 5 of the *Second Treatise* is a whirlwind, to be sure: Locke begins with the simplest, least controversial premise – the moral equality of all persons, each entitled to comfortable self-preservation – and from it derives the characteristic institutions of the modern world: private property and wage labor. If we believe in freedom, so this line of thinking goes, we must also accept a quintessentially bourgeois catalog of rights – to appropriate private property without end, and to sell our labor for wages on the open market. Of course, with these rights and liberties in place, the community is likely to become a radically economically inegalitarian place: this Locke acknowledges and accepts. Indeed, in his mind, the commitment to freedom leads inexorably to inequality; thus have men agreed to "a disproportionate and unequal possession of the earth" (§50). On the one hand, Locke steadfastly believes that the poor are still better off as a result of their association with the economically prosperous: recall that a "day-labourer in England" is better fed and better clothed than a "king of ... the Americans" (§41). But he also recognizes the inevitability of class resentment and conflict, and it is this fear, more than anything, that animates his theory of government and citizenship.

## 2

The state of nature figures prominently in the opening chapters of the *Second Treatise*. Like Hobbes, Locke believes that we can develop a better sense of the proper role and responsibilities of the state only if we have an image of social life without it (§4). And, at first, it is difficult to see why, according to Locke, we need government *at all*: in chapter 2, Locke describes the state of nature as a state of goodwill and mutual aid; every individual, he says, is under a moral obligation to "preserve the rest of mankind" (§6) and to treat others with "justice and charity" (§5). The state of nature does indeed have "a law of nature to govern it, which obliges every one," and that law, knowable to all "rational creature[s]" (§12), "teaches ... [that] no one ought to harm another in his life, health, liberty or possessions" (§6). Occasionally, there will be some who transgress the rules of "reason and common equity" (§8) – endangering the "life, liberty, health, limb or goods of another" (§6) – and who, in turn, must be punished, as far as "calm reason and conscience dictate" (§8). And yet, for the most part, Locke says that, even without government and the concomitant threat of legal punishment, the law of nature, "which willeth the peace and preservation of all mankind," will "be observed" (§7).

But this is not the end of Locke's story about life without government. Indeed, the very next chapter of the *Second Treatise* paints a much different picture of the state of nature: there, Locke describes the "state of war" – a state of mutual "enmity and destruction," in which the rule of reason, which dictates peace and the preservation of all humankind, has been usurped by naked "force and violence" (§16). In such a state, self-preservation is permanently insecure: we are constantly threatened with robbery, slavery, even death (§17). And when faced with such threats – when faced with the violence of those who would deprive us of our freedom, property, and lives – the only rational response is to return that violence in kind: "He who makes an attempt to enslave me, thereby puts himself into a state of war with me.... And therefore it is lawful for me to ... kill him if I can" (§§17 and 18). Suddenly, we are transported back to Hobbes's *Leviathan*, and to an image of the state of nature characterized by permanent, widespread fear and anxiety – a relentless war of all against all (*Lev* 1.13.62).

At first sight, Locke steps back from the Hobbesian abyss: in chapter 3, he is careful to retain the distinction – the "plain difference"

(§19) – between the state of nature and the state of war; the former, he says, is a state of "peace, good will, mutual assistance and preservation," while the latter is a state of "enmity, malice, violence and mutual destruction" (§19). And yet, over and over, Locke effaces the difference between the two: he emphasizes the inconveniences and danger of every person having executive power over the laws of nature (§13; see also §90); and he also describes how, in the state of nature, "wherein there is no appeal but to heaven, ... even the least difference is apt to end" (§21) in a state of war, and that the omnipresent possibility of such conflict means that the state of nature is "full of fears and continual dangers" (§123). But the most decisive consideration, according to Locke, relates to private property, which is "very unsafe, very insecure" (§123) in the state of nature: individuals are compelled to enter political society – to live under promulgated law (§124) and to grant sole executive power of the law to the state (§126) – to make possible the "secure enjoyment of their properties" (§95).

What we might say, in the end, is that Locke is sympathetic to Hobbes's portrayal of the state of nature, but does not fully endorse it: he recognizes the obvious perils of lawlessness, to be sure; but he *also* emphasizes the pacific dimensions of human nature – our capacity to recognize, and willingness to abide by, the laws of nature – and the way this enables property and wealth accumulation despite the absence of codified law or a state. Indeed, by the end of chapter 5, Locke had described the emergence of a quite advanced commercial society – with reasonably secure private property, hard currency, and competitive markets in goods and labor – *before* the state has come into being (§45). According to Hobbes, by contrast, conditions in the state of nature are antithetical to even modest accumulation: without government, he says, there is no "place [for] Industry, ... no Culture of the Earth" (1.13.62), and thus no prosperity. This is the very heart of the Hobbesian argument: the absence of a strong state negates the possibility of productivity, progress, and prosperity.

This is an argument that Locke ultimately rejects: his state of nature is characterized by genuine economic dynamism, whereas Hobbes's is, on principle, static. But Locke does not reject Hobbes *in toto*: although the accumulation of property is possible in the state of nature, it is ultimately "unsecure" and becomes even more so over time (§123). Indeed, as we have already seen, and as Locke candidly admits, the institution of private property is always – necessarily – accompanied by potentially quite radical economic inequality: the "industrious and rational" will always have more than the "quarrelsome and contentious" (§34); there is nothing morally objectionable about this (§46). What *is* morally objectionable, though, occurs when the "fancy or covetousness of the quarrelsome and contentious" imperils the property of the "industrious and rational." Clearly, Locke regards this as inevitable: he describes how, just before the advent of civil society, the "enjoyment of [private property] is very uncertain, and constantly exposed to the invasion of others," "the greater part" of whom are "no strict observers of equity and justice" (§123).

Here we encounter Locke's greatest fear and the main impetus for government: as time passes, and as society becomes more economically unequal, the immediacy of the law of nature, which enjoins us to respect the "lives, liberties and estates" of others (§123), gradually fades away. This is precisely why Locke can speak of persons as *both* fully "oblige[d]" by the law of nature and, later, as "no strict observers of equity and justice" (§123): when we are in an equally penurious condition, abstaining from the property of others is easy; no one possesses anything of value! By contrast, when property comes to be distributed very unequally – when society is divided into haves and have-nots – such abstinence becomes much more difficult and therefore much less likely. In other words, the reason that "mankind ... [is] quickly driven into [political] society" (§127) is class conflict: "The great and *chief end*, therefore, of men's uniting into common-wealths, and putting themselves under government, *is the preservation of their property*. To which in the state of nature there are many things wanting" (§124).

## 3

What sort of government is best able to secure this, the "chief end" of political society? Locke begins by ruling out the Hobbesian option: "*Absolute monarchy*," he says, "which by some men is counted the only government in the world, is *inconsistent with civil society*" (§90). Why, exactly? According to Locke, civil society is the antithesis of the state of nature: in the latter, by virtue of the absence of government, each of us possesses the right to make the rules for ourselves – to determine whether an offense has been committed against us, the proper punishment for that offense, as well as how to go about the execution of that punishment (§128). With the establishment of civil society, though, these rights are transferred to the state: private justice and private vengeance – the two main destabilizing "inconveniences of the state of nature" (§90; see also §125) – are replaced by "*established*, settled, known *laws*" (§124). These are the "public" (§88), "promulgated" (§131) rules of private property – how it can be obtained and alienated, what constitutes theft or trespassing, and the appropriate punishments for such violations (§88; see also §129).

This emphasis on "*settled standing laws*" recurs throughout the *Second Treatise*: it is essential for Locke that the rules governing private property are made fully public – that they are plainly "*stated*" – by the legislative branch of government.[8] Publicity, for him, eliminates the possibility of "absolute power" (§137): it forces the state to declare its guiding purpose and to show the governed that particular legal enactments further that overarching aim – that its rules are limited by and advance the "public good of the society" (§135). The important contrast, here, is between "promulgated law, known to the people," and rule by "extemporary decrees" (§131) and "undetermined resolutions" (§137): when the people invest the state with the latter sort of power, they have "disarmed themselves, and armed [the monarch], to make a prey of them when he pleases" – to engage in the arbitrary and therefore unpredictable expropriation of private land (§138) or the raising of taxes without the consent of the taxed (§140). All of this explains why Locke thinks that absolutism is "no form of civil-government at all" (§90): it runs fundamentally counter to the very purpose for which government was created in the first place. In fact, Locke regards absolutism not merely as unjust, but as incompatible with the demands of reason; after all, "no rational creature can be supposed to change his condition with an intention to be worse" (§131).

Locke then goes further in constraining the power of the state: in a direct repudiation of Hobbes, for whom the powers of law-making and law enforcement must be in the same hands (*Lev* 2.18.91–2), the *Second Treatise* endorses the strict institutional separation of the legislative and executive branches of government (§144). No one is above the law, says Locke, including those responsible for writing it; such persons ought not be in a position to craft the laws to advance their interests, or to apply them idiosyncratically – or, more likely, not apply them at all – in cases related to their property (§143). Despite this separation, the legislature is the "*one supreme power*" (§149) of the state: the executive branch of government does not have discretionary power; when it acts, it is "directed by [the] antecedent, standing, positive laws" generated by the legislative assembly (§147; see also §§150 and 153).[9] And when the interpretation of those laws is in doubt – when the two aforementioned branches of government come into conflict – the decision rests with independent, "indifferent and upright judges" (§131).

Locke's institutional vision is thus characterized by an imperative of power diffusion: contrary to Hobbes, no single institution ought to have the power to make, execute, and interpret the laws; this is the recipe for tyranny, for such concentrated power is "too great a temptation to human frailty, [always] apt to grasp at power" (§143). Indeed, in Locke's mind, the *state itself* is the greatest threat to our liberty and our property; this is why we have to arrange its institutional inner workings so as to prevent it from acting with too much unity and decisiveness (§166).[10] In later chapters of the *Second Treatise*, Locke gives us two additional safeguards against governmental tyranny: first, he says that the legislative assembly must be a reflection of the "assistance" that various "cities ... and counties" (§157) "afford to the public" (§158); in other words, those who represent the wealthiest regions of the political community populate the legislature "in higher numbers" (§158) and are thus better positioned to protect the interests, and property, of their constituents. And second, failing all these diverse, intricate institutional checks on state power, the people always possess an irrevocable right to revolt against the state: "The legislative [power] being only a fiduciary power to act for certain ends, there remains still *in the people a supreme power to remove or alter the legislature*, when they find the legislative acts contrary to the trust reposed in them" (§149; see also §§227 and 243).

This emphasis on popular sovereignty – and the concomitant emphasis on state power as resting on public trust, which is to say, on the always revocable consent of the people – is the heart of the Lockean political enterprise: the purpose of government is to advance the fundamental interests of the governed – to ensure, first and foremost, the "preservation of the properties of [the] people" (§199). And so, when the state fails to do so – when, say, it engages in the arbitrary expropriation of property through excessive taxation – the people can, and ought to, invoke their right to "dissolve the government" (§205) and to subsequently reconstitute it, "such as they see fit" (§222). "Force," says Locke, "is to be opposed to ... unjust and unlawful force" (§204). In fact, when their lives and property are threatened by the state, the people cannot possibly *do* otherwise: "How they will be hindered from resisting illegal force, used against them, I cannot tell," says Locke (§209; see also §168).

In the final chapter of the *Second Treatise*, Locke says that the people always possess, and cannot ever alienate, this right to take up force against the tyrannical state: when "the legislative acts" of the state "endeavour to invade the property of the subject ... the people ... are thereupon absolved from any farther obedience, and are left to the common refuge, which God hath provided all men, against force and violence" (§222). In other words, the right to revolution is a direct outgrowth of our God-given, natural right to prosperous living; much like the institution of private property, it is built into the moral fabric of creation. But Locke is also adamant that the people have a deeply ingrained preference for the status quo and are thus disinclined to invoke this right: "Such revolutions happen not upon every little mismanagement in public affairs" (§225; see also §§161, 208, and 10). Though Locke repeatedly stresses that these revolutionary upheavals will be rare, he is equally vehement that, when they do occur, the state, not the people, is to blame – that the state has put itself "into a state of war with [the] people" by exceeding its narrow mandate" (§163; see also §§218 and 226–8).

# 4

Like Locke, Hobbes's political thought is characterized by its emphasis on commodious living: throughout *Leviathan*, he offers counsel to those in power on how to craft laws that will facilitate prosperity (*Lev* 2.24.127 and 2.30.181) and thus elicit the ongoing satisfaction and consent of the governed (see, e.g., *Lev* 2.21.108). But Hobbes is not naive: he acknowledges the inevitability of rebellion when the sovereign imperils citizens' self-preservation or, more likely, indulges in the arbitrary seizure of their property (see, e.g., *Lev* 2.21.111–14). But – and this is key – Hobbes does not, and cannot, ever speak of a *right* to rebel: the regime of secure private property, he says, depends upon the total relinquishing of citizens' rights vis-à-vis the state (*Lev* 2.18.89–90; see also 2.29.167–8). And this total dependence on the state is built into the very structure of the social contract itself: the act that institutes civil society takes place between those subject to power, not between those subject to power and those who wield it (*Lev* 2.17.87–8); the state thus stands outside the social contract and, because of this, citizens do not have claims of justice against it (*Lev* 2.18.90; see also 2.18.94). Justice, after all, is a property of contracts: performance is justice, nonperformance injustice (*Lev* 1.15.71). Citizens may fight the state, but they are institutionally powerless to do so: in such cases, they exercise might without right. Locke cannot accept this: give people the power to oppress you, he retorts, and you can be sure that they will use that power swiftly and precisely for that purpose; such is the weakness of human nature (§143). This is perhaps *the* central lesson of the *Second Treatise*: that you cannot merely counsel the state to use its power in the public interest; no, you have to design the proper institutional checks on the exercise of state to prevent it from doing otherwise. The design of the system surely matters more to Locke than the individuals occupying powerful offices within it.

But, more than anything, it is the vigilance of the people that prevents the state from descending into tyranny: though forgiving of ineptitude, the people are constantly alert to encroachments on their liberty and property, and this makes them permanently suspicious of state power (§225). And the people are also keenly aware of their ultimate right to judge the state and, when necessary, reconstitute it in order to more effectively advance their interests (§240). In this light, it is easy to understand the strong preference for Locke, over Hobbes, among the propertied class of seventeenth-century England: he invests the nascent English bourgeoisie with exclusive access to, and reins on, the instruments of political power; and he thus ensures that the state will always act in the service of wealth protection and limitless accumulation. Hobbes had given them no similar guarantee. And so now, absolutism is decisively off the table as a legitimate mode of political organization. Instead, the modern state – the Lockean state – is characterized, first and foremost, by its limitations – by its limited capacity to act, and by the limited nature of its guiding mandate.

# 4

## "A Course Intended by Nature": Smith and Kant on the Overwhelming Benefits of Commerce – Domestic and International

The *Second Treatise* was written with a specific, limited purpose in mind: to justify a particular constitutional revolution against an absolute monarch, James II, in the hopes of replacing him with a sovereign whose power would be limited by a parliament of property-owners.[1] But there is an implicit theme in Locke's work that caught the attention of many writing after him: that the impulse to accumulate, and protect, wealth and property leads to many things that we have good reason to want – the rule of law, economic development, prosperity. From the foundational desire for comfortable self-preservation – built into our nature, and thus endorsed, by the Creator – emerges the complex infrastructure of modern market society: property rights, contract enforcement, wage labor, and even popular sovereignty and limited representative government.

In the two centuries after Locke, philosophers and economists focused much more explicitly on the salutary effects of self-interest: the commercial impulse came to be widely accepted as the agent of political and social progress too. And yet, the distance between Hobbes and Locke, on the one hand, and Smith and Kant on the other – not in historical time, mind you, but rather in mentality – is striking. For Hobbes and Locke, the animating impetus is to crawl our way out of the state of nature – a dreaded, because lawless, condition, antithetical to lasting happiness – and to thus eke out a living from the withholding natural world; for them, economic prosperity is a remote possibility for the future, pending the quite radical – and therefore deeply uncertain – reorganization of our present political institutional arrangements. For Smith and Kant, by contrast, such prosperity is very much on the fore-seeable horizon *despite* some potentially very wrong-headed decisions by legislators; the productive energy of profit-hungry entrepreneurs has been fully unleashed, and the ensuing radical transformation of the world simply cannot be arrested. And, as we shall see, this is, for the most part, a cause for celebration: the individual's desire for betterment leads to a generous increase in society's general level of well-being, to good government, and even to lasting peace between states. Indeed, it is in the pages of Smith and Kant that something like recognizably modern capitalism comes into view, and in those same pages that that system receives its first important, spirited, persuasive defense.

# 1

No thinker is more closely associated with this intellectual movement than Adam Smith, whose account of human nature provides the foundational intuition and starting premise of much of eighteenth- and nineteenth-century thought.[2] Human beings, Smith teaches, possess the innate "propensity to truck, barter and exchange one thing for another" (*WN* 1.2.1), and so, eventually, "every man ... lives by exchanging, or becomes in some measure a merchant, and the society itself grows to be ... a commercial society" (*WN* 1.4.1). In such a society – in a society in which the social coordinating mechanism is the market – individuals are, quite naturally, obsessed with whatever capital – whatever time, energy, and wealth – they have at their disposal. They want to invest their capital wisely – in products and services in high demand (*WN* 4.2.7), thus maximizing their return. And they also want to keep their capital close to home, preferring to invest in nearby "domestic industry" rather than the "foreign trade of consumption" or, worse, because farer away, "the carrying trade" (*WN* 4.2.5). Indeed, Smith treats this capital-obsessiveness as a kind of automatic instinct: "individuals," he says, are "*continually exerting*" themselves in the pursuit of "advantage," always "*endeavour*[ing]" (*WN* 4.2.5) "to find out the most advantageous employment for whatever capital [they] can command" (*WN* 4.2.4; see also 2.2.28). *And that's a very good thing*: the drive to invest wisely – and to keep a close and watchful eye on the progress and eventual fruits of those investments – leads to the satisfaction of the needs of others (*WN* 4.2.11), and to maximal infusion of capital – and, with it, "revenue [for the state] and employment" (*WN* 4.2.6) – into local economies. Self-interest, in other words, is salutary: when individuals act for the sake of profit, they "naturally, or rather necessarily, prefer that employment which is most advantageous to society" (*WN* 4.2.4 and 8), even though no one consciously "intends to promote the public interest" (*WN* 4.2.9).

Of course, this is not immediately obvious, and especially so for the advocates of the ancient and Christian traditions discussed in chapter 1. Recall that, for Plato, Aristotle, and Aquinas – and their countless followers too – self-interest is antithetical to the public good: the more we care about debits and credits, the less we care about civic virtue and sacrifice. Smith disagrees, and strongly so: self-interest is a healthy and productive force for the community, at least when it is effectively harnessed by and channeled through markets. It is precisely the competition unleashed by markets that prevents citizens from holding their fellows hostage: if a manufacturer tried to take advantage of customers by charging more than its competitors, they would take away its trade; workers who asked for more than the going wage would not be able to find work; landlords who sought to exact a rent steeper than another with land of the same quality would get no tenants. In other words, competition prevents any single individual or firm from exacting a higher price than that set by the market (see, e.g., *WN* 1.7.5–33). And the market *also* takes care of the types and quantities of goods produced and services offered: firms will enter the markets with high demand, and they will exit markets with low demand. As a result – as markets with high demand entice new entrants, and therefore generate more competition – goods and services tend toward the lowest possible prices – and therefore the greatest possible benefit – for wage-earning (as opposed to property-owning) consumers (*WN* 1.7.15).

Smith is careful to emphasize that all of this – the satisfaction of the needs of all members of our society – happens unconsciously and spontaneously: no one intends to pursue the public good or to satisfy the needs of others; no, all are pursuing profit for themselves. "It is not from the benevolence of the butcher, the brewer or the baker that we expect our dinner," writes Smith, "but from their regard to their self-interest. We address ourselves not to their humanity, but to their self-love, and never talk to them of our necessities, but of their advantages" (*WN* 1.2.2). And yet, despite the ubiquity of self-interest – and the concomitant lack of interest in the needs of others – the needs of all are still met, and the public good of society – its collective interest in economic development, productive employment, ever-rising purchasing power, and concomitant standards of living – advanced.

Conversely, the conscious desire to advance that public interest typically does more harm than good. Here, Smith criticizes the activist "statesman" (*WN* 4.2.10): when states attempt to stimulate domestic industry through artificial policy instruments – "by restraining, either by high duties, or absolute prohibitions, the importation" (*WN* 4.2.1) of foreign goods – they inadvertently deny other, potentially more profitable industries of resources.[3] Capital, after all, is finite and therefore zero-sum: when it is directed to certain productive channels – artificially or not – it is unavailable for others, potentially at the expense of greater productivity and profits (*WN* 4.2–3). According to Smith, spontaneous market signals, not artificial incentives created by the instruments of public policy, should determine capital allocation. After all, there is no guarantee that the protected areas of the economy are the most efficient and therefore most profitable ones: duties may in fact be a sign of powerful merchants exercising undue influence on the government (*WN* 1.7.26–8). Just because an industry is protected, that is, does not mean that that industry maximizes the well-being of the entire society; the protective tariff may actually be a sign of corruption – a sign that the state has been captured by the "clamour and sophistry" (*WN* 1.10.80) of a particular class of merchants and manufacturers.

In many ways, this is the heart of Smith's purpose in writing the *Wealth of Nations*: to show political actors that they ought to refrain from exercising control over prices, production, and international trade. Better, he says, to let individuals decide for themselves "in what manner they ought to employ their capitals" (*WN* 4.2.11). After all, it is individuals, not legislators, who possess the requisite information about the supply and demand for specific markets, as well as the appropriate motive – profit – to put that information to effective use; that is why "every individual, it is evident, can, in his local situation, judge much better than any statesman or lawgiver can do for him" (*WN* 4.2.10).

In other words, "perfect [economic] liberty" (*WN* 1.10.1) – the free movement of goods, services, capital, and labor – is the path to the kind of "*universal* opulence [that] extends itself to the lowest rank of the people" (*WN* 1.1.10).[4] But such "universal opulence" is by no means inevitable: to the extent that states interfere with the free operation of markets – to the extent that organized economic interests are able to insulate themselves from competition through public policy (*WN* 4.2.43) – the wealth of the nation is depressed and the well-being of its inhabitants compromised.

Here, Smith is hopeful but far from certain: for him, "kings and ministers" are characterized by their "capricious ambition" (*WN* 4.3.48), and by their too frequent willingness to make use of the "partial and oppressive" instruments of a beggar-thy-neighbor "political economy" (*WN* 4.9.28). In fact, at times, Smith expresses a kind of hopelessness about the prospects of improvements in governance: "The violence and injustice of the rulers of mankind is an ancient evil, for which, I am afraid, the nature of human affairs can scarce admit of a remedy" (*WN* 4.3.38). Thankfully, though, political progress is not a prerequisite of economic development: "the natural effort of every individual to better his condition ... is so powerful a principle," says Smith, that it is capable of "surmounting a hundred impertinent obstructions with which the folly of human laws too often encumbers its operations." The result, of course, is the "wealth and prosperity" of society *in spite of* the actions of those who control the instruments of political power (*WN* 4.5.82). And eventually – as the "silent and insensible operation of ... commerce and manufactures" (*WN* 3.4.10) advances, inexorably – the gradual introduction of "order and good government, and with them, the liberty and security of individuals" is more and more likely, though not necessarily inevitable (*WN* 3.4.4).[5]

2

If Smith's thought is characterized by a kind of guarded optimism – the future is bright, he teaches, so long as statesmen and legislators refrain from arresting the progress generated by economic liberty – his German disciples, Kant the most important among them, draw much firmer, more confident conclusions from the theory of the "invisible hand" (*WN* 4.2.9). Indeed, according to Kant, a clear-sighted observer will "discover a *purpose in nature* behind this senseless course of human events" (*IUH* 42); elsewhere, he speaks of "*a regular progression* among freely willed actions," and of "a *steadily advancing*" (*IUH* 41), "*definite* plan" (*IUH* 42) for human beings put in place by "the design of a wise creator" (*IUH* 45; see also *PP* 108 and 112).[6] And that plan is gradually actualized, unconsciously, by the self-interested activity of individuals: "Individual men ... little imagine that, while they are pursuing their own ends, each in his own way and often in opposition to others, they are unwittingly guided in their advance along a course intended by nature. They are unconsciously promoting an end which, even if they knew what it was, would scarcely arouse their interest" (*IUH* 41). Nature is not "an aimless, random process," governed by "the dismal reign of chance"; it is a "teleological" process tending toward definite and discernable ends (*IUH* 42). And human beings are the agents of this plan, though they do not know it; their agentic status does not change their motives, or actions, in any way.

And what are those ends, exactly? First, Kant speaks of the cultivation of reason: man, he says, "is the only rational creature on earth," and because "all natural capacities are destined sooner or later to be developed completely," "nature's original intention" is the complete development of reason. But "reason does not work instinctively: ... [it] requires trials, practice and instruction" (*IUH* 42); reason is a "germ implanted by nature in our species," and, like any such seed, is in need of careful nurturing and nourishment (*IUH* 43). And the essential source of such nourishment, somewhat counterintuitively, is struggle: man's "insight and circumspection and the goodness of his will ... the highest degree of [his] skill, [the] inner perfection in his manner of thought, [even his eventual] happiness" – all, says Kant, are the by-product of conflict with nature and competition with others (*IUH* 43). At first, human beings must overcome their original, "utmost barbarism" through ingenuity, cleverness, and will; nature, after all, exercised "the strictest economy" in the sparing design of our "basic animal equipment" – no "bull's horns [or] lion's claws [or] dog's teeth [for us], but only hands" – and so, for whatever well-being and comfort we have heroically scraped from nature, the credit belongs entirely to us (*IUH* 43).

And this dual refinement and expansion of reason is accelerated by living together. Here, Kant's argument rests on what he calls our "unsocial sociability" – our "inclination to *live in society* ... but also to *live as an individual*" (*IUH* 44). We are inexorably drawn to living in communities, that is, *but at the same time* find that others are constantly thwarting our will "to direct everything in accordance with [our] own ideas" (*IUH* 44); we regard others as necessary to our well-being, but also, often, as impediments to our happiness. Such is nature's plan: "It is this very resistance," says Kant, "which awakens all man's powers" (*IUH* 44); it is "the desire for honour, power, or property ... that drives [man] to seek status among his fellows, whom he cannot *bear* yet cannot *bear to leave*" (*IUH* 44). And such status-seeking and wealth accumulation require "that [man] abandon idleness and inactive self-sufficiency, and plunge instead into labour and hardships"; hence Kant's belief that "all human talents would remain hidden forever in a dormant state" without "social incompatibility, enviously competitive vanity, and insatiable desires for possession" (*IUH* 45).

In some ways, this argument can be traced back to Smith: "Commerce," he says, "encourages every man to apply himself to a particular occupation, and to cultivate and bring to perfection whatever talent or genius he may possess for that particular species of business" (*WN* 1.2.3). And, for Smith, commerce also *disciplines* this process of self-realization, because it *necessarily* develops the desirable, productive habits of "economy, industry, discretion, attention, and application of thought ... prudence, vigilance, circumspection, temperance, constancy, firmness" (*TMS* 7.2.3). After all, in a market society, where every person "becomes in some measure a merchant" (*WN* 1.4.1), all must respond to, and diligently satisfy, the needs and desires of their "customers" (*WN* 1.10.86); and success in this endeavor depends on "solid professional abilities, joined to prudent, just, firm, and temperate conduct" and on "the favour and good opinion of ... neighbours and equals" (*TMS* 1.3.3). In other words, a society dominated by the pursuit of self-interest *also happens to be* a moral society; once again, the market channels the *potentially* socially destructive pursuit of wealth and status into the socially beneficial pursuit of deserved esteem and solid, honest reputation (*TMS* 1.3.2).

But our innate sociability and need for the approbation of others – both actualized by commerce – do not absolve us of the need for a state. Quite the opposite: without a legitimate and capable state, says Smith, "liberty, reason, and the happiness of mankind" cannot "flourish" (*WN* 5.1.213). After all, without a state, commerce cannot function properly; think, for example, of the state's provision of the requisite market-supporting infrastructure, what Smith calls the "public works and institutions for facilitating the commerce of society": armies and fleets for external defense, systems of transport (too expensive to be delivered by private firms), a judicial system to resolve internal disputes, state institutions capable of enforcing complex tax regimes and punishing defectors, and so on (*LJ* 239).[7] In fact, the entirety of book 5 of the *Wealth of Nations* is devoted to a detailed analysis of the proper functions of government, as well as how to pay for them; without these "public works and institutions," that "universal opulence" simply is not possible. Luckily, though, a well-functioning market economy generates enough wealth – and taxation revenue – to ensure the effective provision of this infrastructure.

Kant too emphasizes the crucial distinction between natural and civil freedom. The presence of others, and our natural competitive desire to best them, provides the necessary spur to productive activity and the concomitant development of our talents. But the "continual antagonism" (*IUH* 45) that characterizes social life also presents a problem: we are also perpetually fearful of others, whose "unrestrained freedom" is a menace to our own freedom, happiness, and property; "It is impossible" for creatures like us, says Kant, "to exist side by side for long in a state of wild freedom" (*IUH* 46; see also *TP* 73). The solution, of course, is to "renounce this brutish freedom and seek calm and security within a law-governed constitution" (*IUH* 49), the purpose of which is to provide "the most precise specification and preservation of the limits of freedom" among equals (*IUH* 45; see also *PP* 112–13 and *TP* part 2). In fact, for Kant, civil society is the essential precondition of the "development of all natural capacities": without the freedom secured by law – without "a civil society [that] can administer justice" – "all the culture and art which adorn mankind" simply cannot exist; lawless freedom makes us grow "stunted, bent and twisted" (*IUH* 46). And civil freedom is the precondition of prosperity too: without law to govern our interactions, "the vitality of business in general and hence also the strength of the whole are held in check" (*IUH* 50).[8] That is why Kant speaks of the establishment of "a society [that secures] freedom under external laws" as "the highest task which nature has set for mankind" (*IUH* 45); it is also "the most difficult" (*IUH* 46).

## 3

As we have seen, the *Wealth of Nations* – and especially book 4 – is a thoroughgoing attack on the assumptions, and practices, of European trade in the eighteenth century. Smith is trying to expose what is in his view a deeply mistaken belief that international trade is a zero-sum game: "Each nation," he says, "has been made to look with an invidious eye upon the prosperity of all the nations with which it trades, and to consider their gain as its own loss" (*WN* 4.3.38). Prosperity, according to this "mercantile system" of thought, consists in "the depression of all ... neighbours" (*WN* 4.8.1); it requires, for one, that domestic merchants and manufacturers be insulated from foreign competition through protectionist measures, such as high duties, tariffs, and even outright prohibitions on imported goods (*WN* 4.2.1). And, in many cases, powerful economic actors are insulated from domestic competition too. Here, Smith cites the counterproductive colonial policies of Europe's powerful states: the state-sanctioned monopolies possessed by the East India Companies of Holland, England, and France disadvantage consumers at home (*WN* 4.1.33) and also undermine the development of productive markets abroad (*WN* 4.7.95).[9]

Instead, Smith wants to show that, through trade, *we can all get rich together*: "Commerce," he says, "ought naturally to be, among nations, as among individuals, a bond of union and friendship" (*WN* 4.3.38). After all, open borders lead to the ramping up – the gradual globalization – of the division of labor. Here, Smith discusses the productive, mutually beneficial specialization that takes place when nations trade freely: if the French can produce a better, cheaper bottle of red wine, Smith asks, why shouldn't we Scots trade our better, cheaper wool for it (*WN* 4.2.15)? Why not get rich together by selling to each other the things that we are each the best at making? What is the point of developing the ability to rival French wine? This is bound to be an extremely expensive, laborious, time-consuming process, a process that will direct capital away from more productive, more efficient, and therefore more profitable enterprises. Why not employ our capital in the most effective way?

Why not focus on raising the fattest sheep and producing the highest quality wool in the world? The market, in other words, ought to be a pacific force in the lives of states: it is very bad business, after all, to wage war upon and kill your customers.

This is a prominent theme in Kant's political philosophy too: that, much like the path to reason and to good government, the possibility of lasting peace – the "end to all hostilities" between states, *in perpetuity* (*PP* 93) – is neither "fantastic [nor] overstrained" (*PP* 108); perpetual peace is *not* "an empty chimera" (*PP* 114). But to achieve this aim, there are certain active commitments that all states must undertake: they must negotiate the cessation of hostilities in good faith (*PP* 93), refrain from levying punitive, unsustainable rates of interest on foreign debts (*PP* 95), refuse to employ "dishonourable stratagems" that interfere with the internal political affairs of other states, such as "the instigation of treason" or the "diabolical" use of "spies, assassins [and] poisoners" (*PP* 96–7), and, perhaps most demandingly, gradually abolish standing armies, the existence of which "spur on states to outdo one another in arming unlimited soldiers," and thus "make peace more oppressive than a short war" (*PP* 94).[10]

Kant is not naive, though: "each state," he says, still "sees its own majesty precisely in not having to submit to any external legal constraint," such as these requisite articles of peace. In other words, sovereignty is still believed to encompass the right to declare and wage war, and to undermine the cohesion and stability of one's enemies. Thankfully, though, Kant believes that perpetual peace is, in the end, not the outcome of conscious moral choices by politicians; the cause of peace, rather, is advanced by the "self-seeking inclinations" (*PP* 112) of individual citizens: it is through trade, says Kant, "that nations first entered into *peaceful relations* with one another, and thus achieved mutual understanding [and a] community of interests,... even with their most distant fellows" (*PP* 111). And it is through trade – what Kant later calls "the spirit of commerce, [which] sooner or later takes hold of every people" (*PP* 114) – that the cause of perpetual peace is advanced, however inadvertently and unconsciously. After all, productive commerce "cannot exist side by side with war" (*PP* 114), which requires "increasingly high expenditure on standing armies," leads to a steady rise in "the price of all necessities [without] any proportionate increase in metal currencies," saps all those "resources saved during [peace]," and eventually redirects revenues toward the servicing of "national debt" (*TP* 90; see also *PP* 100). War, simply put, is bad for business, and so "states find themselves compelled to promote the noble cause of peace, though not exactly from motives of morality" (*PP* 114).

Of course, there is an important political precondition at work here: that the state is well-ordered, in a very specific sense – that "citizens"[11] have "the right to vote on ... legislation"[12] and, as a result, that the laws reflect "the will of the entire people" (*TP* 77). Kant calls such a regime "republican" (*PP* 99): its "public laws" pass "the test of rightfulness," because they "guarantee everyone his freedom," and also advance "the commonwealth's prosperity" (*TP* 79–80). The contrast, here, is to "despotism" (*PP* 101), the regime committed solely to the ruler's "desire for aggrandisement" (*TP* 91). In such a state, "war actually costs nothing" (*TP* 90) for the person with the power to declare and wage it: "War will not force him to make the slightest sacrifice so far as his banquets, hunts, pleasure palaces and court festivals are concerned" (*PP* 100); its burdens fall on the people, who must "[do] the fighting, [supply] the cost of war from their own resources, painfully [make] good the ensuing devastation, and, as the crowning evil, take upon themselves a burden of debt which will embitter peace and which can never be paid off on account of the constant threat of new wars" (*PP* 100). In a well-ordered republic, by contrast, where "the consent of the citizens is required to decide whether or not war is to be declared" (*PP* 100), violent conflict is comparatively very unlikely: the people know that they will be the ones to bear its costs – personally and financially – and so "they will have great hesitation in embarking on so dangerous an enterprise" (*PP* 100). Peace is thus produced, says Kant, by "the love of each age for itself" (*TP* 90–1).

## 4

And yet, Kant and Smith *are* also plagued by lingering moments of doubt. Kant, for example, recognizes that the drive to accumulate wealth can become all encompassing, drawing us away from more exalted human pursuits, such as the development and refinement of our moral and aesthetic sensibilities (see, e.g., *IUH* 45; *TP* 89; *PP* 106; and *MM* 149). And in book 5 of *The Wealth of Nations*, Smith expresses a similar sentiment: he laments the mind-numbing, soul-crushing drudgery to which a growing majority of wage-laborers must submit; and he raises important concerns about the socially and politically destructive consequences of work under capitalism (see, e.g., *WN* 5.1.78; and *LJ* 253–9). For example, when a man spends his "whole life ... performing a few simple operations," as is typical under the workshop division of labor, "he has no occasion to exert his understanding ... [he] becomes as stupid and ignorant as it is possible for a human creature to become" (*WN* 5.1.10). This is very bad for the worker, of course: labor is the source of misery, not the self-realizing development of the talents, as it ought to be (and actually is for some). But this *also* constitutes a profound loss for the wider society too: when the majority are reduced to thoughtless automatons, there is a precipitous decline in the prevailing levels of "intellectual and social virtue" (*WN* 5.1.10). Workers may own leather shoes and woolen coats – and they may drink tea on the way to work, during their breaks and after supper – but the general well-being of society is *not* improved in any meaningful sense (cf. *WN* 1.1.10).[13]

No wonder, then, that Karl Marx, to whom we turn in chapter 7, found much to admire in Smith's thought. In fact, Marx's account of alienated labor can be traced directly to *The Wealth of Nations*![14] And yet, at bottom, Marx surely found that discussion deeply unsatisfying: what Smith says, in the end, is that the solution to the monotonous and stultifying division of labor is universal access to "those most essential parts of education," financed and promoted by the state (*WN* 5.1.182). Without accessible public schooling for children, that is, "gross ignorance and stupidity" would spread among, and "benumb," the ranks of working people (*WN* 5.1.10).[15] With such access, by contrast, even workers will be able to make "proper use of [their] intellectual faculties," despite the heavy mental burden of repetitive work (*WN* 5.1.10). As we shall see, Marx offers a much more radical solution to the problem of alienated labor – to put it mildly! Indeed, Smith's discussion of state education is, in the end, part of his attempt to show that market society *does* constitute progress – political, economic, *and* moral – and that its benefits *can* still be democratized. What is required to achieve that *universal* opulence – a rise in the standard of living *for the majority* – is calculated and intelligent (not excessive and overbearing) intervention by the state.

# 5

# "Make Money Contemptible and, if Possible, Useless": Rousseau on Modern Discontent

In his *Theory of Moral Sentiments*, Adam Smith describes the sorts of "inferior virtues" that tend to proliferate in commercial societies: because merchants need to attract and retain customers in a competitive environment, they must practice "prudence, vigilance, circumspection, temperance, constancy, firmness" (*TMS* 7.2.3.15). Elsewhere, he speaks of the "less violent and turbulent passions" that merchants must cultivate and exhibit to succeed: "decency, modesty, and moderation ... industry and frugality" (*TMS* 6.3.13). Such behavior is hardly "dazzling," Smith concedes; we may not love or even admire this system of values, not the way we would the courage and fortitude of, say, the ancient Romans. But it *is* deserving of our "esteem," however "cold" that esteem may be (6.1.14). After all, a commercial society is likely to be a tranquil society: its inhabitants are wholly absorbed in their private concerns – family and health, reputation and wealth – and so are content to leave "the public business" of government to be managed by others; they want only to "walk in the humble paths of private and peaceable life" (*TMS* 6.3.13 and 6.1.13). *That* is why market society possesses a novel and desirable solidity: it is devoid of zealous, destabilizing political ambition, and it is overstuffed with the sort of private, calculating ambition that knits us into sturdy, tangled webs of buyers and sellers.

Such a view is familiar to us, of course, though many of Smith's contemporaries experienced this retreat into private life as a profound loss.[1] For example, in his *Essay on the History of Civil Society*, Adam Ferguson celebrates the civic harmony of the ancient world and laments the atomism of modern market society. Greek and Roman citizens, he says, thought of themselves, first and foremost, as "part of a community" (*EHCS* 2.3.3); for them, "the individual was nothing, and the public everything" (*EHCS* 1.8.19). Under such psychic circumstances, the essential source of lasting happiness is contributing to the common good (see, e.g., *EHCS* 1.8.18 and 1.9.3). For modern citizens engaged in commerce, by contrast, "the individual is everything, and the public nothing" (*EHCS* 1.8.19). Twenty-three years later, in his *Reflections on the Revolution in France*, Edmund Burke expresses a similar sentiment: there, Burke blames the destructive "spirit of money-jobbing and speculation" for the eventual dissolution of France's political institutions; the impulse to accumulate wealth, he says, is incompatible with the virtues and character necessary for good government (*RRF* 160 and 258–69).[2]

The most famous voice in this critical chorus is Jean-Jacques Rousseau: the guiding thread of Rousseau's oeuvre is his belief that commercial society ultimately destroys human happiness; it does so by nurturing and greatly increasing the unnecessary wants to such an extent that we become incapable of lasting satisfaction. And this pervasive, all-encompassing dissatisfaction in turn destroys the possibility of good citizenship: the more dominant our interest in personal gratification – the more relentless our desire for "all those vicious ornaments" of fashion (*FD* 7) – the less we care about the well-being of others.[3] It is only modern man, laments Rousseau, who can "say in secret at the sight of another suffering: 'Perish if you will; I am safe'" (*SD* 54). In Rousseau's mind, such indifference to the plight of others represents a radical departure from – a dulling, a disfiguring of – human nature: we are *good*, he says, *naturally* good, and it is modern society that makes us bad. How did we fall so far?

## 1

The *Discourse on the Origins of Inequality* begins in a strange and unexpected place: the primeval forest – Rousseau's version of the state of nature.[4] There, we encounter "savage man": he is recognizable to us – he walks on two feet, he uses his hands as we use ours, he has no talons, no claws, no fur – but he is still more animal than human; he possesses no language, no permanent home, no lasting connections. One moment, he satisfies his "hunger under an oak tree"; the next, he quenches "his thirst at the first stream" he finds; at night, he makes his "bed at the foot of the same tree that supplied his meal" (*SD* 47). And thus, adds Rousseau, "*all his needs are satisfied*," easily so, by the earth's massive plenty (*SD* 47). There *are* dangers in the state of nature, to be sure: inclement weather, ferocious beasts, the inevitable injuries of a rough-and-tumble life. But savage man is strong, robust, agile: his body is not enervated by easy access to axes, slings, and ladders (to say nothing of doctors and medicine). And he is clever too: he observes and imitates all the other animals – constantly acquiring new ideas and new skills in the process – and he knows when to fight and when to flee. Savage man, in short, is *healthy*. And this is true not only of his body, but of his mind too.

Here, we encounter the reason for – and payoff of – Rousseau's odd anthropology:[5] savage man does not want anything he cannot easily obtain – nourishment, shelter, rest, temporary companionship, all are omnipresent, all abundant. And this has important psychic consequences: savage man is happy, satisfied, *whole*; his needs and desires are perfectly commensurate with his abilities and with what is available to him, and he cannot imagine their expansion. He is, to use a modern idiom, fully *present*: "His soul, agitated by nothing, is given over to the single feeling of his own existence, without any idea of the future" (*SD* 55). Clearly, we are not describing a "full-fledged philosopher": savage man has no need for, or interest in, metaphysics, abstraction, language even (*SD* 56). *But that is a key part of his happiness*: a central theme of the *Second Discourse* is that cleverness – the emergence and development of "cultivated reason," ingenuity, the ability to project a future, to compare ourselves to others – is the cause of our misery (*SD* 61). And "what kind of misery could there [possibly] be," Rousseau asks, "for a free being whose heart is at peace and whose body is in good health" (*SD* 60)?

Inevitably, savage man will come across others. But these encounters are infrequent, fleeting, and pacific: savage man has no interest in community, but neither does he have any interest in hurting or subduing those he meets; he possesses a natural well of repugnance for the suffering of all sentient creatures (*SD* 62).[6] He is solitary but not lonely, vulnerable but self-sufficient, primitive but humane, simple but happy. *This* is the demanding ideal against which Rousseau measures his contemporaries – "the pure movement of nature prior to all reflection" (*SD* 62). And modern man – *reflective* man, *social* man – looks awful in this light: the further away he falls from nature – from the noble, placid life of the savage – the less happy he is likely to be. How *did* this fall happen?

Savage man is animal-*like*, certainly, but there is, according to Rousseau, one *very* big difference: animal nature is static, human nature is dynamic; animals are forever slaves to their instincts – a cat will starve "atop a pile of fruit or grain" (*SD* 52) – but man is *free* – free to ignore his instincts, free to change, free to improve and perhaps even perfect himself, but also free to fall away from goodness. In other words, our dynamism introduces an element of danger into our history: the more we change, the further we move away from simplicity and, with it, wholeness; hence the *apparent* inevitability of our misery – this combination of our cleverness and our plasticity.

For example, in part 2 of the *Second Discourse*, Rousseau describes the "first revolution," the invention of tools, "hatchets made of hard, sharp stones," which are used to "cut wood, dig up the soil and [later to] make huts [of] clay and mud" (*SD* 71). And the settlement revolution, he adds, changes *us*. No, *we* change *ourselves* by settling down – our bodies *and* our minds. Settlement makes us *soft*: the leisure facilitated by technology withers our once-strong bodies; in fact, the more advanced our technology, the more enslaved we become to the division of labor and the more alienated we become from our real *human* powers. And, perhaps worse, we suddenly *need* things we did not need before – property, comfort, distinction – the absence of which we now experience as deeply painful (*SD* 72).

Now, there *are* certain consolations for this unexpected dependence on people and on things: as we settle and form communities, we also develop the bonds of genuine love – for our family and the members of our tribe. This can be meaningful and indeed very pleasant. In fact, Rousseau calls this early tribal phase of human history the "happiest epoch" (*SD* 74). But this era is also pregnant with something sinister: when we live with others, we also tend to become dependent on them. According to Rousseau, this is true in two distinct senses: first, we become *materially* dependent on others – as necessary links in the division of labor, as suppliers of the things we now anxiously crave. Of course, *this* form of dependence becomes more acute as society grows more technologically advanced and more commercial – a theme to which we return below. We *also* come to depend on others for our *emotional* needs – for affection, for recognition, for respect.

This is a crucial step in Rousseau's argument – the rise of *amour-propre*.[7] The more time we spend around others, he says, the more apt we are to notice differences – to draw comparisons – between them: we see that some are strong, smart, and productive, others are weak, dim-witted, and lazy; some are beautiful, others are ugly; some have perfect pitch, others are tone deaf (*SD* 73). And each of us desperately wants to be "the most highly regarded," no matter the metric of comparison (*SD* 73). In fact, this becomes an all-consuming need: we find that we cannot be happy *without* the high regard of others. "As soon as men had begun to mutually value one another," says Rousseau, "and the idea of esteem was formed in their minds ... it was no longer possible for anyone to be lacking it with impunity" (*SD* 73).

Thus, we are no longer able to provide entirely for ourselves (as we once were): our material (so-called) needs are now too complex and multifaceted for a single person to master; and we also need to be seen, and esteemed, by others in order to feel good and whole. This latter form of (emotional) dependence is especially debilitating. If we are lucky, we may have enough money to buy (or resources to barter for) whatever we happen to want at any given moment (the satisfaction from the accumulation of *things* never lasts). But we can never *really* control *how* other people see us or *whether* they see us at all, no matter how hard we try. In other words, our emotional happiness – once easily and independently secured simply by *being* alive – *now* depends on something evasive and inchoate – the fluid and ephemeral economy of esteem. And our solid sense of self disappears too – a satisfying feeling of knowing ourselves, a feeling of true *being*, of real authenticity. We now live only to please others – we are obsessed with *seeming to be* whatever merits their esteem – even though we find such recognition difficult to gain and impossible to keep.

According to Rousseau, this indicates something structurally problematic about social life itself: living with others *can* be the source of genuine pleasure and deep meaning, *but this paradise rarely lasts*; and living there, temporarily, puts our heirs at grave risk for real suffering. Indeed, social life eventually and typically – *perhaps* inevitably – makes us very bad and very unhappy: anxious and insecure, desirous and dissatisfied, preening and vain, vacillating and inauthentic. Nowhere is this easier to see – nowhere is the distinction between seeming and being more apparent and more consequential – than in the marketplace; that is why the nadir of Rousseau's sorry history is the full flowering of commercial (bourgeois) society. Merchants, he says, *by their very nature*, are actors and hypocrites, all desperately trying to carve out some "advantage" – money, influence, power – by selling people whatever they happen to want (*SD* 77). To succeed, they must convince others that "they are of useful service to them"; they must employ "grandiose ostentation [and] deceptive cunning," while wearing "the mask of benevolence" (*SD* 77). They may, in the process, become "rich" (*SD* 77). But that wealth is purchased at the price of their freedom! After all, even the most successful merchant becomes a "slave ... to his fellowmen": his "consuming ambition" – the infinite "zeal for raising the relative level of his fortune" – means that he depends on others – as customers, as employees, as the sources of envy – and must orient his persona to attract them (*SD* 77).[8] In other words, commercial man is the complete antithesis of savage man: the latter is *incapable* of artifice, the former is *all* artifice.

*This* is where we encounter the real depth of Rousseau's critique of bourgeois society: it is not *just* that commercial societies are chock full of silly, pointless things to buy – the sorts of things that vain people want in order to incite the very real jealousy of their equally vain peers. That is true, of course, but it doesn't take a genius to see this. In fact, what Rousseau is saying is that commerce leads to the total loss of genuine selfhood. There is simply no *there* there: "Everything is reduced to appearances, everything becomes factitious and deceptive ... in the midst of so much ... politeness ... we have only a deceitful and frivolous exterior" (*SD* 91). This is equally true of rich and poor, employers and employees, producers and consumers. What is worse, adds Rousseau, is that we don't even realize that this is happening: we *think* we are free – to buy and to sell, to live and to work – but the reality is that we are now *wholly constituted* by outside forces beyond our control – for our sense of self, for our desires, for our well-being. "We are always asking others what we are," says Rousseau, "and never dare to question ourselves on this matter" (*SD* 91). Of course, this puts the introductory discussion of this chapter in a strange new light: there, Adam Smith looks at the marketplace and sees it teeming with upstanding, hardworking entrepreneurs, all keenly attentive to the needs of their fellows and diligently trying to fulfill them. Rousseau sees something *very* different, something dark and depraved: soulless, empty shells – totally unaware of their soullessness and emptiness – waiting to be filled and emptied and refilled by the day's passing fancies.

## 2

In the *Second Discourse*, Rousseau traces our misery to the (somewhat surprising) willingness to *work*: savage man, he says, "has a mortal hatred" of labor, the antithesis of his easy-going freedom (*SD* 57). And yet, he allows himself to be domesticated by it – first by settlement, then by agriculture, and later (because of a truly improbable sequence of events) by metallurgy (*SD* 75). Why? Because "man realized that it was useful for a single individual to have provisions for two" (*SD* 74). A simple yet fateful realization. This desire for more, and for better, requires that the ambitious conscript the help of others. Soon, the dense, rewarding bonds of familial love are dissolved by new relations – owner and worker – and nature's once public plenty is appropriated by labor: "vast forests transformed into smiling fields ... watered with men's sweat" (*SD* 75). Indeed, this pathological drive – activated, and then accelerated, by the increasingly pressing need for esteem – generates the whole oppressive constellation of modern institutions: private property and the division of labor, commerce and prosperity, inequality and class conflict, justice, law, and (finally) statehood.

It is here, in the discussion of property and work, that we encounter the fundamental aim of the *Second Discourse*: to "trace the source of the [present] inequality among men" (*SD* 39). In the state of nature, inequality exists, Rousseau concedes, but the effect of such inequalities is nil: because there are no lasting relations, and all are self-sufficient, differences in intelligence, strength, and ability simply do not matter; such natural inequalities have no bearing on individuals' ability to survive or be happy (*SD* 91). Of course, in settled society, things are *very* different: once the land has been divided up – "to the point of covering the entire landscape and of all bordering on one another" (*SD* 77) – survival and happiness are permanently insecure. Of course, this is true of the wage-earning poor, who must now subject themselves to "domination and servitude ... subjugation and enslavement" in order to survive (*SD* 78). But, in Rousseau's telling, the land-owning rich do not fare very well either: they live in perpetual fear of "violence and thefts" – of the "acts of brigandage" by roving "troops of bandits" (*SD* 78).[9] And their anxiety is ramped up even more by the tenuousness of their claim to the land: the rich, says Rousseau, know full well that their property was acquired "merely by force" and that, by extension, their ownership of it is established "on nothing but a precarious and abusive right" (*SD* 78). What is established by force can always be taken away by a greater force.

The solution to this quandary is the state, of course, which, by fixing the present distribution of land as *private property*, protected by the full force of the law, transforms the "adroit usurpation" of the past into an "irrevocable right," now and in perpetuity (*SD* 79). Hence Rousseau's belief that the state, "the most thought-out project that ever entered the human mind," *had* to be "finally conceived" by "a rich man" (*SD* 79). He soon goes further than that: law-governed civil society is not *just* a profound idea; it is a profound *con job* perpetrated *on* the poor *by* the rich who promise peace, justice, and liberty for all; all they ask, in exchange, is for the post hoc legitimation of their past crimes – their appropriation of the commons without the unanimous consent of all affected parties (*SD* 78). Why would those with nothing to protect agree to such a bargain? Simply because men are "easily seduced": they "ran to chain themselves" to the obligations of citizenship "in the belief that they secured their liberty" (*SD* 79).[10] What they received, instead, was "new fetters," a life of "labour, servitude, and misery" (*SD* 79). Indeed, the legal regime to which they must now submit does not *abolish* inequality, as it claims to do, by protecting the equal liberty of all. No, the social contract *institutionalizes* the reign "of property and of inequality"; it makes "the profit of a few ambitious men" the purpose and exclusive aim of social life, at the expense of the well-being of everyone else (*SD* 79).

According to Rousseau, such a regime is remarkably, disappointingly stable: the people "allow themselves to be oppressed" – by a king, an aristocracy, a parliament even, whatever the case may be[11] – for they too are driven by "blind ambition," by the vain hope that they can one day join the ranks of the masters (*SD* 87). In other words, Rousseau once again traces our misery to the frenzied need for distinction: "We consent to wear chains," he says, "in order to be able to give them in turn to others" (*SD* 87). And we know that this longing for mastery – a longing born of slavery – has grave psychological consequences: it extinguishes the desire for liberty altogether; the longer we have a master, the less we experience our oppression as oppressive. "The value [of liberty] is felt only as long as one" is free, says Rousseau; we lose "the taste for [it]" when we are reduced to slavery (*SD* 82). This is fertile ground for "despotism" – for the assumption of "arbitrary power" – after which "the people no longer have leaders or laws, but only tyrants" (*SD* 89). Indeed, it is no surprise, says Rousseau, that we "see oppression continually increase ... the rights of citizens and national liberties gradually die out, and the protests of the weak treated like seditious murmurs" – the inevitable result of living with others *as dependents* (*SD* 88). Thus ends the *Second Discourse*, with "the final stage of inequality," which, ironically, is a return to equality: "all private individuals become equals again," laments Rousseau, "*because they are nothing*" vis-à-vis the state that dominates them (*SD* 89; italics added).


# 3


Is freedom possible *in* society? Can we live with others *and* be happy? Based on the arguments of the *Second Discourse*, the answer is, *probably not*: there is, it seems, something about living with others that activates a latent, pathological, all-encompassing desire for esteem; this desire is present – *lurking* – in all of us, and it leads us to inequality, domination, subservience, and, finally, tyranny. At bottom, then, Rousseau's argument bears a striking resemblance to the Christian doctrine of original sin: the theological principle that man is an irredeemably evil creature – badness is built into his very being – and that salvation is an exclusive property of the life to come. In fact, Rousseau explicitly rejects this conclusion: man *is* naturally good, he says, and it is his social relations that determine his character. Change those relations, *and you change man with them*. In other words, our present misery is not necessary or inevitable; it *is* possible to imagine a radical reconstruction of social life and, with it, human nature.

Rousseau gestures toward this argument in part 2 of the *Second Discourse*; there, he traces the history of despotism and finds its source at the founding moment of civil society: because the social contract reflects, and legitimizes, prevailing inequalities (of wealth), it sets in motion relations of mastery and servitude, domination and dependence – with all the accompanying psychological and political drawbacks.[12] In other words, a faulty foundation makes an unsound house: "Because it had been badly begun," says Rousseau, not even "the labours of the wisest legislators ... could ... repair the vices of [that] constitution" (*SD* 81). It is therefore necessary, he immediately adds, to "[clear] the air and [put] aside all the old materials, as Lycurgus did in Sparta, in order to raise a good edifice later on" (*SD* 81). A fascinating and important passage: when our political institutions are based on, and perpetuate, inequality, they permanently extinguish our natural goodness – our ability to live well and happily with others. Now, this surely make us lament our bad luck course in the past: natural man *is* good and was unlucky to be thrust into a situation that drew out his worst self. But Rousseau's emphasis on starting over should *also* make us hopeful for the future: if we engage in the (very) radical redesign of our political institutions, it *is* possible to revive, harness, and give full vent to the salutary natural composition of the human sentiments.

*This* is the task of political philosophy: not to critique the status quo, though Rousseau spends quite a lot of time and energy on that! No, the key task of political philosophy is *constructive*, not *critical* – to outline the political institutional arrangements conducive to stability *and* to the genuine, lasting happiness of individual citizens. This is no easy thing: Rousseau's *Social Contract* repeatedly emphasizes the need to fundamentally reprogram – *denature* – man in order to make him fit for political life (*SC* 2.7).[13] Human beings, after all, are constitutionally self-centered: they are *not* the sort of creatures who find happiness or satisfaction in being immersed in collectives; this is true of *both* savage and civil man. Rousseau accepts this: he takes "men as they are" as the basic building block of his scheme, and he also acknowledges that dislodging that natural solipsism is the hardest thing to do.

As we have already seen, Rousseau's model is the ancient city-state, especially Sparta: what is required to transform human nature, first and foremost, he says, is *public education*. This Lycurgus knew well: Spartan law "kept watch chiefly over the education of children [which] established mores that *nearly* dispensed with having to add laws to them" (*SD* 87; italics added).[14] But education alone is not enough, not anymore: in his dedicatory letter of the *Second Discourse* – addressed to his fellow citizens of Geneva – Rousseau also stresses the necessary material conditions for stability. For example, the "possibility of being well governed," he says, depends on a small, homogeneous population: "All private individuals [must be] known to each other," otherwise "the obscure maneuvers of vice" can be hidden from "the judgement of the public" (*SD* 31).[15] It is also essential that the division of labor – and with it, the economy – remain primitive and underdeveloped: we must not get *too* rich, warns Rousseau, lest our city become riven by class conflict from within – by its antagonistic division into rich and poor – and a tempting target for conquest from without (*SD* 35).

It is here, in his discussion of the damning effects of market society, that Rousseau's pessimism drifts back up to the surface: the selfish inclinations can never be *fully* eradicated, he implicitly concedes, no matter how rigorous and well-designed our public pedagogy; and so the self-regarding inclinations must also be tamed by – are perhaps most effectively tamed by – the legal and punitive force of the state. For example, Rousseau suggests the implementation and strict enforcement of sumptuary laws; luxury, after all, is "the worst of all evils in any state whatever" (*SD* 103).[16] And he also emphasizes the need for careful state censorship of the arts and (especially) advances in the sciences, without which ambitious citizens may try to monetize, and profit from, breakthroughs in knowledge and technology (*SC* 4.7). The essential purpose of these laws is to discourage economic development and, with it, a commercial ethos, both of which nurse individual self-interest and so threaten communal feeling.[17] In precisely this spirit, Rousseau draws a distinction between those virtuous *citizens* of ancient republics and self-seeking, politically apathetic modern *bourgeois*: the former are animated by public-spirited courage, while the latter are wholly absorbed by selfish pursuits (*SC* 1.7).

But more than patriotism is at stake here: our freedom is too! After all, we have already seen the psychological and political consequences of unrestrained selfishness: inequality, dependence, despotism. In Rousseau's mind, these threats must be answered with the full force of the law: citizens, to use his famously enigmatic formulation, must be "*forced to be free*" (*SC* 1.7). The law, in other words, must protect citizens from themselves – from their basic inclination to *prefer* themselves, to institutionalize that preference in the legal relations that govern social life, and to thus set in motion social and political processes that end in their servitude (and indeed in the servitude of all). Hence, Rousseau's firm, unrelenting emphasis on the need for *complete and total legal equality*: when our legal institutions generate (and validate) hierarchical relations – relations of rulers and subjects – we are all reduced to slavery (even the masters); when, conversely, legal relations are characterized by strict equality – when the law applies equally to all *citizens* – our liberty is secure, for no one can amend the laws in the hopes of enslaving others. A law rooted in equality, says Rousseau, "cannot harm one of the members without attacking the whole body"; hence his confident claim that "the force of the state [i.e., the law] *creates* the freedom of its members" by securing them "against all personal dependence" (*SC* 1.7 and 2.12; italics added).[18]

In Rousseau's mind, the gravest threat to such equality is economic *in*equality: it is always the richest members of the community, he warns, who try to evade the laws, who see themselves as exempt from – indeed, *above* – the law, who try to deform the law into an instrument of their own profit (*SC* 3.10). It is therefore essential, he says, that the law is *inviolable* and *unlimited*: that no citizen – no matter how wealthy or influential or powerful – can bend the law to better suit his interests (or break the laws that run counter to them), and that no domain of human life stands outside the legislative reach of the state. As an example of such absolutist powers, consider Rousseau's discussion of the pressing need to carefully regulate the economy and the distribution of wealth: for civil society to be stable and "advantageous" for *all* its members, he says, it is essential that "they all have something and none of them has too much" (*SC* 1.9). To achieve this – to secure relative economic equality – it is essential that "the state is master of all [citizens'] goods" (*SC* 1.9).

A striking and controversial claim. Rousseau *does* have his Lockean moment in the *Social Contract*: he emphasizes, and celebrates, the way that civil society transforms (mere) "possession," which in the state of nature is insecure, into "legitimate ownership" (*SC* 1.8–9). But, unlike Locke, Rousseau believes that there *are* important limits to rightful accumulation; he thinks that unlimited accumulation (by *some*) negates the purpose of the social contract – the abolition of all relations of dependence. To avoid this – to avoid the reemergence of mastery based on wealth – "each private individual's right to his own land [must be] subordinate to the community's right" to limit, and redistribute, property in order to preserve (relative) economic equality among its members (*SC* 1.9). According to Rousseau, this does *not* require complete and total economic equality. Indeed, he stresses circumspection in the appropriation and redistribution of private property: "The sovereign cannot impose on the subjects any fetters that are of no use to the community" (*SC* 1.4). And yet, it *is* essential that the law prudently moderate economic inequality – that "the force of legislation" should ensure that "no citizen should be so rich as to be capable of buying another citizen, and none so poor that he is forced to sell himself" (*SC* 2.11). Otherwise, "two estates" will emerge and the idea of "a common good" shared by them will die; in such divided societies, "public liberty becomes a matter of commerce" (*SC* 2.11).

Of course, this generates another (obvious) problem: isn't this merely a new form of dependence – dependence on law, as opposed to dependence on others? Rousseau sees this objection, and his answer to it has two parts: first, he says, dependence is an ineliminable aspect of human life, and the only salutary, sustainable form of it is dependence on *things*, not people – things like the impersonal law, things that can be (relatively easily) controlled (*E* 2:85). And second, it is essential that the law is made *democratically* – that the law is produced by the most direct democracy, which is to say, by an assembly of all citizens, each of whom has an equal say in its crafting and adoption;[19] in such cases, dependence on the law is, at bottom, a form of self-reliance (*SC* 2.6).[20] In fact, this takes us directly to the heart of Rousseau's political enterprise: to free us from dependence on others by making us dependent on law alone, on the law that we give to ourselves as citizens with equal standing. Only then – when we confront others as equals, with the law we give ourselves operating in the background – can we approximate the (seemingly lost) independence of savage man; only then can we be free, happy, and whole while also living with others, knowing full well that our status (as free and equal) is reflected in, and protected by, the legal structure of our society. Hence Rousseau's belief that *only* the civil society of the *Social Contract* harnesses and puts to effective use man's natural inclinations: in an egalitarian democracy, our benign preference for ourselves, implanted in us by nature, leads – *can only lead* – to the freedom of all.[21]

## 4

Rousseau is not naive: he frequently acknowledges that the establishment,[22] stability, and vitality of these republican institutions is difficult, demanding, even unlikely. And so, throughout the *Social Contract*, he suggests a host of supplementary measures necessary for effective institutional functioning. The most important of these supplements (to institutional well-orderedness) is a keen attention to moeurs, to the cultivation of a fervent patriotic "sensibility common to all its members" (*SC* 3.1). "Without virtue," warns Rousseau, no state can "subsist" (*SC* 3.4). To cultivate such virtue, as widely and deeply as possible, Rousseau emphasizes the need for both civic education and, more ambitiously, a distinct civic religion: a stable regime, he says, *must* have its own "sacred cult," a cult in which the demands of virtue and good citizenship wholly overlap (*SC* 4.8).[23]

Despite these suggestions, the *Social Contract* is ultimately characterized by its deep pessimism: Rousseau gives us many hints – some subtle, some not – that republican institutions are simply too burdensome to last, that citizenship ultimately requires too great a virtue for self-interested creatures like us. After all, every citizen possesses an "absolute and naturally independent existence" – this no patriotic education (or civic cult) can ever *fully* extinguish; and this ineluctable "private will" may often be different from "the general will" of the political community (*SC* 1.7). Of course, this is a permanent danger to political stability and cohesion: this disconnect – ideally mostly dormant, but probably inevitable – "can cause [those who experience it] to envisage what he owes the common cause as a gratuitous contribution" (*SC* 1.7). The decisive statement, though, comes in book 3, where Rousseau explicitly acknowledges the inevitability of fatal decay; death, he says, is the iron law of political life: the usurpation of the general will by the private will of powerful citizens "is the *inevitable vice* that, from the birth of the body politic, tends *unceasingly* to destroy it, just as old age and death destroy the human body" (*SC* 3.10).[24] If Rome and Sparta fell, what hope can there be for us?[25]

And so, if (lasting) freedom under law is not possible – if even the best regimes are destined to fall – then solitude is the only tenable solution to the problem of human misery. If we can't rely on our legal institutions to preserve our happiness, then we can only rely on ourselves; we must retreat from social life altogether – to the lake,[26] to the mountain,[27] to the forest.[28] Unfortunately, such solitude does not suit many people: it is very difficult for us to live with others, as we have seen, but now it is just as difficult to live *without* them; we cannot turn the clock back on our corruption. Only an exemplary person – someone in possession of extraordinary genius and a profound strength of soul, *someone like Rousseau* – can find lasting happiness in solitude, independence, withdrawal. And indeed he does: when alone, Rousseau finds he can think, enjoy, laze, simply *be*.[29] "I am not made like any of the [people] I have seen," he confesses. "I dare to believe that I am not made like any that exist" (*Con* 5). Have truer words ever been written?

# 6

## "The Reason Which Shines Through": Hegel on the Ethical Dimensions of the Market

Kant's philosophy is undergirded by an idiosyncratic – and to us moderns, anachronistic – worldview: he believes that nature is purposive and rational, not random and anarchic. Nature, Kant teaches, desires the fullest realization of the highest human capacities – reason chief among them – and arranges things so that this gradually occurs over time, though typically through bitter antagonism (*IUH* 44). "If we assume a plan of nature," as Kant does, then "we have grounds for greater hopes ... [that] the human race [will eventually] work its way upward to a situation in which man's destiny can be fulfilled here on earth" (*IUH* 52). Reason, in other words, is a slow-going process, one requiring "trial, practice and instruction" (*IUH* 42); it is immanent in our nature and only gradually actualized over countless generations. In Kant's mind, this gives history itself a "disconcerting" – even tragic – aura: "The early generations seem to perform their laborious tasks only for the sake of the later ones ... [and] only the later generations will in fact have the good fortune to inhabit the building on which a whole series of their forefathers had worked without themselves being able to share in the happiness they were preparing" (*IUH* 44). Perhaps, Kant muses, there are some "inhabitants of other planets" whose "nature" is such that "each individual can fulfil his destiny completely in his own lifetime"; not so for us humans: "Only the species as a whole can hope for this" (*IUH* 47).

As an example, here, Kant discusses our political and legal institutions: for much of our history, human beings lived in a state of "wild," "unrestrained," "purposeless," and "savage" freedom; such a condition is antithetical to both moral and economic progress: our intellectual resources are too single-mindedly devoted to bare survival – in "isolation" we grow up "bent and twisted," like trees deprived of "air and sunlight" – and the fruits of our productive economic labors too susceptible to invasion by others (*IUH* 46). "Man," says Kant, "is [therefore] an animal who needs a master" (*IUH* 46). Eventually – only after "great experience" and "many unsuccessful attempts" (*IUH* 47) – this insight is accepted and put into political practice: despite our natural aversion to submission, human beings come to recognize the necessity of "a law [that] impose[s] limits on the freedom of all" (*IUH* 45). But many still yearn for their lost freedom, and such persons "exempt [themselves] from the law where [they] can" (*IUH* 46). That's why Kant speaks of the establishment of a "public justice" to which all willingly submit as the "most difficult of all tasks,"[1] especially for independent creatures like us, constitutionally "so enamoured with [our now lost] unrestrained freedom" (*IUH* 46).

But it is *also* "the highest task which nature has set for mankind" (*IUH* 45). In Kant's mind, the fulfillment of our rational destiny – our destiny as nature's uniquely rational beings – explicitly requires certain political and legal conditions: namely, "the greatest *freedom under external laws*" (*IUH* 45). After all, the development of reason depends on a wide and protected sphere of noninterference, guaranteed by law and by the sorts of executive, judicial, and punitive institutions that give the law teeth: we must be free, that is, to make choices, exercise judgment, develop our talents and tastes, execute and revise our plans; and none of this is possible without the "irresistible force" of the state (*IUH* 45). In fact, it is *only* after we "enter into a civil constitution" that "all [our] dormant capacities [can] be developed," and that we move along the path to moral maturity (*IUH* 49).[2]

This is the right moment to transition to Hegel, whose moral and political thought owes a massive debt to Kant: like Kant, Hegel believes that reason operates behind our backs, and that nature's desires for us are realized through long, often quite painful historical processes. And like Kant – whose *Idea for a Universal History* is "a philosophical attempt" to draw out "a plan of nature," and thus give us "greater hopes" for the future, despite the *apparent* chaos and senselessness of human history – Hegel also believes that the purpose of philosophy is to make plain reason's cunning: without a clear sense of the character-forming function of our history – as well as our present political institutions and our social and economic practices – we cannot be fully reconciled to it (*PR* preface 11).[3] In other words, Hegelian philosophy is not aimed at giving instruction about what the world ought to be like; instead, it is aimed at understanding what *is*. If something exists, there must be a reason for its existence; and this reason, hidden and elusive as it may be, must be brought out into the open by philosophy. As we shall see, Hegel's analysis of the market is an example: the casual observer who looks at the workings of civil society sees chaotic, uncoordinated, socially unproductive, self-seeking behavior; when philosophers look – especially those under the influence of Adam Smith, as Hegel was[4] – they see something wholly different: a secret harmony, one that advances the interests of both individual participants and the political community at large. If civil society exists, so this line of thinking goes, it must serve some rational function – it must advance the development of reason and, with it, the cause of human freedom.

This was hardly apparent to Hegel's influential precursors and contemporaries, many of whom believed that market society was antithetical to human flourishing and happiness. We have already encountered this critique in the previous chapter: Rousseau there draws our attention to the psychologically and socially toxic combination of frivolous luxury and ever-expanding desire, while Ferguson laments the decline in civic virtue characteristic of the modern bourgeois milieu, which contrasts so unfavorably to the self-effacing, willing sacrifice of the ancient Greeks and Romans. And Hegel's German contemporaries added a new avenue of concern to this plaintive chorus: they believed that the sort of specialization characteristic of work under capitalism – precisely the sort of specialization, and the concomitant division of labor, that Smith celebrates in the *Wealth of Nations* (see, e.g., *WN* 1.1.1–4) – leads to a debilitating psychic and spiritual fragmentation. Here, the work of Friedrich Schiller provides a representative example. In his *Letters on the Aesthetic Education of Mankind*, Schiller complains that modern men "[develop] but one part of their potentialities, while of the rest, as in stunted growths, only vestigial traces remain.... Everlastingly chained to a single little fragment of the Whole, man himself develops into nothing but a fragment; everlastingly in his ear the monotonous sound of the wheel that he turns, he never develops the harmony of his being, and instead of putting the stamp of humanity upon his own nature, he becomes nothing more than the imprint of his occupation, of his specialized knowledge" (*AEM* 32–5).[5] One of the central purposes of the present chapter is to lay out Hegel's deep disagreement with this line of thinking.

# 1

For Hegel, modernity is, first and foremost, the epoch of reason: in the past, individuals were content to rely on the wisdom and authority of their superiors, political and religious. After Luther,[6] though, and especially after the (failed but still immensely consequential) French Revolution,[7] a higher standard was set in place: now, Hegel says, our institutions and practices are in need of *rational* justification, without which they are experienced as illegitimately coercive and, by extension, an unjust impediment to our inviolable autonomy. And this is precisely what Hegel hopes to provide: an account of how our institutions and practices came to be and, more importantly, how they advance our freedom, our sense of self, our feeling at home in the world. If we can see and accept all this – if we have a clear and persuasive sense of how our political and social world makes possible and enhances our freedom, our individuality, as well as our sense of belonging – we can overcome the alienation and feelings of resignation that many of Hegel's Romantic contemporaries felt so keenly.[8] But, again, the route to reconciliation goes through critical reason, not the irrational, ecstatic surrender to, and subsumption within, some higher force – nature, God, the *Volk* – a force capable of giving meaning to an otherwise isolated and therefore meaningless existence.[9]

Indeed, in the preface to the *Philosophy of Right*, Hegel directly attacks his Romantic contemporaries, specifically for their conception of freedom. Freedom, for them, was understood as radical authenticity, measured by "the extent to which [the individual's way of life] diverges from what is universally acknowledged and valid and manages to invent something particular for itself" (*PR* 12). We are most free, according to this line of thinking, when our choices, and ensuing actions, are *idiosyncratic* – distinctive, novel, and unexpected; we are most free when we can choose to do *anything* we like (§15). In Hegel's view, this is a naive, superficial, and deeply mistaken understanding of freedom: certainly freedom requires the act of choosing; the abstract, possible self requires particular instantiation: the individual must transition "from undifferentiated indeterminacy to *differentiation, determination, and the positing* of a determinacy" (§6; see also §§13A and 14). But if the options available are arbitrary – if we are forced to choose between *whatever* "drives desires and inclinations" (§11) that *happen* to strike us at any given moment – we are not free in any meaningful sense: we are pushed to and fro by forces that we do not understand and cannot control (§§15–17). In other words, the Romantic conception of freedom leads not only to a kind of despondent rootlessness, a permanent sense of dissatisfaction and a concomitant yearning for change; it leads to the loss of freedom altogether.

What is required, instead, is that we *systematize* those ideas, impulses, and inclinations: that we have a clear and persuasive sense of why we are doing what we are doing when we are doing it, as opposed to being wholly "determined by [the arbitrary and therefore freedom-denying] natural drives" (§18; see also §145). Freedom, in other words, requires structure – a stable, predictable *pattern* that gives our choices rational grounding and, by extension, our life stability, coherence, and lasting satisfaction (§142). And the source of this pattern is the social and political world; the source of solid (not arbitrary or contingent) reasons for action is our standing as family members, workers, and citizens.

Hegel calls this ensemble of practices and institutions "ethical life," and he devotes part 3 of the *Philosophy of Right* to it: the "ethical substance" (§33) of our reasons and decisions – all those choices we make, which give expression to our individuality – are determined by and made knowable to us as participants in, concrete social, economic, and political practices – the family, civil society, and the state (§§144–8). It cannot be otherwise: we are the sorts of creatures *made by* our institutions; our values, preferences, and choices, says Hegel, cannot transcend the social and political context in which they are made – they are *determined by* those circumstances (§§29–30). Elsewhere, Hegel refers to "the absolute value of *education* ... [in the] cultivation" of free thinking (§20).

At first glance, Hegel's own view seems to be a renunciation – the antithesis – of freedom: if we are worked upon by social and political institutions – and if in turn those institutions have the effect of determining our preferences, our character, our actions, and our way of life – then how can we rightly be described as free? Aren't we merely being pushed to and fro by the historical forces of the past and the social forces of the present? How, exactly, is Hegel's own view of freedom an improvement on the shallow, and so discarded, Romantic conception?

The Hegelian response to such critical questions is twofold: first, modern human beings have a keen sense of their status as free; they have been educated to such an idea – the *fact* of their ends-status – by their political institutions, which recognize and protect a comprehensive catalog of liberal rights (see, e.g., §§37, 41, 45–7, 121–3, and 209R).[10] This idea of our ends-status is not immanent in our consciousness: it is, to the contrary, a product of history (§20).[11] And our having access to such an education (to autonomy) leads to a certain kind of relationship to our obligations: that they are freely chosen by us, and so give meaningful expression to our identity as *free agents* (§23). Our commitments – as family members, workers, and citizens – cannot "exclude thought" (§21R) or critical "reflection" (§20); we cannot be forcibly conscripted into them as a result of ideology, deception, or the threat of violent reprisal (§268). In fact, it is *only* when our commitment to others passes the test of "self-conscious reason" (§31) – when we freely choose those commitments – that we are able to wholly identify with our social and political roles, willingly fulfill the obligations associated those roles, and derive lasting satisfaction from the fulfillment of those obligations (§149).

Freedom, in other words, does not require complete independence – the total withdrawal from social and political life; this is precisely the error made by the Romantics, whose theory leads us into slavish arbitrariness. Instead, freedom is instantiated in carefully considered and then conscientious identification with something *other* – a nuclear or extended family, a collection of like-minded colleagues, an assembly of citizens – and with the willing performance of the requisite social responsibilities that make these associations stable, happy, and productive: "The *Idea of freedom*," says Hegel, "has ... its actuality through self-conscious *action*" (§142). As an example, here, Hegel discusses love and marriage: the family, he says, is the first "moment" (§157) of ethical life – the first site of our moral education – and its binding force is "love" (§158). According to Hegel, love is something of a contradictory force. On the one hand, our desire to be loved activates our independent sense of self: we desire the recognition and reciprocal affection of another (§158A). And our eventual entrance into marriage is another essential moment in the development of self-consciousness: we give our "free consent to *constitute a single person*" (§162); *this* is what makes marriage "an *ethical* relationship" (§161A; italics added) – the role it plays in awakening our autonomy.[12]

At the same time, though, love *also* dissolves our desire for independence: when it is absent from our lives – when we are alone – we feel "deficient and incomplete" (§158A); we are the sorts of creatures that naturally desire "the sharing of the whole of individual existence" (§162). And this desire for community – combined, at least in small part, with the dread of isolation – inclines us to make personal sacrifices to enhance the stability, cohesiveness, and (economic and spiritual) prosperity of the family. This requires, to start, the dedicated accumulation of economic resources through "work and struggle [in] the external world," as well as careful guardianship of "family piety" and the enforcement of morally salutary "discipline" for children (§§166 and 174; see also §171).[13] But, again, Hegel speaks of these obligations as "a self-limitation" (§162), which is to say, freely chosen by those who possess them.

Hegel's depiction of family life draws our attention to (what in his mind constitutes) a significant advantage of the ethical theory outlined in the *Philosophy of Right*: that our moral duties are instantiated in concrete social institutions, and there is therefore no ambiguity about what their performance requires; we know what we need to do to ensure, say, the family's flourishing, because the family is a living practice: the needs of its individual members – and, more generally, the needs of the whole – are on close and perpetual display, and so knowable, for us (§§134–5A and 150). "In an ethical community," says Hegel, "it is easy to say *what* someone must do and *what* the duties are which he has to fulfill in order to be virtuous. He must simply do what is prescribed, expressly stated, and known to him in his situation" (§150R; see also §156A).

Of course, the actual content of these moral obligations is only a part of Hegel's story: what matters even more for him is that we freely choose them for ourselves – that our participation in these institutions and practices gives expression to our freedom of choice and action. Without my duties as husband and father, so this line of thinking goes, I am, for all intents and purposes, *nothing* – a *potential* self, awaiting *actualization through freely chosen practice*. That is why Hegel speaks of virtue itself "as a second nature" (§151): it is only through the rational, willing (not coercive) adoption and performance of obligations to others over time that the freedom to choose – and to act in the light of those choices – is fully realized; hence, "the individual ... finds his liberation in duty" (§149).

This is a counterintuitive formulation, to be sure, but Hegel's meaning is reasonably clear: the liberation he describes here is the liberation from the radical indeterminacy of abstract agency; and this liberation is effected through uncoerced, fully self-conscious participation in social (in this example, family) life (§162R). That is why our obligations to others, he says, are not a "limitation" (§149) on our freedom, or a burdensome imposition on our independence. Quite the contrary: we *become* ourselves *in and through* productive participation in concrete social practices. "The ... ethical laws ... [are] not something *alien* to the subject," says Hegel. "On the contrary, the subject bears *spiritual witness* to them as to its own essence ... – [our] relationship [to our *duties*] is immediate and closer to identity than even a relationship of *faith* or *trust*" (§§146–8; see also §153A). My relationship to my family makes me *me*; in fact, there is no *me* without the obligations that I have to my loved ones, colleagues, and fellow citizens (§106). And this brings us to the second clear advantage of Hegel's ethical theory: that the fulfillment of those ethical duties is *also* the source of satisfaction; there is therefore no insuperable tension between the performance of duty and the achievement of personal happiness, as many others – Kant chief among them[14] – had previously taught (§§121–3 and §187R). Being good to my family – adding to its cohesiveness and its animating feelings of love – makes me good *and* happy.

## 2

The family, though, is only the first "moment" (§157) of ethical life: eventually, its substantial unity gives way to the competitiveness – and *apparent* atomism – of civil society. In many ways, this is inevitable: the survival and vitality of the family requires secure access to "financial resources, food, costs of education, etc.," which are primarily obtained (by the husband, at least according to Hegel's depiction of the division of spousal responsibilities[15]) in the external world of work (§159). But, as always, Hegel wants to transcend the fact of necessity; he wants to discover "the reason which shines through" the sort of instinctive self-seeking behavior, and ensuing competition, characteristic of modern market society (§182A). And, according to Hegel, civil society is ultimately rational, because of the essential contribution it makes to two moral aims: first, individual participants gain a keener sense of their individuality and ends-status – an awareness of themselves as beings with skills and relationships in need of development and desires deserving of satisfaction; and, second, participants also come to recognize their essential interdependence – the fact that each of us "cannot accomplish the full extent of [our] ends without reference to others" (§182A).

Indeed, civil society is, on the surface, the domain of rampant individualism: in it, we are treated, first and foremost, as fully "self-sufficient individuals"; we have our own specific needs and desires, and their satisfaction is made possible by the existence of a "legal constitution," which provides us with "security for persons and property" (§157; see also §§182A and 187). For Hegel, the secure possession of private property – as well as the associated right to alienate that property on the market – represents a crucial stage in the history of human freedom and in the education to selfhood. Physical property, after all, is a concrete instantiation of my individuality: my sense of self is, on the one hand, "something internal"; but it *also* requires "something external, an *existent world*," and this is the role that Hegel attributes to "external objects" (§33R). "If it is not to remain abstract," says Hegel, "the free will must first give itself an existence, and the primary sensuous constituents of this existence are things, i.e. ... *property*" (§33A). That is why it is so important, for Hegel, that the "*modern*"[16] (§124) state is committed to the protection of private property: the fact that something is securely *mine* is recognition of my individuality (§154; see also §§45–9).

And secure possession advances our sense of selfhood in another key sense: to work upon "to supersede the thing and transform it" – and to thus "appropriate" it as private, as *mine* – "means basically ... to manifest" not only the existence but "supremacy of my will in relation to the thing" (§44A). Here, Hegel emphasizes the importance not only of possession but of productive activity too: what matters, for him, is not merely secure ownership, though of course that is crucial; *work matters too*: by laboring upon and thus transforming my property – and, in the process, increasing its value (as a salable commodity) – "I give [it] a soul other than that which it previously had; I give it *my* soul" (§44A; see also §197). In other words, property instantiates not only our universal right to appropriate; it *also* manifests our particular talents and abilities: that is why Hegel says that "civil society is the sphere ... in which all individual characteristics [and] all aptitudes ... are liberated" (§182A). Working – and earning a living by working – is one of the most important ways in which we develop a clear sense of our independence and individuality.

At first glance, then, civil society is the domain of atomistic, competitive self-assertion. But for Hegel, of course, things are not always what they seem. There is, he says, a hidden rationality at work in the market (§189R): what appears to us as "contingent arbitrariness and subjective caprice" (§185) is *actually* "a system of all-around interdependence" – a "system" in which "the subsistence and welfare of the individual" are "interwoven with, and grounded on, the subsistence welfare, and rights of all" (§183). Clearly, Hegel is deeply influenced by Adam Smith, whom he mentions by name in the *Philosophy of Right* (§189R): like Smith, Hegel believes that the market tames potentially destructive self-interest by forcing us to be social – to consider the needs and desires of others, and to labor toward the satisfaction of those needs and desires (§192).[17] "In civil society," says Hegel, "each individual is his own end, and all else means nothing to him. But he cannot accomplish the full extent of his ends without reference to others" (§182A; cf. *WN* 1.2.2). Prosperity explicitly requires that we recognize, address, and satisfy the needs of others; as a result, "each individual, in earning, producing and enjoying on his own account, thereby earns and produces for the enjoyment of others" (§199).

Of course, the Rousseauvian rejoinder is obvious: these needs are not natural or necessary; they are wholly artificial, invented by the profit-seeking labors of others. In fact, these artificial desires – for luxury, especially – are *the* crucial impediment to lasting human happiness and social solidarity: their pursuit renders us incapable of satisfaction and indifferent to the plight of our fellows. Hegel acknowledges that market freedoms can lead in some cases to "boundless extravagance" (§185A) – they lead to "deprivation and want" (§185A) too – but he ultimately rejects Rousseau's argument: *most* human wants, he says, are not natural; rather, they are, instead, the product of human effort, ingenuity, culture, and imagination (§§190–1; see also §194R). And, in fact, this is desirable, not only because it increases the scope of individual choice and expression; the construction and growth of our desires also further knits us into morally salutary webs of social and economic interdependence (§192A).

For example, as desire becomes more expansive and also more refined, processes of production become more specialized, the division of labor is advanced, and the opportunities for work proliferate (§§196–8 and 200–1). For Hegel, as for Smith, though ultimately for different reasons,[18] this is a cause for celebration: work, after all, is an essential source of dignity, self-respect, and individuality; without it – without the opportunity to "[support] oneself by one's activity and work" – "that feeling of … integrity and honour" is lost (§244; see also §206). And work, adds Hegel, is the source of autonomy too: in our working lives, we incur a dense network of professional obligations, and our conscious identification with, and willing performance of, those obligations is another important instantiation of our agency. That is why Hegel describes civil society as the second site, or "moment," of ethical life: as with our choice of spouse, our choice of occupation invests abstract agency with the content – the responsibilities, practices, modes of collaboration, and standards of success characteristic of each profession – necessary for rational (not arbitrary or contingent) action. At work, we know what is expected of us – we know what the performance of our duties requires, because these duties are explicit in the daily practices of our professional life – and in the fulfillment of these freely chosen expectations our identity *as free* is on full display (§251; cf. §147).

This is also an important part of Hegel's argument against Rousseau: our embeddedness in professional communities of practice – Hegel calls them "estates" (§201) – is the most effective antidote against the sort of vapid, fruitless, irrational consumption described in the *Second Discourse* (§185 and §187R). After all, these estates provide concrete models of the well-lived, productive, successful life, including the appropriate levels of consumption for such a life (§253A); and its members, naturally drawn to something outside themselves, are desirous of the approbation of their colleagues, without which they cannot feel truly at home at work (§207). "Despite their selfishness," says Hegel, "private persons find it necessary to have recourse to others" (§201A; see also §253). And receiving the admiring recognition of others requires "merit" (§206) and "rectitude" (§207) – the self-determined fulfillment of the characteristic "ethical disposition" of one's profession, as well as the performance of one's professional tasks "with diligence and skill" (§207; see also §150). It is no wonder, then, that Hegel speaks of the estates as "a *second* family for its members" (§252); "it is necessary," he says, "to provide ethical man with a universal activity in addition to his private end" (§255A).

## 3

The chief task of the *Philosophy of Right* is to show the (hidden but still present and operative) freedom-guaranteeing infrastructure of modern market society: the chaos and competition, says Hegel, is only *apparent*; lurking beneath its surface is reason: "Free thinking ... does not stop at what is given ... [instead] the *truth* ... needs to be *comprehended* as well, so that the content which is already rational in itself may also gain a rational form and thereby appear justified to free thinking" (*PR* 11). For Hegel, we must have a clear sense of the contribution that our family and professional lives make not only to our individuality but to freedom too; only then can we "feel at home" amidst others (§§382–5). But Hegel's aims are not *exclusively* moral or philosophical: *Philosophy of Right* is *also* rooted in political debates of Hegel's own day. Indeed, beginning in the second half of the eighteenth century, Prussia's reformist civil service – under the influence of the philosophy of Adam Smith[19] – initiated a campaign of political and economic modernization: they hoped to replace Prussia's feudal-agricultural order, dominated by local princes and the landed aristocracy, with a modern commercial economy fueled by the profit motive.[20] Clearly, Hegel supported these reforms, many of which are specifically justified and endorsed in the *Philosophy of Right*, including the freedom of occupation (§206), the right to a fair and public trial by jury (§§219 and 228), universal eligibility for the civil service and military (§§271, 277, and 291), and estates-based representation in the legislative institutions of government (§§298–314). A social world with these rights, opportunities, and institutional arrangements could be a home for human beings.

But a *rational* social world is by no means a *perfect* world: modern civil society is the path to freedom, independence, self-realization, and community for many; but it is also the path to ruin for many more. Indeed, Hegel repeatedly emphasizes the systematic tendency of market society to produce extremes of wealth and poverty: the greatest profits come from the employment of the cheapest possible labor, after all (§§243–4; cf. §200). And so those with nothing to sell but the energy of their bodies inevitably fall below the level of subsistence – they are reduced to a "rabble" (§240A). This is both unfortunate *and wrong*. In the modern world, individuals have developed a legitimate sense of entitlement: they have a *right* to a decent livelihood and, by extension, dignity and self-respect (§236A). And when those rights are denied (or ignored altogether), suffering ensues: those reduced to poverty know themselves to be excluded from the material and psychological benefits of modern life, and their resentment – their sense of having been wronged – grows (§241). This, warns Hegel, is a combustible situation: as class conflict becomes more acute, the community's feelings of solidarity, togetherness, and patriotic pride wane; and so too does respect for law and order: "That feeling of right, integrity, and honour which comes from supporting oneself by one's own activity is lost.... This in turn gives rise to ... rebellion against the rich, against society, against the government" (§244A).

What, then, is the solution? To begin, Hegel rejects private charity, the extensive need for which is a reflection of the failure of the public institutions that regulate civil society (§242 and §245). Poverty, after all, represents the violation of a right; therefore, addressing it is the obligation of the state – what Hegel calls "the police" (§236A). And so, in addition to the provision of essential infrastructure – "street-lighting, bridge-building ..., and public health" (§236A) – the state is also responsible for the maintenance of "the increasingly impoverished mass at [society's] normal standard of living" (§245). But this is no easy feat. Ultimately, Hegel's treatment of the problem of poverty is characterized by its pessimism and by a deep, abiding sense of resignation: first, he rejects public welfare without the accompanying demand for work; remunerated work, after all, is an essential precondition of meaningful, lasting self-respect (§245). And Hegel also rejects the provision of unnecessary work to the poor by the state, which would lead to the production of goods without accompanying demand (§245).[21] Because poverty is the necessary and inevitable effect of the free operation of markets, it is a necessary and inevitable aspect of civil society (§245). To the problem of the "rabble," then, there seems to be no persuasive solution. And Hegel refuses to provide an unpersuasive one: "The important question of how poverty can be remedied is one which agitates and torments modern societies especially ... despite an *excess of wealth,* civil society is *not wealthy enough* ... to prevent an excess of poverty and the formation of a rabble" (§§244A–5). If a penurious, hostile, socially destabilizing rabble is a constitutive element of civil society, then perhaps civil society – and, with it, the free operation of the market – must go?

# 7

# "Free, Conscious Activity": Marx on Alienation and the Path to Human Emancipation

Hegel lived and worked in turbulent political times. Throughout his career, Prussia was lurching toward political and economic modernity: power was gradually funneled away from society's feudal elements – the autocratic Junkers in the country, and the protective, exclusionary guilds in the towns[1] – in the hopes of creating a productive economy that diffused wealth more evenly throughout the nation.[2] And the agent of these reforms was the civil service: the Prussian merchant class was relatively weak vis-à-vis the landed aristocracy, and so commerce- and market-friendly initiatives were undertaken on their behalf by the bureaucracy.[3] Karl von Hardenberg, Prussia's first minister beginning in 1810 and the leader of this movement, defined the purpose of reform as "a revolution in a positive sense, one leading to the ennoblement of mankind, to be made not through violent impulses from below or outside, but through the wisdom of government."[4] Economic liberty was thus implemented and enforced from above: Prussia's civil servants, deeply under the influence and sway of Adam Smith, were desirous to represent the economic interests of the entire political community, not just the entrenched economic interests of its richest members. "Freedom," wrote B.G. Niebuhr in 1815, "depends much more on the administration than the constitution."[5]

Clearly, Prussian bureaucratic activism made an impression on Hegel too: throughout the *Philosophy of Right,* he describes the civil service as "the *universal* estate" – the estate that has "*the universal interests* of society as its business" (§205). In a modern market society, that is, most people are motivated, first and foremost, by self-interest (§§288–9A); it is therefore essential, says Hegel, that there exists a class motivated by the public good – by the "proper interests of all individuals" (§297). That class, he adds, must be populated by society's ablest citizens – regardless of race, religion, or class status – and its members must regard their labor in the service of the state as a "vocation," as opposed to a mere source of income (§291; see also §294A). Indeed, it was essential for Hegel that civil servants be immunized from market and financial pressures: an individual's appointment to the civil service "provides him with resources, ... and frees his external situation and official activity from other kinds of subjective dependence and influence" (§294). But education, adds Hegel, is even more important than economic security: the development of a bureaucratic culture characterized by "dispassionateness, integrity, and polite behaviour" depends on "direct *education in ethics and in thought*" (§296); otherwise, the bureaucracy risks being transformed into "an instrument of profit and domination" (§297A).

This is the right moment to turn to Karl Marx. In 1836, Marx transferred to the University of Berlin and soon began a "review of the Hegelian philosophy," which was so dominant there at the time (4).[6] On 10 November 1837, he wrote to his father, "I got to know Hegel from beginning to end, together with most of his disciples" (8). And in the foreword to his doctoral dissertation, Marx describes Hegel's thought as an essential "nodal point ... in the history of philosophy" (10). Despite his initial admiration, though, by the early 1840s Marx's attitude toward Hegel had become deeply "critical" (4); what was needed, now, was the "ruthless ... criticism of the old" philosopher (13). And it was Hegel's account of the bureaucracy that was a special target of Marx's critical labors: in his "Contribution to the Critique of the Philosophy of Right," Marx rejects the Hegelian civil service's claim to universality. The truth, he says, is that, much like the members of civil society, bureaucrats are animated by a "crass materialism" – by the self-interested "*chasing after higher posts, the making of a career*" (24); hence, "it goes without saying that the bureaucracy is a web of practical illusions" (23).

In many ways, this gets us to the heart of Marx's intellectual purpose, at least during the early phase of his career: to show that everything in the modern state *looks* different from its *true* character. The bureaucracy operates under the banner of universality – under the banner of the common good – but actually pursues the private interests of its individual members. To fail to see this, says Marx, is to possess a "mystical consciousness" – to live in a "dream," in a state of alienation (15). What is needed, instead, is to "clarify consciousness" through the critical analysis of the "political form[s]" to which citizens are subject (15). Marx actually sees this as a continuation of Hegel's work: "Mankind begins no *new* work," he says, "but consciously accomplishes its old work" (15). The goal of the *Philosophy of Right*, after all, is to show the contribution that the modern state makes to individual freedom, and to thus reconcile citizens to their political and social world. Marx too endorses freedom as the goal of philosophy, and he also thinks, with Hegel, that the world can be a home for human beings. But Marx ultimately regards the institutional arrangements of Hegel's rational state, including the bureaucracy, as antithetical to that goal: "*German political science*," he says, "expresses the *imperfection of the modern state itself, the degeneracy of its flesh*" (60). And so, the first step to genuine freedom requires recognition – exposing – of the freedom-denying character of the social and political status quo. "Our motto must therefore be," says Marx (in 1843), "*reform of consciousness*" (15).

## 1

Just as Marx was deeply critical of Hegel's image of the state, so too was he critical of Hegel's vision of civil society. This critique is the central theme of Marx's 1843 essay "On the Jewish Question." There, he asks, should the Jewish citizens of Prussia be politically emancipated, which is to say, granted the political rights of full citizenship, including the right to participate in political affairs as members of the bureaucracy (41)? For Marx, this question is deeply misled: "*Political* emancipation," he says, "is not the final and absolute form of human emancipation" (32). Why not? Because political emancipation (alone) leaves civil society in place: insofar as we lead private lives as "shopkeeper[s], day-labourer[s], landed proprietor[s]," and so on, we are "*separated* from the *community*...

and from other men" (35; see also 42). After all, civil society is the "sphere of [universal] egoism and of the *bellum omnium contra omnes*" (35); it is populated by individuals conceived as "self-sufficient monad[s]," and its guiding spirit is "differentiation," privacy, competition (42). Of course, the characteristic right of civil society is the right to accumulate, and alienate, private property – "the right to enjoy one's fortune and to dispose of it as one will; without regard for other men and independently of society. It is the right of self-interest" (42; cf. *PR* §§41–53). And yet, *at the same time*, at least in the modern state, we *also* possess the status of citizen, endowed with the "spiritual" (34) responsibility of advancing "the *general* interest" (35). As a result, "man leads, not only in thought, in consciousness, but in *reality*, in *life*, a double existence. He lives in the *political community*, where he regards himself as a *communal being*, and in *civil society*, where he acts simply as a *private individual*, treats other men as means, degrades himself to the role of a mere means" (34).

For Marx, this "double existence" (34) – this "contradiction," this "division of man into the *public person* and the *private person*" (35) – is the quintessential form of alienation in modernity (39). We are torn between our "celestial" lives as citizens and our "terrestrial" lives as earners (34), plagued by the nagging feeling that the latter is more *immediate* and yet also somehow *less important* than the former. Here, Marx draws an analogy with religion, which for him is another striking example of human alienation: for believers, the eternal life *to come* is somehow *more real* – more sacred, more important – than our temporary, profane, and therefore lesser material existence. "The political state, in relation to civil society," says Marx, "is just as spiritual as is heaven in relation to earth" (34; see also 53). In fact, these two forms of alienation are tightly linked: "The members of the political state are religious," says Marx, "*because of* the dualism between ... the life of civil society and political life" (39; italics added). Belief, according to this line of thinking, is a symptom of the suffering and psychological discomfort – guilt, even – wrought by the seemingly insuperable tension between our political and economic lives: the more we shirk our public responsibilities to others, the more likely we are to retreat into the domain of private religiosity (54).

This feeling of having been "lost ..., alienated" (39) is exacerbated by the fact that the profane sphere of life eventually takes precedence over the sacred sphere; the tension between the economic and political domains dissolves, and the former "finally" (46) comes to dominate the latter. Here, Marx describes the typical catalog of modern liberal rights – "*equality, liberty, security, property*" (42). What is conspicuous, here, says Marx, is the individualist orientation of this catalog: political emancipation is in actual fact *nothing more than* the assertion, and ultimate privileging, of the needs and interests of "egoistic man" (43); political participation, by extension, is *nothing more than* the "mere means for preserving these so-called rights of [bourgeois] man" (43; see also 62). In this sort of political milieu, the "frenzied" (45) pursuit of wealth becomes the sole source of meaning and purpose in human life. "Money dominates [us]," says Marx, "and [we] worship it" (50; see also 93 and 101–5).[7] The social instincts and inclinations, once dulled, are now effectively – though not permanently – extinguished (49).

Things need not be so. Marx yearns for – and believes in the possibility of – a kind of psychic integrity or "whole[ness]" (59): it *is* possible, he says, to achieve "*real* happiness" (54) – to feel at home, here, in the world, with ourselves and with others. But the transcendence of alienation – or, to put it in Marx's terms, "real, practical" (not merely political) emancipation – requires something truly radical: namely, the total overhaul of the "organization of society," an overhaul designed to "abolish ... the rule of private property and money" (48 and 50). What Marx is describing here, of course, is the abolition of civil society altogether: the market is characterized by the interaction of "atomistic, antagonistic individuals" (51), each out to accumulate as much "interest and profit" as possible, and thus "become richer than his neighbour" (49). But this rampant competitiveness leads to isolation and alienation. For Marx, this indicates the path to existential calm and satisfaction: "Human emancipation will only be complete," he says, "when as an individual man, in his everyday life, in his work, and in his relationships, ... has recognized and organized his own powers as *social powers*" (46).


## 2


What would it mean to recognize, and organize, our *individual* powers as *social* powers? When we work and produce things, says Marx, those objects are "the direct embodiment of [our] individuality" (85). We come to know ourselves, as productive and creative beings, in possession of transformative powers, in concert with nature, through labor – an insight that Marx no doubt owes to Hegel. But Marx mines this insight to further depths. Work, he says, sets in motion a dialectical movement: as processes of production become more refined and more sophisticated, we too become more refined and more sophisticated; the more we work, the more our "essential powers" (88) – "seeing, hearing, smelling, tasting, feeling, thinking, being aware, sensing, wanting, acting, loving" (87) – are cultivated. In other words, work results not only in the transformation of nature; work transforms *us* too: the things we produce not only "confirm and realize [our] individuality" – "*man himself* [also] becomes the object" (88).[8] That is why "the history of industry" is "the *open* book of *man's essential powers*" (89).

According to Marx, most philosophers and historians fail to see this: they relegate the history of our productive labors to the inconsequential domain of "*need, vulgar need,*" and focus instead rests on "religion ..., politics, art, literature, etc." (89–90).[9] The reality, retorts Marx, is that our "essential powers" can be understood only by the "*true* science," natural science, which aims to provide the history of the production of "*sensuous, alien, useful objects, ...* [by] *ordinary material industry*" (90). And this history, adds Marx, has an essentially social character: we shape the needs and desires of others through our productive activity, just as our needs and desires are shaped by the productive activity of others; hence, "man produces man – himself and the other man" (85). Even when we work in complete and total isolation, says Marx, we are still social: after all, what, and how, we produce is "the result of the movement" of history – of the efforts, ingenuity, and needs of previous generations" (85). That is why *all* human "activity and consumption ... are *social* production and *social* consumption" (85). After all, my activity as an individual is "given to me as a social product" and therefore reflects "the *living shape* [of] the real community, [its] social fabric" as it has been woven, over time, by my predecessors (86).

The concept that Marx uses to capture all of this is "species-being": unlike animal activity, which is determined by the impelling, necessary force of instinct, human activity is "free, conscious activity." "Man produces," adds Marx, "when he is free from physical need," and it is precisely in this freedom – in this transcendence of the natural needs of the body – that "man's species character" is on full display (76).

As an example, here, Marx discusses art and aesthetics – the fact that man "also forms things in accordance with the laws of beauty" (76). This is important and illuminating for him, not only because art is, strictly (physiologically) speaking, unnecessary; rather, when we create, and then step back to contemplate our act of creation, only then do we become keenly aware of our special status as free producers and of the world-creating power of our productive activity (76). A world with *this* (or that) standard of beauty is a world that we brought into being through our activity; we live in this world – this world of our own making – and so have the power to recreate it too. But, again, this freedom does not exist in a timeless vacuum; it has a history: we are both inheritor and contributing member of a common, cooperative project, a project that extends over the whole history of the species. Marx calls our contribution to this ongoing history our "species-activity" (90; cf. *IUH* 44); and he calls the awareness of our necessary immersion in this history "consciousness of species" (86).

In this light, it is easy to see why capitalism is so deeply antithetical to self-realization and, more generally, human happiness: modern factory labor is characterized by its "wretchedness" (70); it "does not affirm [the worker] ... [or] develop freely his physical and mental energy ... [work] mortifies [the] body and ruins [the] mind," producing "deformity, idiocy, cretinism" (73–4; see also 94–5).[10] Workers are thus alienated from their nature as species-being: the act of producing is no longer an expression, and affirmation, of our "essential powers" – work is dreaded toil, necessary for bare physical subsistence, and the source of "privation" (73). After all, we no longer confront the objects we make as a testament to our productive powers – our individual creativity and ingenuity; those objects are instead experienced as *"something hostile and alien"* – a testament to our suffering, "the loss of self," the reassertion of the animal needs (74). We produce only to earn and to survive: "Labour does not appear as an end in itself but as the servant of a wage" (79).

But this is not the full extent of alienation under capitalism: we are estranged from others too. As we have already seen, social life under capitalism is not characterized by its cooperative quality, as befits our true nature; civil society is the domain of "avarice" and sets in motion a *"war amongst the avaricious – competition"* (71). And the most destructive competition, adds Marx, is the competition between "propertyless *workers*," the class that grows and grows and grows under capitalism. The result, of course, is a surge in labor supply and a concomitant decline in wages: "The worker sinks to the level of a commodity ... [and] the necessary result of competition [for work] ... [is that the worker] becomes indeed the most wretched of commodities" (70). We no longer regard others as ancestors and partners in generations-spanning processes of cooperative production; they are simply competition, driving our wages down, eventually below the level of subsistence. And the same goes for our relationship to our employers: because the owner of the means of production is "the master of [the] object[s produced by our labour], ... [labour is] performed in the service, under the dominion, the coercion and the yoke of another man" (78).

Things need not be so. Capitalism itself, says Marx, is the result of a series of "fortuitous circumstances"; it is *not* a natural or "necessary course of development," as the economists of Marx's day would have us believe (70–1; see also 95–7). It is therefore possible to imagine the transcendence of alienation – from our nature, from the products of our labor, from each other – through the reorganization of society's political and economic institutions. The essential change, here, of course, is the "[annulment] of private property ... [what Marx calls] communism" (82). After all, "wages and private property," says Marx, "are identical" (79); and so the abolition of the latter necessarily leads to the abolition of the former and, as a result, the "transcendence of human self-estrangement" and the recovery of the possibility of genuine human emancipation (84). Of course, adds Marx, this does not mean the end of work or the necessity of labor: "The category of *labourer* is *not* done away with," he says; rather, it is "extended to all men" (82).[11] Only then – when the "antithesis of *propertylessness* and property ... *labour* and *capital*" (81) is overcome – will productive activity regain its social dimension as species-activity (84–5); only then will work be undertaken as a form for pleasure and the path to self-realization and existential satisfaction (87); only then will nature be experienced as a rich repository of beauty, not a useful resource to be exploited for profit (88–9).

How will this revolution take place? Who is responsible for bringing this new, better, egalitarian world into being? Here, Marx gestures toward the redemptive future of working-class wage labor: "A class must be formed," he says, "which has *radical chains*, ... a class which is the dissolution of all classes ... [and] the negation of private property ... this ... is the *proletariat*" (64–5). There is a great irony at work here, Marx gleefully notes: the emergence of this revolutionary, liberating class is the necessary "result of the industrial movement" (64) – of the commodification of labor, the resultant swelling of the army of factory workers, and the gradual, though inevitable, reduction of wages to "the barest and most miserable level of physical subsistence" (95). In other words, the owners of the means of production bring into being – by the necessary dynamics of capitalist wage labor – "the liberating class *par excellence*" (63). But Marx also acknowledges that this is no quick and easy process: the proletariat, he says, currently "lacks the logic, insight, courage and clarity, ... generosity of spirit ... [and] revolutionary daring" to say, "*I am nothing and I should be everything*" (63). Workers are atomized and so disorganized; they fail to recognize the full extent of the exploitation to which they are subject, succumbing to rampant, unnecessary, distracting consumerism – enjoyment, under capitalism, says Marx, is a form a "*self-stupefaction*" – and drowning their sorrows in "the English gin-shops ... [and hollow] Sunday pleasures" (98).

This is precisely the task of philosophy – "to unmask human self-alienation" (54), and to expose the owners of the means of production as "the oppressing class" – as the perpetrators of "*notorious crime*[s]" against "the whole society" (63). But theory alone is not enough: "It takes *actual* communist action to abolish actual private property" (99). This is, in part, a veiled criticism of Hegel, for whom the world is rational, and so only needs to be recognized and understood as such. For Marx, by contrast, the world does not yet conform to the demands of reason, and so requires active transformation: "The philosophers have only *interpreted* the world, in various ways; the point, however, is to change it" (145). And the material force of change is the proletariat, of course, roused to action by the philosophical vanguard, which exposes injustice and points the way toward (earthly) salvation. There is, in other words, a necessary partnership – a unity – between philosophy and politics, theory and practice: the goals of philosophy – reason, freedom, *self-realization for all* – can be realized only through the practical (revolutionary) reorganization of economic and political life. "Just as philosophy finds its *material* weapons in the proletariat," says Marx, "so the proletariat finds its *intellectual* weapons in philosophy" (65).

## 3

Thus far, our focus has been on Marx's early writings. His "Contribution to the Critique of Hegel's Philosophy or Right," "On the Jewish Question," "The Economic and Philosophic Manuscripts," and the "Theses on Feuerbach" were all written before the spring of 1845 – when Marx was twenty-six years old.[12] It is quite striking, then, that we already have in place the complete constellation of Marx's core ideas, the ones that animated his thinking throughout his long, engaged, productive life: his confident belief that the task of philosophy is to expose false consciousness, and transform it into revolutionary consciousness; that the modern state is the source of oppression, exclusively reflecting the interests of the owners of private property; that work is the source of alienation, and that wage labor is the source of exploitation and immiseration; that the proletariat is the class that will bring about the revolutionary transformation of society's economic and political institutions; and, finally, that communism – the abolition of the institution of private property and the capitalist state that protects it – is the solution to all of these problems. But, again, at this point in his career, these ideas were not rooted in economic (historical) analysis; they were, rather, formulated as a result of Marx's engagement with, and thoroughgoing critique of, Hegelian political philosophy. Eventually, though, Marx came to regard this exclusively philosophical approach as one-sided and insufficient: his foundational claims needed to be rooted in scientific fact, not philosophical speculation. And so, beginning in 1849, after having been expelled from France, Marx sequestered himself in the lonely confines of the British Museum Reading Room, anxious to master modern political economy, despite that discipline's complicity with the capitalist status quo.[13]

But Marx did not retreat from public life altogether: quite the contrary. In 1847, he, with Engels and other German intellectuals, founded the Communist League, a political party devoted to stirring the once dormant, now raging revolutionary consciousness of the Western

European proletariat. And a year later, again with Engels, Marx published a manifesto outlining the new party's guiding ideals and vision for the future. That document – *The Communist Manifesto* – is notable for its conspicuous abandonment of the obscure, Hegel-inflected philosophical jargon of Marx's youth: the task of "[settling] accounts with [his] erstwhile philosophical conscience" (5) was now complete, and the new task was a creative act of destruction – to bring about the "dissolution of modern bourgeois property" (471). But, first, workers must be made to see that, under capitalism, they are subject to "naked, shameless, direct, brutal exploitation" (475) and so have "nothing to lose but their chains" (500); what was required, first, was a revolution in workers' consciousness, aided, of course, by that "portion of the bourgeoisie ... who have raised themselves to the level of comprehending theoretically the historical movement as a whole" (481).

Again, for Marx and Engels, there is a delicious irony at work here: the bourgeoisie, they claim, has prepared the way for this revolution. In the recent past, exploitation was difficult to see: feudal relations of production were "veiled by religious and political illusions" – by "the most heavenly ecstasies of religious fervour, of chivalrous enthusiasm, of philistine sentimentalism" (475). With its political ascendance, though, the bourgeoisie has "put an end to all feudal, patriarchal, idyllic relations ... the motley feudal ties that bound man to his 'natural superiors' ... have been drowned ... in the icy waters of egotistical calculation"; all that is left is "naked self-interest, the callous 'cash payment'" (475). And, for Marx and Engels, *that is a good thing*. For one, the oppression to which workers are subject is laid bare for all to see, no longer obscured by the community of care and feelings of mutual indebtedness that existed between lord and serf: "All that is holy is profaned, and man is at last compelled to face with sober senses, his real conditions of life, and his relations with his kind" (476). And what is more, it exposes a characteristic feature of capitalist society: the relentlessness of the social, political, and technological upheaval always occurring within it – "All that's solid melts into air" (476). This shows the proletariat that nothing is sacred and everything is mutable, including the economic and political status quo; hence, the bourgeoisie "has played a most revolutionary part" (475) in making the postcapitalist society possible. And this is true in another crucial sense. According to Marx and Engels, the bourgeoisie has *also* put in place the productive infrastructure that makes possible the forthcoming just society:

> During its rule of scarce one hundred years, [the bourgeoisie] has created more massive and more colossal productive forces than have all preceding generations together. Subjection of Nature's forces to man, machinery, application of chemistry to industry and agriculture, steam-navigation, railways, electric telegraph, clearing of whole continents for cultivation, canalisation of rivers, whole populations conjured out of the ground – what earlier century had even a presentiment that such productive forces slumbered in the lap of social labour? (477)

The bourgeoisie has "conjured up gigantic means of production" (478), capable of generating a heretofore undreamed of level of abundance. And yet, in the midst of this once impossible affluence, the masses are reduced to destitution and misery, "daily and hourly enslaved by the machine" (479) and sinking "deeper and deeper [into] pauperism" (483). At times, workers have revolted against this glaring inequality: "they smash to pieces machinery, they set factories ablaze" (480); some even organize into political parties, fighting legislative battles through pacific constitutional avenues (481). But, according to Marx and Engels, a more fundamental line of attack is necessary – not against "the instruments of production themselves," but against the principle that undergirds their use and the distribution of the value created by their operation – the "mission" of the proletariat "is to destroy all previous securities for, and assurances of, individual [private] property" (482).

Such a revolution is by no means historically novel: "The French Revolution, for example, abolished feudal property in favour of bourgeois property" (484). But the proletariat revolution *would* have a historically novel element: whereas the French Revolution produced the class antagonism between bourgeois and proletariat – the institutions of private property and wage labor were left in place, after all – the forthcoming workers' revolution leads to the abolition of classes – and, as a result, class conflict – altogether. Marx and Engels do not step there, of course: the abolition of private property leads inexorably to the abolition of the state too; after all, the purpose of the modern (bourgeois) state is, first and foremost, the protection of private property: the disappearance of the latter therefore leads to the obsolescence of the former.

Of course, the withering away of the state takes time; here, Marx and Engels acknowledge the need for a temporary interlude – what they will later call the *"revolutionary dictatorship of the proletariat"* (538).[14] During that period, the working class "makes itself the ruling class" and uses "its political supremacy" to expropriate the private property of the bourgeoisie; the proletariat must "centralise all instruments of production in the hands of the State" and then proceed to "increase the total productive forces as rapidly as possible" (490–1). After all, a social world genuinely conducive to the "free development of all" (491) depends on the quite radical degree of material plenty wrought by (capitalist) technological advancement; hence, Marx and Engels's disdain for all those "utopian" socialists who fail to acknowledge the "economic [and technological] conditions" necessary for true and lasting "emancipation" (497).

In fact, there are no "ready-made utopias to introduce *par décret du people*" (635). The bourgeois epoch is indeed "pregnant [with] the new society," but the realization of that society will require that the current generation passes "through long struggles" in order to make possible "that higher form to which present society is irresistibly tending by its own economical agencies" (636). In other words, "the first phase of the communist society" (531) does *not* constitute a *radical break* with capitalism – it is *accelerated* capitalism *without* capitalists! There is simply no getting around this, says Marx, and those who believe that this socialist interlude can be skipped are deluded. "Right," after all, "can never be higher than the economic structure of society" (531). This is also the main theme of Marx's 1852 political pamphlet "The Eighteenth Brumaire of Louis Bonaparte": "Men make their own history, but they do not make it just as they please; they do not make it under circumstances chosen by themselves, but under circumstances directly found, given and transmitted from the past. The tradition of all dead generations weighs like a nightmare on the brain of the living" (595).

## 4

On the basis of Marx's own writings, it's difficult to say what, exactly, the postcapitalist (communist) society looks like. After all, Marx's main interest was stoking the revolutionary consciousness of the proletariat by demonstrating the injustice of the status quo: the material conditions of production transform history, he says, not ideas about how our productive activities *ought* to organized; it follows that *any* description of the coming communist future amounts to idle speculation at best, and destructive, indulgent utopianism at worst. That, in any case, was the official line. In actual fact, though, Marx's writings – the later ones, especially – are littered with evocative hints about postcapitalist economic and political life. For example, in his "Critique of the Gotha Program," Marx describes "a higher phase of communist society" (531). In such a society, the productive infrastructure initially developed by the bourgeoisie has become the "common property of society," and so too has the "total social product" generated by the interaction of labor and the expropriated means of production (528). The entire society now owns the value created by the individual labor of its citizens: "capital" is no longer "personal" power, as it was in the bourgeois economic milieu; it has been reclaimed as "a social power" (485).

Notice an important assumption at work here: that the communist society does not abolish the need for labor – for "actual material production" – altogether; we cannot ever transcend what, in volume 3 of *Capital*, Marx calls "the realm of necessity" (441). But there *is* a crucial distinction between necessary and exploited labor: the latter enriches (exclusively) the owner of the means of production (at the expense of the laborer's livelihood and general well-being), whereas the former adds to society's capital. And the essential purpose of this shared social power, adds Marx, is "to widen, to enrich, to promote the existence of the labourer" (485). This is the heart of the Marxist argument for communism: in it, society's capital is no longer hoarded by individual members of the bourgeoisie, all of whom are engaged in fruitless, socially destructive competition. Instead, society's capital is common property – carefully "regulate[d] upon a common plan," and redistributed in the interest of the maximal enlargement of the consumption power and freedom of all (635). That is why it is so important to harness and maximize the efficiency of society's productive infrastructure: this generates a plenty and also minimizes necessary labor time, creating leisure and, with it, the possibility of genuinely free self-development. "Freedom," says Marx, "can only consist in ... the least expenditure of [*necessary*] energy and ... [so the] shortening of the working day is its basic prerequisite" (441).

After all, compulsory labor – labor as a commodity, labor as a means to subsistence – is antithetical to our nature (as species-being); such labor attests only to our animal needs and ignores our (uniquely human) creativity. Only free labor – labor freely undertaken, labor as the source of "all-around" self-development and the expression of our energy and creative powers – is genuinely self-realizing (531). And the very possibility of such labor depends, quite simply, on *free time*: it is only once we are free from the yoke of necessity that we have space for experimentation, "to do one thing today and another tomorrow, ... just as I have a mind" (160). *This* is what nonexploitive work is like; *this* is the means of escape from the intellectually and spiritually stultifying division of labor characteristic of work under capitalism (531). And *that* is why Marx speaks of communism as "the riddle of history solved" (84) – because of the way it makes possible the transcendence of *both* exploitation and alienation. We are not exploited when, at bottom, we work for ourselves – when we possess an equal share of society's shared capital and have a meaningful say in and benefit from its use, distribution, and investment. And we have overcome alienation – from ourselves, from nature, from each other – when our activity is *free* and self-affirming, and so the source of genuine, lasting pleasure.

8

# "A Dozen Wise Men": Lenin on the Revolutionary Vanguard

In the revised preface to the 1882 edition of *The Communist Manifesto,* Marx and Engels celebrate the recent rise of the Russian proletariat: "In December 1847," they write, "the proletarian movement still occupied ... a limited field.... [At that time, tsarist] Russia constituted the last great reserve of all European reaction" (471). Now, less than forty years later, "Russia forms the vanguard of revolutionary action in Europe" (471). Marx and Engels acknowledge, however subtly, that this development is a counterintuitive and surprising one: as they imagine it, the proletarian revolution would take place *only after* the intense ramping up of capitalist industrial production. This process would lead to the immiseration of the working class, and then to its inevitable radicalization and mobilization. This process was essential for another reason: the tenability of the communist future depends on a secure and predictable plenty, which in turn demands the advancement and maximal efficiency of the productive infrastructure first developed by the profit-hungry bourgeoisie.

Engels says much the same thing in his 1874 letter to the Russian radical Pyotr Tkachov: "The revolution which modern socialism strives to achieve is ... the victory of the proletariat over the bourgeoisie.... This requires not only a proletariat ..., but also a bourgeoisie in whose hands the productive forces of society have developed so far that they allow the final destruction of class distinctions" (666). Engels calls this revolutionary pathway "the ABC of socialism" (666). In Russia, though, it *seems* that this path is blocked: the institution of private property is less well established there, and society's economic resources are less well developed as a result. For example, "more than half the land [is] owned in common by the peasants," and that land is typically less cultivated and therefore less productive than "bourgeois landed property" (471–2; see also 667 and 673).[1] For Marx and Engels, this raises an obvious and difficult question: Can Russia achieve "the higher form of communist common ownership" on the basis of the prevailing "primeval common ownership of land" (472)? Or "must it first pass through the same process of dissolution as ... the West" (472)?

In the 1882 preface, Marx and Engels endorse the former possibility, though tepidly, half-heartedly, with obvious reservations: "The present Russian common ownership of land," they write, "*may* serve as the starting-point for a communist development" (472; italics added). This is such a fraught path to revolution because the "*obshchina*" – and with it, the accelerated development of society's economic resources – is "greatly undermined" by the political status quo: as Engels thoroughly documents in his 1874 letter, the Russian state reflects, protects, and advances the economic interests of the "big landowners" at the expense of peasant farmers; the latter pay higher taxes for less fertile land and are also subject to usurious rates of interest by state agricultural industries (667–8). In fact, large-scale Russian landowners – the "big bourgeoisie of Petersburg, Moscow, Odessa" (668) – pay an infinitesimal share of taxes vis-à-vis the quantity and quality of the land they own (667). The result, says Engels, is a "capitalistic parasitism [that] covers and entangles the whole country," and the reduction of the mass of peasants "into a most miserable and wholly untenable situation" (667–8).

In some ways, though, this is also the source of hope: one of the prominent themes of the *Communist Manifesto* – and of Marxist thought in general – is precisely that revolutionary fervor is most effectively fomented in the deepest depths of despair – that the most oppressive situations are also the most combustible, that revolutions occur when "the proletarians have nothing to lose but their chains" (500). And this is, in many ways, the case in Russia: "Her financial affairs are in extreme disorder. Taxes cannot be screwed any higher.... The administration, as of old, corrupt from top to bottom.... The whole held together with great difficulty and only outwardly by an Oriental despotism" (675). That is why Engels says that, despite its economic backwardness, "a revolution is in the offing in Russia": "The condition of the Russian peasants since the emancipation from serfdom has become intolerable," he says, "and cannot be maintained much longer" (668). But Engels also admits that the possibility of revolution depends on the development of an urban, educated, *bourgeois* revolutionary vanguard: "The Russian peasant lives and has his being only in his village community.... This is so much the case that in Russia the same word, *mir*, means, on the one hand 'world' and, on the other, 'peasant community'" (672). Such isolation and inwardness lead directly to "tsarist *despotism*" and, by extension, the continued exploitation and immiseration of the rural masses. The only effective antidote to such oppression, says Engels, is "a growing recognition among the enlightened strata of the nation concentrated in the capital that this [situation] is untenable.... [This] revolution which, started by the upper classes of the capital, must [then] be rapidly carried further, by the peasants" (675).

But even that is not enough. In his 1874 letter, Engels concedes that "communal ownership in Russia is long past its period of florescence" (673). After all, this mode of production has been, and continues to be, steadily undermined by the state. If, then, communal ownership is to act as the foundation for "a higher ... form of society ... without [having] to go through the intermediate stage of bourgeois small holdings" – as it must, given Russia's prevailing industrial underdevelopment[2] – then the productivity of the "whole agricultural system" must be greatly enhanced, and soon (673). From whence does Engels expect the money, technology, knowledge, and support needed for such a boost? From the Western European proletariat: "If anything can still save Russian communal ownership and give it a chance of growing into a new, really viable form, it is a proletarian revolution in Western Europe"; it is from the West's sense of solidarity that the Russian peasant should expect the advance in "material conditions ... requisite for [the] transition" to communism (673). And so, in the end, Marx and Engels's assessment of the revolutionary possibilities in Russia is striking in its pessimism: the productive infrastructure there is conspicuously underdeveloped, and the possibility of its advancement – itself the essential precondition of stable communism – is in turn contingent on revolutionary success – and sustained international consciousness – in the more developed West. An intellectual vanguard alone is not enough, adds Engels, and "a premature attempt at insurrection" spurred ahead of schedule by it is doomed to fail (675).

# 1

In his early political pamphlets, Lenin echoes Engels's belief in the necessity of an intellectual vanguard: revolution, he concurs, radiates outward, from the affluent, educated cities to the poor, illiterate country. But Lenin's assessment of the Russian situation differs from Marx and Engels's in one essential respect: his German forefathers overlook a key aspect of the Russian situation – its nascent industrialization. In "The Tasks of the Russian Social-Democrats," written in 1897 while Lenin was in Siberian exile,[3] he writes of "the enormous progress that Russian capitalism has made in recent times": "Industry is 'prospering' ... business is brisk ... factories are working at full capacity ... and countless new factories, joint-stock companies, railway enterprises, etc., etc., are springing up like mushrooms" (2.346).[4]

As in Western Europe, such a situation is pregnant with revolution: a "fairly sharp crash" is "inevitable" – "one need not be a prophet to foretell" it; and so it is essential, when that crash comes, that the Russian factory proletariat is "more class-conscious, more united, [and] able to understand [its] tasks" (2.346; see also 9.47–50, 9.55–6, and 9.112). This is precisely the role – the main *task* – of Lenin's Russian Social-Democratic Party: consciousness-raising. The party, he says, must spread "*by propaganda* ... among the workers a proper understanding of the present social and economic system"; it must "help workers understand [capitalism], [and] draw [their] attention to [its] most important abuses" (2.329; see also 5.400–1, 5.413–14, 5.470, and 9.111).

This emphasis on the leadership role of intellectuals is a recurring theme in the early phase of Lenin's career as a politician and polemicist. In his 1902 essay, "What Is to Be Done?," Lenin emphasizes the essential guiding role of "professional revolutionaries," who are responsible for the formulation of "the most advanced theory": this is necessary, he adds, because "without revolutionary theory, there can be no revolutionary movement" (5.369 and 5.464). Without theory, that is, workers' demonstrations and strikes are "spontaneous," uncoordinated, and so ultimately ineffective; they only represent the revolutionary "consciousness in an *embryonic form*" (5.374; see also 5.384 and 9.58). What is needed, instead, is the dedicated, thoughtful guidance of "a dozen wise men, ... developed from among students or working men" (5.464), whose wisdom provides vision and coherence to isolated and discrete events, and who transform workers' unconscious, inarticulate "outbursts of desperation and vengeance ... [into] class *struggle*" (5.375; see also 5.475 and 7.412). It is therefore essential, Lenin adds, that bridges be built between the intelligentsia and workers.

In order to facilitate this, Lenin suggests the organization of "study circles among workers, to establish proper and secret connections between them and the central group of Social-Democrats," as well as the publication and widespread distribution of "working-class literature ... leaflets and manifestos" (2.329; see also 5.422, 5.490, and 5.499).[5] Inevitably, adds Lenin, this will have an agitating effect on workers: with this newly acquired knowledge about the mechanics of capitalism, and the sort of exploitation at its heart, workers will make demands for shorter working days, better wages, and safer working conditions (5.425).[6] Indeed, in Lenin's mind, "urban factory workers" are the heart of this movement, the target of the vanguard's activism, and the source of hope for those longing for justice: the urban proletariat, he says, are "most susceptible to Social-Democratic ideas, most developed intellectually and politically, and most important by virtue of their numbers and concentration in the country's largest centres" (2.330; see also 5.373 and 5.429–31). But that does not mean that the party should ignore the "rural proletariat" altogether – "the many millions of regular farm workers and day labourers, and also ... ruined peasants who ... cling to their miserable plots of land" (2.330). Quite the opposite, though the practical task of enlightening and educating "handicraftsmen and rural labourers" falls, in the end, to the "Russian factory worker," who frequently "comes into close contact with the rural proletariat" (2.330; see also 5.422).

At first, Lenin imagines the workers wringing "partial concessions from their enemy," here and there effecting surface-level improvements to "their economic condition," thanks in large measure to party-led organization, discipline, and training (2.332; see also 5.375). Eventually, though, he endorses the possibility of something much more radical:

the reconstitution of the Russian state altogether. According to Lenin, these two modes of activism – economic and political – are "inseparably" linked together: "every strike, ... agitation against the restriction of the rights of workers as Russian citizens" is a political act – an exposure of the "class content ... [of] absolutism" and of the need "to overthrow it" (2.332). In fact, it is simply not possible to wage "a successful struggle for the workers' cause without achieving political liberty and the democratisation of Russia's political and social system" (2.332). Russia's economy cannot be made more just, that is, until the state is made more democratic; hence, Lenin's belief that "economic agitation" goes hand in hand with "political agitation" – that they are, in fact, "two sides of the same metal" (2.332). In this endeavor – political agitation – the workers have a host of unlikely allies: all those classes "persecuted by the autocratic government," including the bourgeoisie, who "cannot help but realise that industrial development is being retarded by the autocracy" (2.333). Even Marx and Engels "themselves belonged to the bourgeois intelligentsia" (5.375)! But it is essential, adds Lenin, that this partnership be "temporary and conditional": "the Social-Democrats support the progressive classes against the reactionary class," to be sure; but this support is undermined by the knowledge that, in the end, the bourgeoisie want to limit democracy exclusively to the property-owning classes (2.334; see also 5.361–2).

This is also a prominent theme of "What Is to Be Done?" Lenin begins the essay by excoriating what he calls "practical Bernsteinism":[7] the recent decision by socialist parties in Germany and France to abandon orthodox Marxism in favor of political cooperation with conventional (i.e., bourgeois) parties, within the confines of constitutional democracy, in order to gradually reform capitalism (5.354). Of course, Lenin abhors this "slavish" complicity with the status quo, and he pulls no punches with those who advocate for it: how, he asks, can these so-called socialists "remain in cabinet even after the shooting-down of workers for the hundredth and thousandth time" (5.354)? How can such "opportunists" be content with "pompous *projects* for miserable reforms" in the face of real suffering (5.354)? Why are they so willing to be reduced to a mere "appendage of the liberals" (5.363)?

Over and over, Lenin rejects (gradual) reform altogether: *genuine* socialism is, by its very nature, "the *most revolutionary*" doctrine (5.373); it aims at nothing less than "the most far-reaching historical task ...

the overthrowing of the autocracy ... [and] the achievement of political liberty ... for the working class in Russia" (5.376; see also 5.421). True socialists therefore cannot be content with merely "alleviating the distress to which [workers'] condition gives rise" through constitutional measures, such as the right to strike and form unions, as well as laws against child labor and dangerous working conditions (5.387; see also 5.404). Instead, they are committed to "the abolition of the social system that compels the propertyless to sell themselves to the rich" (5.400). And, again, this movement requires stable intellectual leadership by professionals – a "compact core of the most reliable, experienced, and hardened workers ... connected by all the rules of strict secrecy" – not spontaneous mass demonstration by workers (5.459).[8] In fact, Lenin explicitly defines socialism as "*a fierce struggle against spontaneity*": it is essential, he says, that revolutionary activity be undertaken in accordance with "a systematic and carefully thought-out and gradually prepared plan for a prolonged and stubborn struggle" (5.442); hence, "an organisation of revolutionaries [is] an essential factor in 'bringing about' the political revolution" (5.452). The contrast that Lenin draws, here, is to the "amateurish methods" employed by his political and intellectual opponents, who act without adequate training, preparation, discretion, secrecy, or, most likely, some toxic, self-defeating combination thereof (5.443).

What, then, *is* to be done? Here, Lenin calls for the decisive abolition of spontaneity and, by extension, the development of a cadre of specialized, secretive revolutionaries: it is essential, he says, "to have a strong [centralized] organisation of tried revolutionaries ... professional agitators, organisers, propagandists, literature distributors ... [leaders with] experience and dexterity ... without which the proletariat *cannot* wage a stubborn struggle against its excellently trained enemies" (5.469). And this task, adds Lenin, falls to the Social-Democratic Party: its members must constantly be on the lookout for those "gifted and promising ... worker-agitators"; the party must ensure that its leaders – present and future – are "not left to work eleven hours a day in a factory" – that they are adequately supported and so able to "go underground in good time ... [where they can] enlarge their experience, widen their outlook, and are able to hold out for at least a few years in the struggle against the gendarmes" (5.472).[9] And often, this will lead trained revolutionaries to programs beyond "what is 'accessible' to the masses" (5.473).

Well and good, says Lenin: the vanguard is precisely that, and so must shed its "fear of rising too high above mere attendance on the immediate and direct requirements of the masses" (5.472). But this ought not be a cause for concern: the party is "boundlessly devoted" to the cause of revolution and it, in turn, enjoys "the boundless confidence of the widest masses of the workers," despite the latter's inability to fully grasp the ideas and actions of those who fight in its name (5.472; see also 5.511–12). To the question, how does the necessity of a furtive, militant vanguard square with his equal insistence on the democratic character of the socialist revolution, Lenin gives no satisfying answer. The "urgent tasks of the moment," he says, combined with "the gloom of the autocracy and the domination of the gendarmerie," justify "the strictest secrecy and strictest (consequently, more restricted) selection of members" (5.478; see also 9.86).

## 2

In "Two Tactics of Social-Democracy," written in the summer of 1905, Lenin candidly admits that the influence of his Social-Democratic Party on "the masses of the proletariat ... is as yet very, very weak ... quite insignificant" (9.57; see also 23.238). But Lenin is also optimistic: "Revolution unites rapidly and enlightens rapidly. Every step in its development rouses the masses and attracts them with irresistible force" (9.57). Since 1905, the fledgling autocracy has been massively helpful in this respect: its ineptitude, its willingness to conspire with the big landowners and urban bourgeoisie, its "atrocious" cruelty toward Jews, its willingness to "systematically and unswervingly" employ "bayonets and rifle butts" to pacify workers – all have created deep resentment and "widespread ferment" (9.132, 23.238, and 23.250).[10] In fact, "within a few months" of the first revolutionary thrust in the streets of St. Petersburg, "the picture changed completely [and] dormant Russia was transformed into a Russia of a revolutionary proletariat and a revolutionary people" (23.238; see also 23.247–8).

Indeed, in his "Lecture on the 1905 Revolution," Lenin describes a "wave-like rise" of mass strikes, beginning among the metal workers of St. Petersburg, Riga, and Warsaw, then cascading down to the textile factories and even to the rural peasantry (23.240). And eventually, there began a series of mutinies in the army and the navy too. Here, Lenin relates the story of a sailor named Petrov who "with one shot killed [his superior officer] Captain Stein of the Belosk Regiment" – a microcosmic reflection of the fact that the "major questions in ... life ... are settled only by force" (23.244 and 9.132). So too with the (in Lenin's mind) inevitable, "decisive victory over tsarism": no such victory can take place without reliance on "military force, on the arming of the masses ... [with] rifles, revolvers, knives, knuckledusters, sticks, rags coated in kerosene for starting fires, barbed wire, nails, etc., etc." (9.56 and 9.420; see also 11.61–8).

Here, Lenin describes "the establishment of the *revolutionary-democratic dictatorship of the proletariat and peasant*," the essential task of which is "to destroy the remnants of the old institutions" (9.56 and 9.132). This regime "*must* act dictatorially" and avoid reactionary half-measures: "constitutional illusions and school exercises in parliamentarism" constitute "the bourgeois betrayal of the revolution" (9.132). According to Lenin, this is Marx's view as well: in a series of 1848 articles on the workers' uprising in Berlin, Marx laments the new regime's unwillingness to "immediately smash up" the institutions of imperial Prussia, preferring instead the ("boring") gradualist strategy of working through its toothless democratic assembly (quoted in 9.131–2). Clearly, Lenin takes this lesson to heart: the most important task of any newly established workers' regime, he says, is "defence against counter-revolution and [by extension] the actual elimination of everything that contradicted the sovereignty of ... the proletariat and the peasantry" (9.133; see also 24.370). And, of course, the revolutionary wave of 1905 ultimately fails this test: the assembly established that year is simply a continuation of tsarist despotism – the successful pacification of powerful elements of the bourgeoisie by incorporating their voice and their interests into the organs of the tsarist government (23.247).

Even after Nicholas's abdication in 1917, Lenin still refuses to accept the legitimacy of the provisional government left if in its wake.[11] Despite its superficial constitutional facade, the Lvov regime is, at bottom, indistinguishable from its autocratic predecessor – it even continued the capitalist war, conducting secret agreements with imperialist Britain and France (24.259; see also 25.413)! Hence, upon his arrival at Finland Station, Lenin promptly declares his unwillingness to support the provisional government (24.21–2).[12] Instead, all power should belong to the soviets – "the *only possible* form of revolutionary government" (24.23). These soviets were first formed in the wake of the 1905 uprising; they were made up of "delegates from all factories," and promptly usurped the government authorities, forming a network of "small local 'republics'" (23.248).

Lenin celebrates the direct democratic character of this "peculiar mass organization": unlike the "parliamentary bourgeois-democratic republic of the usual type," the soviets exercise power "on the direct initiative of the people from below, ... *not on a law* enacted by a centralised state power" (23.249 and 24.38; see also 25.373 and 28.247–8). In this, they resemble the Paris Commune of 1871, which Marx also celebrates in his "Civil War in France" (24.39; see also 631–6). Unfortunately, Lenin concedes, these soviets are still "weak and incipient" vis-à-vis the provisional government; but they *do* "exist" alongside it, and they are "growing" (24.38). It is the responsibility of the party vanguard to accelerate the class-consciousness of these soviets, and thus facilitate the complete usurpation of "the bourgeoisie by the *second* government – the Soviet of Workers' Deputies" (24.40; see also 24.373–4).

# 3

In chapter 1 of *The State and Revolution*, Lenin outlines the "prime task" of the work: "to *re-establish* what Marx really taught on the subject of the state" (25.391). This is necessary, he adds, because many of his contemporaries – self-identified Marxists, though "petty-bourgeois ideologists" in actual fact – "omit, obscure or distort the revolutionary side of [Marx's] theory" of the state; they reinterpret that theory so that it "seems acceptable to the bourgeoisie," when that theory *actually* necessitates the "*destruction* of the apparatus of state power" altogether (25.392).[13] After all, the state is, first and foremost, an instrument of class domination: its purpose is to legitimate and protect the bourgeoisie's exploitation of the proletariat; as that exploitation becomes more extreme, and class conflict becomes more acute, the need to ramp up the state's repressive apparatus – its police, its army, its prisons – becomes more pressing (25.394; see also 25.412). Hence, the vast majority of those subject to its power regard the state as a source of alienation – a distant, inscrutable, parasitic network of violence-wielding institutions that stand outside and above social life (25.397). This complex of institutions will be decisively "*abolished* by the proletariat in the course of the revolution" (25.402; see also 25.373).

The first step, here, after the usurpation of political power, is the rapid, violent, public expropriation of the once private means of production: the postrevolutionary dictatorship of the proletariat is a "special coercive force for the suppression of the bourgeoisie" (25.402). Of course, the necessary expropriating infrastructure is already in place: the state, by its very nature, is "an organization of violence for the suppression of some class" and, in the wake of the revolution, that organization is redirected away from the proletariat – its target under capitalism – toward "the exploiting class, i.e., the bourgeoisie" with the stated aim of "completely removing it" (25.407–8). Here, Lenin invokes the Marxist principle, outlined most explicitly in "The Eighteenth Brumaire of Louis Bonaparte," that history sets us only eminently solvable tasks: the overthrow of the bourgeoisie is possible, he says, because that class unknowingly set in place, and then "perfected," the centralized coercive infrastructure needed to do so – the bureaucracy and the standing army (25.410–11 and 25.470; see also 25.595). Eventually, though, "the state machine ... must be broken, smashed" (25.411); the expropriating dictatorship of the proletariat is, by its nature, temporary, fleeting, designed to wither away.

What takes the place of the state machine? First, Lenin calls for the "abolition of the standing army," in favor of a people's militia made up of workers and peasants (24.182). And he also calls for the radical transformation – the "socialist reorganization" – of the bureaucracy: "Officials," he says, must "be elected and subject to recall ..., their wages reduced to the level of ordinary 'workmen's' wages'" (25.424 and 25.426). *This* is what *real,* "fuller" democracy looks like: the state machinery is no longer the exclusive domain of a "privileged minority (privileged officialdom, the chiefs of the standing army)"; instead, "the majority itself can fulfil all [state] functions," and the more involved the people are in the exercise of political power, the less alien the state becomes (25.424–5). Like Marx before him, Lenin makes sure to note the irony at work here: "Capitalist culture," he says, "has *created* large-scale production, factories, railways, the postal service, telephones, etc., and *on this basis* the great majority of the functions of the old 'state power' have become so simplified and can be reduced to such exceedingly simple operations of registration, filing and checking that they can be easily performed by every literate person" (25.425–6).

This is the heart of Lenin's argument for the possibility of stateless communism: capitalist institutions and processes of production are so technologically and bureaucratically advanced that they are characterized by a kind of splendid automaticity (25.431). Here, Lenin discusses the postal service, "an example of the socialist economic system" and a blueprint for the organization of post-state economic institutions: the inner workings of the organization are so thoroughly routinized, he says, that the need for expertise is negated; minimal literacy is the full extent of the administrative and practical talents needed to make the operation function well (25.431; see also 25.477–8). And much the same can be said about industrial production more generally: an initial plan or goal is set for each firm, and a vast, complex mechanism is set in motion, each constituent part of which – each technician, foreman, administrator, accountant, and so on – has a well-defined sense of purpose and responsibility (25.431). They key issue, of course, is who has the power to set the plan, and who benefits from its efficient completion. Under capitalism, benefits accrue (exclusively, spectacularly) to the bourgeoisie, while workers are paid a piddling wage – exploitation in a nutshell. After the expropriation of the means of production, though, benefits accrue to society as a whole.

In the early stages of socialism, decisions regarding production, investment, and redistribution are made by "the armed vanguard of all exploited and working people" (25.430; see also 25.438–9). Indeed, Lenin is adamant that the centralized bureaucratic state does not, and cannot, disappear overnight; he does not endorse, or long for, some freewheeling anarchist utopia (25.440 and 25.466). For socialism to function well – for the postrevolutionary society to retain, and increase, the high level of productivity that characterized the capitalist epoch – the state must establish a careful economic plan: "a reserve fund ... must be deducted from ... the social labour of society," a fund for "the expansion of production, ... for the replacement of the 'wear and tear' of machinery, and so on"; then, "from the means of consumption must be deducted a fund for administrative expenses, for schools, hospitals, old people's homes, and so on" (25.469; see also 25.329 and 27.241). And the state must also implement that plan with "strict, iron discipline backed up by the state power of armed workers" (25.431). This is the responsibility of self-governing, "genuinely democratic ... Soviets of Workers' and Soldiers' Deputies" (25.475). Work remains "socially necessary," in other words, and the prospect of force omnipresent, but the experience of state-sanctioned discipline at work is conspicuously different: work is no longer a form of exploitation and a source of alienation; now, it contributes to society's shared capital, which, in turn, makes possible the satisfaction of the needs of all (25.470–1; see also 25.474–8).

But this vanguard must still set in motion the "*gradual* abolition of all bureaucracy"; *this* is the stated, ultimate "*aim*" of "the *temporary* dictatorship of the oppressed class" (25.470–1, and 25.441; italics added). This is a "lengthy process," to be sure, and it is impossible to specify, with any precision, "the moment of the [state's] 'withering away'" (25.462; see also 25.473–4). But a communist society – a just and happy society – is a stateless society; in Lenin's mind, there is no ambiguity about this: only under communism, he says, "when the resistance of the capitalists has been completely crushed, when the capitalists have disappeared, when there are no classes, ... *only* then [quoting Engels's letter to Bebel] 'the state ceases to exist,' and 'it becomes possible to speak of freedom'" (25.467).

Once again, the model, here, ironically, is the private firm under capitalism: the simplification, routinization, and ensuing democratization of the levers of industrial power means that the role of employees is gradually (but surely) pared down "to that of simply carrying out ... instructions as responsible, revocable, modestly paid 'foremen and accountants'" (25.431). According to Lenin, much the same can be said about the bureaucracy: "The functions of control and accounting, becoming more and more simple, will be performed by each in turn, will then become a habit and will finally die out as the *special* functions of a special section of the population" (25.431). Society, *as a whole*, achieves that splendid automaticity, which is possible only in postcapitalist modernity. With the inexorable advance of technology, the need for the directing bourgeoisie and for the specialized bureaucracy has evaporated: control of the state apparatus has become "universal, general and popular" (25.479).

At this point, adds Lenin, it is only a matter of time before the arrival of communism, though in the end he refuses to say exactly how much: "From the moment that all members of society ... have learned to administer the state *themselves*," he says, "the need for government of any kind begins to disappear altogether" (25.479). Of course, Lenin acknowledges the persistence of isolated acts of violence – a "scuffle" here and there, the occasional "assault"; these are inevitable, he concedes, and must be dealt with by the force of "the armed people themselves" (25.469). But this does *not* necessitate some "special machine," some "special apparatus of suppression"; this is necessary only under capitalism, with its class domination, radical, widespread deprivation, and ensuing criminality (25.469). With the disappearance of the "want and poverty" created by the "exploitation of the people" by the bourgeoisie – and with the establishment of an economic system characterized by *inclusive* opportunity and prosperity, and by the commitment to satisfy the needs of all – "people will gradually *become accustomed* to observing the elementary rules of social intercourse ... without violence ... without force, without coercion, without subordination, *without the special apparatus* for coercion called the state" (25.467; see also 25.461).

## 4

Not long after the October Revolution, Lenin acknowledges the realities of the Russian situation: if the democratization of "accounting and control" is the essential precondition of the withering away of the state, then statelessness remains a distant prospect indeed.[14] After all, these areas are still the exclusive domain of "bourgeois experts," who must be paid top dollar for their services to the state – without doubt, Lenin concedes, a violation of the socialist commitment to equality, and so "*a step backward* on the part of Soviet power" (27.249; see also 31.44). This is merely the first of a seemingly never-ending series of setbacks, delays, and concessions to the bourgeoisie: the nationalized People's Bank is still unable to attract deposits, property and income taxes remain underreported and therefore uncollected, and essential monopolies – in grain and leather, especially – are routinely undermined by "bribe-takers and crooks"; the establishment and enforcement of "compulsory labour service" for the rich has also been more difficult than expected (27.252). And, perhaps most worryingly of all, the productivity of Russian industry lags far behind that of Western Europe: without major advances in "the development of the production of fuel, iron, the engineering and chemical industries," without the installation of "the Taylor system" of industrial production, without an educational and cultural revolution among Russian workers, the vast majority of whom are still suffering from a "hangover from serfdom," the eventual transition to communism cannot sustainably take place (27.257–8).[15]

It is therefore no surprise that, in the end, Lenin came to share Marx and Engels's assessment of the Russian situation. In a 1918 letter to American workers, for example, he acknowledges that, although Russia was "the first country to *break* the convict chains of the imperialist war," the continued success of her revolution depends on "help from ... the European proletarian revolution" (28.74–5; see also 31). Russia, after all, is still characterized by an "exceptional backwardness" and is therefore in need of help from the more economically and technologically developed West (28.74–5). But Lenin also candidly admits that he does not expect the workers' revolution to "flare up within the next few weeks" (28.74–5). The spirit of the Western proletariat is "maturing, growing, gaining more strength," to be sure; but revolutions do not arrive "on a *definite* and early date" (28.74–5). Russia must therefore wait, "in a besieged fortress ... for the other detachments of the world socialist revolution to come to our relief" (28.74–5).

But this wait need not be wholly passive: the Russian proletariat must actively form intellectual and political "alliance[s] with the revolutionaries of the advanced countries" (25.87). And so, in his 1920 pamphlet, "Left-Wing Communism: An Infantile Disorder," Lenin does his best to efface the seemingly "enormous difference between backward Russia and the advanced countries of Western Europe" (31.21; see also 31.31). In fact, he says, "certain fundamental features of our revolution have a significance that is not local, or peculiarly national, but international" (31.21). What is needed, more than anything is a "proletarian vanguard" characterized by "its tenacity, self-sacrifice and heroism" and driven into action "by a correct revolutionary theory" (31.24–5; see also 31.41). With this plea for persistent, disciplined, and (for the most part) uncompromising leadership by the professional intelligentsia, Lenin's intellectual career comes full circle, never having come close – not remotely – to the promised land.

9

# "The Function of Industry": Tawney on the Demands of Equality and the Need for Democracy

Reading Lenin's political philosophy is a plaintive affair: the promises of workplace democracy, genuine equality, and the gradual dissolution of the state all come to naught; what emerges, instead, is a totalitarian grotesquerie. Indeed, the outlines of Stalinism – a specter that haunts every word that Lenin put to paper – emerge as early as 1917, as the Bolsheviks begin *consolidating* one-party rule, a process that unfolds with dizzying rapidity.[1] "Members of leading bodies of the [opposition] Cadet Party, as a party of enemies of the people," declares Lenin on November 28, "are liable to arrest and trial by revolutionary tribunal. Local Soviets are ordered to exercise special surveillance over the Cadet Party" (26.351). Two weeks later, on December 7, the Bolsheviks establish the All-Russian Extraordinary Commission for Combatting Counterrevolution, Sabotage, and Speculation, which leads to the shuttering of critical newspapers, mass arrests of political opponents, and even summary executions, all under Lenin's guidance and with his hearty approval (see, e.g., 26.283, 27.518–19, 33.330–3, 44.49, 44.135, and 44.283–4). Finally, on January 6, 1918, the Bolsheviks dissolve the Constituent Assembly, Lenin declaring it "an expression of the old relation of political forces which existed when power was held by the compromisers ... [and so] an obstacle in the path of the October

Revolution and Soviet power" (26.277). With that, the dictatorship of the proletariat *vanguard* was firmly established.

What follows is a series of compromises, reversals, and (mostly) disastrous failures, all rooted in ideological zeal and an accompanying disregard for the constraints of the possible: the expropriation and redistribution of land "from the kulaks and sharks" to the peasantry leads to violent score-settling and chaos in the country (26.515); the forced collectivization of farms leads to widespread corruption and devastating famine (27.348); the state's appropriation of the industrial means of production leads to dictatorial control over factory labor, a wave of strikes and disturbances in response, as well as shortages of essential manufactured goods (27.243); and the elevation of the priority to feed the cities and the military leads to the forced requisition of meager agricultural surpluses, and a cascade of rural anti-Bolshevik resentment, to which the state responds with the creation of a "food army ... [designed to] carry out any instructions that may be given by the People's Commissariat for Food" (27.455; see also 28.339–48). Indeed, the only predictable feature of Bolshevik policy in the early years of its rule – ineptitude aside – was the party's willingness to employ violent force against "the enemies of the people" in the pursuit of whatever policy it happened to adopt at any given moment (26.351; see also 32.183–5 and 32.241–4).

This is not the place to list the crimes and abuses committed by the Russian state under Lenin and then Stalin.[2] It suffices, here, to emphasize that a real and undeniable aspect of Lenin's legacy is his intense drive to centralize the state and to eliminate all organized political opposition, with violence if necessary – a trait that Lenin clearly passes on to his successor. Indeed, there was to be no withering of the state, as promised, before or after Lenin's death on January 21, 1924. Even Lenin's immediate contemporaries were able to foresee – in general contours, not minute detail, of course – the monstrous brutality of the Bolsheviks under and after Lenin. For example, in his 1918 pamphlet "The Dictatorship of the Proletariat," Karl Kautsky calls attention to the dictatorial tendencies of the Lenin regime; he warns against the dangers implicit in rule by a vanguard without law, the "erroneous" ways of the path currently taken by the Bolsheviks and the likelihood of eventual "destruction" of the workers' revolutionary movement (2). Instead, the proletariat must pursue its objectives through democratic channels:

"Socialism without democracy," says Kautsky, "is unthinkable" (6). It is therefore essential, he adds, that the proletariat develop and make use of its political strength within the status quo – that the socialization of the economy come about as a result of "making use of the [political and civil] liberties which [already] exist" as part of the existing constitutional state (9). Democracy, after all, is, at bottom, a numbers game: as the ranks of the working can swell – inevitable under capitalism – the proletariat can seize the instruments of political power *at the ballot box.* Kautsky even cites Marx's authority on the matter: "Marx thought it possible," he adds, "that in England and America the proletariat might *peacefully* conquer political power" (9; italics added).

Lenin's response is swift, brutal, and altogether predictable: he sets out to disprove Kautsky's "renegade sophistries" and accuses him of the ultimate crime – the "complete renunciation of Marxism" (28.229)! Indeed, in Kautsky's hands, Marx himself has been reduced from a genuine revolutionary to – the horror – "a common liberal" (28.241). The proletariat, retorts Lenin, simply cannot renounce the use of "revolutionary violence ... against its oppressors": the political rule of the bourgeoisie is too thoroughly entrenched for even a moment's complicity with its *supposedly* democratic institutions (28.241). Indeed, the inclusivity of democracy is itself mere illusion: "You will see at every turn evidence of the hypocrisy of bourgeois democracy ... [all of which have] loopholes or reservations in [the] constitution guaranteeing the possibility of dispatching troops against workers, of proclaiming martial law, in case of a 'violation of public order'" (28.244). Constitutional parliamentarism must therefore be smashed altogether – it is "a paradise for the rich and a snare and deception for the exploited, for the poor" (28.243). Instead, power must be exercised by the dictatorship of the proletariat: this requires a vanguard of professional revolutionaries, at least at first, and then the gradual devolution of power to the soviets, "the direct organization of the working and exploited people themselves, which *helps* them to organize and administer their own state in every possible way" (28.247).

In his polemic against Kautsky, Lenin celebrates the impressive progress of the soviet system of government since the dissolution of the Constituent Assembly: in the year following the Bolshevik seizure of power, soviet membership has nearly doubled, and "*two* all-Russia congresses of representatives of the overwhelming majority of the population" have taken place – all this despite the fact that Russia remains "a backward country," her impoverished citizens possessing "the least experience, education and habits of organization" (28.270–1). Imagine what could be possible, Lenin implies, in the more affluent, more educated, more technologically advanced West. This is precisely the note on which "The Renegade Kautsky" ends – with a call to revolution, and plea for help from, abroad. This is a familiar refrain in Lenin's polemics – the interconnectedness of domestic and foreign policy. The sustainability of Russia's revolution, Lenin concedes, is not guaranteed without workers' uprisings in the West. Luckily, those workers abroad have been given a blueprint and a wellspring of inspiration: "Bolshevism," Lenin declares, "has actually helped to develop the proletarian revolution in Europe and America.... The workers of the whole world are realising more and more clearly that the tactics of the ... Kautskys have not delivered them from ... wage-slavery.... *Bolshevism can serve as a model of tactics for all*" (28.293).

Of course, the exact opposite turns out to be the case in the West, where Kautsky's moderate view wins the day: in contrast to Russian Marxism, twentieth-century socialism is characterized by its principled renunciation of violence – by the view that the legitimate rise to power must be accomplished, *exclusively*, through constitutional democratic channels. The Regina Manifesto, published in 1933 by the Canadian socialist political party, the Co-operative Commonwealth Federation (CCF), offers a representative example. In many ways, the CCF manifesto recalls Bolshevism in its ideological assumptions and political agenda: the capitalist system is there characterized by "injustice and inhumanity ... domination and exploitation ... waste and instability ... poverty and insecurity." The interests of workers are "habitually sacrificed" to the "predatory" interests of "a small irresponsible minority of financiers and industrials," and, as a result, society "oscillates between feverish prosperity ... and catastrophic depression." Instead, society's productive resources – natural and industrial – must be "owned, controlled and operated by the people," with the ultimate aim of making possible "a much greater degree of leisure and a much richer life for every citizen." With all of this, Lenin and his contemporaries would surely agree. But, in the end, there is one essential difference between Marxism-Leninism and democratic socialism in the postcolonial West: the "social and economic transformation" of capitalism into socialism, reads the CCF platform's preface, must "be brought about by political action, through the election of a government ... supported by a majority of the people. *We do not believe in change by violence.*"

It is quite easy to trace the historical genesis of this attitude toward the pursuit of political power: at the end of the nineteenth century, a wave of British craftsmen and laborers began to pour into Canada, bringing with them a socialist consciousness ripe for implantation in the agricultural and industrial milieu abroad.[3] And English socialism was itself characterized, first and foremost, by its (relative) moderation (vis-à-vis Leninism), by its (again relative) lack of militancy (compared to the Russian proletariat). Indeed, according to Schumpeter, English socialism is an eminently "practical" variety of "progressivism," one that looks to "improvement" within the constraints of the status quo – improvements effected by "parliamentarians" and state "administrators" – not the radical reconstitution of it; the typical English socialist, adds Schumpeter, is not a "straight enemy of the established order," looking to instigate "revolutions and class wars," but is rather a "reformer" desirous to make "economic care a public affair," knowing that this is sure to be "a slow process" (*CSD* 322–4).

This is the intellectual milieu in which R.H. Tawney comes of age.[4] In 1906, he joins the Fabian Society, the heart of gradualist British socialism, and later, at Oxford and then the London School of Economics, sets down a thoroughgoing, engaging, and still powerful critique of Victorian industrialism. Any honest, clear-eyed, sane assessor of the modern English capitalist milieu, he says, over and over, will recognize the sickness of that society, its need for stout medicine. This is indeed a common refrain in Tawney's thought: the altogether obvious flaws of unplanned capitalism – the unfair privileges it creates for the few, the depths of destitution to which it condemns the majority – all plain to see, even for the untrained eye. A person with even a single ounce of compassion will therefore be drawn, inexorably, to socialism.

# 1

Along what lines, then, *ought* the economy to be organized? Of course, "any considerable reconstruction of society" must begin with "an appeal to principles"; the economy cannot be effectively redesigned, that is, without a clear sense "of the deficiency of what is, and of the character of what ought to be" (*AS* 10). And Tawney believes that guiding principles for this industrial reorganization are quite "elementary" – plain for all to see, really (*AS* 12). Industry, after all, is nothing mysterious: it is an association of persons designed to achieve some function or common purpose. And so those in search of principles to guide these associations must begin by asking, What purpose or function is industry meant to serve? What is all this productive activity *for*, exactly? Why are we working so hard, and making so much? What is the *end* of all this feverish effort? Again, for Tawney, the answer to these questions is simple and obvious (though obscured by the theory- and principle-phobic status quo): the purpose of industry, he says, is to "supply man with things which are necessary, useful, or beautiful, and thus bring life to body or spirit" (*AS* 11); "the function of industry," put simply, "is *service*" (*AS* 13; italics added). We work and create, that is, in order to serve others, to satisfy their needs – some basic, corporeal, and essential, others complex, refined, and (strictly speaking) useless; there is, in other words, "a social quality" or "purpose" proper to industry (*AS* 11).[5] And so "service" too is the standard against which production ought to be judged and valued: to what extent do these activities serve the common needs, and advance the "common ends," of society (*AS* 17–19)?

Under capitalism we have clearly lost sight of this. The modern economic milieu is characterized by atomistic self-assertion – "private rights and private interests, ... absolute and indefeasible" (*AS* 18) – and by a relentless obsession with "productivity" – the god of the capitalists, "the first word that rises in their minds" (*AS* 11). In such a milieu, self-interest always trumps the "larger purpose" of society; there are, by extension, "no moral limitations on the pursuit by individuals of their economic self-interest" (*AS* 20). Tawney traces this view of life to John Locke and Adam Smith: first, Locke defends the "indefeasibility of [private] property rights," setting the stage for Smith's fantastic account of the infallible "alchemy by which the pursuit of private ends is transmuted into the public good" (*AS* 20; see also *AS* 51). Tawney concedes that, when read in proper historical context, the new economic philosophy is necessary, heroic even – the enlightened critique of irrational, unjust feudal privileges and the worthwhile democratization of the rights of economic enterprise (*AS* 23 and 52). In an industrial society, though, as private property comes to be concentrated in fewer and fewer hands, none of which actually work, this Smithian alchemy is wholly illusory – the ideological foundation of what he calls "the acquisitive society," the society committed to "unfettered economic freedom ... independent of any service" unconsciously or intentionally rendered to it (*AS* 22 and 25). In such a society, any limit on individual initiative – "a minimum standard of safety and sanitation from the owners of mills," say, or even a basic tax on income and inheritance – is met with howls of opposition (*AS* 26–7). After all, the purpose of human life, according to this (in Tawney's mind, depraved and despicable) line of thinking, is "to give free play to the one of the most powerful human instincts ... the unlimited acquisition of riches" (*AS* 32).

Tawney rejects outright the values and assumptions of the acquisitive society: the pursuit of riches, without limits, he says, is "meaningless" – "the confusion of one minor part of life with the whole of life" (*AS* 35 and 44). This is a conspicuously Aristotelian moment in Tawney's thought: for both, acquisition is – rather, it ought to be – a *means* to happiness, well-being, and the flourishing of close associates, not an end in itself. Under capitalism, though, the relationship is reversed: the pursuit of wealth becomes the ultimate end – all other ends are subordinated to it – and that pursuit, by its very nature, is "infinite" (*AS* 42–3). Hence, Tawney's depiction of capitalist activity as a kind of ceaseless, pathological, and ultimately hollow striving; all individual participants are incapable of lasting satisfaction with their lot (*AS* 42–3). But this individual psychological damage is not the full extent of the damage wrought; capitalism's system of values – and the characteristic disposition of those who endorse it – has social repercussions too: we come to regard others as nothing more than impediments to (or instruments that facilitate) the satisfaction of the ever-expanding desire for wealth, and social life is inexorably transformed "into a scene of fierce antagonisms" (*AS* 40). And there is yet another grave social consequence of this single-minded obsession with wealth: the irresponsible employment of society's productive resources. When market signals alone are the determinant of social production, precious (finite) resources are squandered in the production of those useless and wasteful things desired by the rich – "hotels, luxurious yachts, and motor cars like that used by a Secretary of State for War"; such things "no man can make with happiness," aware that "they had much better not be made, and that his life is wasted in making them" (*AS* 38).

But this attitude toward wealth and productive activity is by no means *necessary*: it is the contingent by-product of an arbitrary historical tide. It is therefore possible to imagine a cultural sea change – a profound paradigm shift, from infinite accumulation to the secure satisfaction of the basic needs of all.[6] And Tawney thinks that this paradigm shift will come about if we look at the present situation with clear eyes and solid common sense: "If the nation desires to re-equip its industries with machinery and its railways with wagons," he asks, "had it not better refrain from holding exhibitions designed to encourage rich men to re-equip themselves with motor cars" (*AS* 39)? Conspicuous consumption, and production oriented by it, is an obvious moral affront: it leads to the gratification of the few, and the degradation of the many. What is required, instead, is careful attention to society's *real* needs – "food, clothing, house-room, art, knowledge" – and the reorientation of production so that they are satisfied; what we need, adds Tawney, are "builders, mechanics, and teachers … not gardeners, chauffeurs, domestic servants and shopkeepers in the West End of London" (*AS* 39). Away from trifles for the rich toward necessities for all – only a thoughtless and uncaring person could privilege the former over the latter.

According to Tawney, this indicates to us a very powerful principle for regulating our productive activity: such activity is meaning*ful* only insofar as it is "subordinated to a social purpose" (*AS* 35) and meaning*less* insofar as it lacks "any end or purpose other than the satisfaction of those engaged in it" (*AS* 40). And this leads, in turn, to another powerful and important regulating principle: that property rights are not absolute and inviolable, as the proponents of the acquisitive society claim (*AS* 40–1). Instead, such rights are "contingent and derivate"; they exist in order to "discharge a social purpose" and can therefore "be justly revoked" when they fail to do so (*AS* 29; see also *AS* 13–14). In other words, productive activity itself is constrained by the existence of limits, limits defined by society's needs of the day.

Tawney is clear-eyed about the implications of his principled belief that not "all economic activity is equally justifiable" – that there *is* in fact "a principle superior to the mechanical play of market forces" (*AS* 40); he acknowledges that it will require a quite radical reorientation – no, the abandonment – of the priorities of the acquisitive economy, and a quite radical degree of intervention by the state against the market mechanism and the institution of private property. But this is necessary and fitting, for as long as social life is conceived as the assertion of the inviolable right to accumulate wealth, wholly divorced from any accompanying obligations to others, the majority will be subjected "to the few whom good fortune, or special opportunity, or privilege have enabled most successfully to use those rights" (*AS* 45).

Society must therefore be recentered on duties: rights, after all, are things that we press upon others, that lead us to assert and "resist" (*AS* 80). Obligations, by contrast, conduce to cooperation: they are rooted in the pursuit of a specific end or purpose along with the assignation of roles, and performance of the animating responsibilities, necessary to achieve it. This focus on obligations forces us to ask, What *is it* that we are trying to achieve? What is the *purpose* of our productive life together? "The purpose of industry," says Tawney, "is to provide the material foundation of a good life" (*AS* 80); it exists "for the service of the public" (*AS* 92). It follows that any policy or institution that draws us away from that purpose ought to be abandoned: first and foremost, here, is the paradigm of private ownership and its accompanying managerial entitlement. When firms are privately owned by those who do not ever set foot in them, workers are "shovelled like raw material into an economic mill, to be pounded and ground and kneaded into human pulp," all in the search for rising dividends for absentee shareholders (*AS* 81). The only way to avoid such a predicament – how can a sane society passively allow such parasitism to continue, Tawney implicitly asks – is to socialize industry and, by extension, to invest planning, organizational, and executive power in "those who work, not those who own" (*AS* 81); the solution, in other words, is an "extension of public ownership," a form of economic organization in which "the worker is free to carry on his work without sharing its control or its profits with the mere *rentier*" (*AS* 82). We must treat the landlords and shareholders, says Tawney, "as Plato would have treated the poets ... crown them with flowers and usher them politely out of the state" (*AS* 86). Notice, here, Tawney's emphasis on politeness; he rejects the revolutionary "nationalization," or the "expropriation [of private property] without compensation" (*AS* 96). Instead, he endorses (comparatively gradual) reform through the formation of solidaristic unions and, more promisingly, legislative channels; it is eminently possible, Tawney says, for the once iron, insoluble bonds of private (total) ownership to be gradually "attenuated" through legal action by the state, paving the way for meaningful workplace democracy (*AS* 97; see also *AS* 112).[7]

In Tawney's mind, these two central imperatives – a renewed focus on service to the community, not escalating dividends for owners, and the democratization of industrial governance – are essentially connected, one the by-product of the other: when the instruments of organization and direction are in the hands of workers, the firm will be animated by a clearer, more specific sense of purpose – not profit, but the maximally efficient satisfaction of the needs of consumers compatible with workers' dignity and well-being. Profit is no longer the guided aim of productive activity – *service is* (*AS* 37). Whenever profits happen to be generated by efficient labor, they belong to the firm as a whole, to be used, redistributed, and invested as workers see fit (*AS* 102–3). It is essential, adds Tawney, that this fund be administered publicly and transparently: industrial finances must be transformed from "an inscrutable mystery," as they are under capitalism, to "a system of *public* costing and audit ... competently managed ... [and always open for] discussion and criticism" (*AS* 105; italics added; see also *AS* 126–7). In fact, when there is a widespread commitment to "publicity as to costs and profits" – when a spirit of "open dealing and honest work and mutual helpfulness" reigns (*AS* 103) – the conditions for speculation and risk-taking are negated: society is able to develop a clear sense of both its needs and its productive capacity, and can work toward a sustainable symmetry between the two; "the surpluses which are the subject of contention" under capitalism thus fade away, and society is delivered from the relentless, never-ending, destructive "industrial war" of all against all (*AS* 40–1; see also *AS* 105–6).

## 2

There are many hopeful signs of this dawning industrial reorganization, all initiated by effectively mobilized trade unions and then implemented by the legislative activity of the state: minimum wages and maximum hours, as well as the abolition of the "power of arbitrary dismissal" (*AS* 139).[8] Enlightened societies, adds Tawney, are now characterized by the dawning sense that workers' livelihood ought not to be "dependent on the caprices of an individual" (*AS* 139). This emphasis on caprice is a characteristic and recurring theme throughout Tawney's oeuvre: vulnerability to *arbitrary* power, he says, is antithetical to liberty; we cannot be free, so this line of thinking goes, if we are subject to an authority that we cannot control or (even less demandingly) constrain (*AS* 14). Of course, this is precisely the predicament that workers typically face under the paradigm of private ownership: possession of the means of production leads directly to the complete and total right to direct those instruments, including the right to determine who can earn their livelihood from their use. In other words, employers exercise a kind of "economic tyranny"; they have permanent recourse to the "terror of unemployment" and, as a result, the reliable compliance of their employees (*AS* 140–1).

This is the guiding theme of *Equality*: that the prevailing constitution of private firms is incompatible with the liberty of workers; and so, any society that publicly professes to care about the liberty of *all* its members must legislate away these industrial fiefdoms (*E* 164). To show this, Tawney begins with a discussion of the nature of power: power, he says, is necessary for all communities, because power is required to get things done – power is another way of discussing agency, the power to act; without it, society would be paralyzed and the talents of its individual members would remain underdeveloped and therefore unproductive for society at large (*E* 165). And, in fact, what is required here is an *inequality* of power: we need those with energy, wisdom, and dedication to guide the course of the community, and to pursue and achieve the goals that society sets for itself (*E* 165). But, of course, we don't want *too much* inequality of power: we *need* a class of leaders, to be sure; but we do *not* want to invest those leaders with the power to oppress us (*E* 165). After all, oppression is always a threat for people who live in communities and who participate in its organizational life: some lead, the rest follow, and the most important task for these groups – the task that makes our association stable, happy, and productive – is to ensure that leaders don't abuse the power at their disposal – that they don't prey upon those they lead.

And that is why, in the sphere of politics, we have developed important institutional innovations: innovations like the rule of law, which sets public, known, settled limits on what the state can (and cannot) do, and the system of constitutional checks and balances, whereby the power of the state is divided among legislative, executive, and judicial branches of government and is thus prevented from being used with too much unity or swiftness. According to Tawney, all of this is all well and good: "The need for [such] precautions is today not disputed," he says. "It is recognized that political power must rest on consent, and that its exercise must be limited by rules of law" (*E* 165). In other words, the need for – and exclusive legitimacy of – democracy is no longer in doubt when it comes to the political lives of states. It is conspicuous, though, that there is no such intellectual consensus on the exercise of *economic* power. Again, the most obvious example is the private firm: in advanced, industrial economies, productive activity is not taken on, primarily, by individuals; it is carried out by corporations – by massive, complex "groups that are endowed by the State with a special legal status" (*E* 166). For Tawney, the quintessential feature of these groups is what he calls the "unity of control": owners, that is, have complete and total discretion to determine "the lines of which the common enterprise is to proceed," as well as "the social environment of their employees" (*E* 166). As a result, those employees "pass their working lives under the direction of a hierarchy ... [a] business oligarchy," and working life is ultimately characterized by a detestable "precariousness" (*E* 166).

Now, as we have already seen, Tawney believes that social life itself, including our working life, is inevitably hierarchical: this is necessary and usually good. But there is an essential caveat here: that those *subject* to the power of their superiors have some meaningful say over how that power is exercised. We have already seen how this is true at the level of politics: lawmakers are democratically accountable to the people, and their actions are also constrained by the legal enactments of their democratically elected predecessors. But the same cannot be said about the capitalist firm: owners own and the rights of ownership give them the liberty to direct; and workers, in turn, must submit or face unemployment and, with it, starvation. Here, Tawney forces us to think precisely about what it means to be free: "Freedom," he says, "is always relative to power," and genuine freedom requires the placement of limits or constraints on that power (*E* 167). That's why "no [*genuinely free*] man [can] be amenable to an authority which is arbitrary in its proceedings, ... or incapable of being called to account" (*E* 166); no one can be called free, in any meaningful sense, when subject to an authority "whose [unpredictable] actions they are unable to modify or resist" (*E* 167). And, in Tawney's mind, this describes the predicament of workers under capitalism: submit or starve. In precisely this spirit, he quotes Louis Brandeis, who called the modern corporation an "industrial absolutism" (*E* 169). Of course, the obvious objection here is simply that the worker can quit and find work elsewhere. But Tawney's reply is equally simple and even more compelling: that this would merely amount to exchanging one unaccountable, unpredictable master for another. The unfreedom of the worker is woven into the organizational fabric of the firm.

So what, then, is the solution? The answer, says Tawney, is the "extension of liberty from the political to the economic sphere"; *this*, he adds, is one of "the most urgent tasks [facing] industrial societies" (*E* 167). What does such liberty (in the economic sphere) look like, exactly? The generous expansion of workplace democracy, "encouraged and accelerated" by the force of law: workers, that is, must have more extensive opportunities to participate in setting the course of their firm's direction, production processes, and social environment – including "matters of health, safety, hours, and wages," as well as decisions related to workplace "discipline, the introduction of new processes, machinery, and so-called scientific management" – and their right to do so must be backed by the punitive power of the state (*E* 167 and 174–9).

As an example, here, Tawney discusses the rapid growth of trade unionism in the early decades of the twentieth century, especially in Great Britain, and the accompanying political demand that matters once regarded as wholly "reserved to the decision of the management" should instead "be settled by negotiation" and "collective bargaining" (*E* 177). Workers, after all, are no less concerned than their employers "with the improvement of technique and organization," and so their representatives ought to have a meaningful and "constructive" say when decisions are made on "projects of the industry ... [and] questions of economic strategy" (*E* 178–9). *This* is what Tawney means when he says that "the control of those aspects of economic life by which all are affected must be amenable, in the last resort, to the will of all" (*E* 168). Ultimately, to retain its legitimacy, power must always be accountable to those affected by its exercise; this, more than anything, is the most effective guarantor against the enslavement of the "economically weak [by the] economically strong" (*E* 168). And this leads Tawney to proclaim the ultimate inextricability of liberty and equality: we cannot have the former, he says, without the latter. Without a commitment to democratic equality within the firm, that is – a commitment lived up to, at least initially, on account of the coercive sanction of the state – economic liberty is a chimera (*E* 181–2). Of course, this principle is true when applied to the wider political society too: without legal constraints on the resources and influence of the strong – without a commitment to prevent "sensational extremes of wealth and power by public action for the public good" (*E* 164) – the liberty of the weak is permanently under threat.

## 3

In his *Religion and the Rise of Capitalism*, Tawney traces our present misery – the waste, deprivation, and unfreedom characteristic of modern industrial society – to the seventeenth century; it is to Locke, he says, that we owe the (wrongheaded) view that the purpose of human association is to protect the private property of its individual members.[9] But what made the Lockean revolution possible? Of course, things have not always been so, as we have seen.[10] Take, for example, the "divines" of the medieval period: they "fulminated" against all forms of economic initiative, from "the uncharitable covetousness of the extortionate middle man" to "the grasping money-lender" to "the tyrannous landlord" (*RRC* 173–4). Such "economic license," they argued, ignited "the greed of individuals [and] the collision of classes"; it was therefore both "hateful to God" and a threat to "social solidarity" (*RRC* 173–4). This emphasis on social solidarity – on cohesion and stability, and on the virtue required to sustain them – runs throughout *Religion and the Rise of Capitalism*: in the medieval period, says Tawney, religion was "the preservative of order"; it emphasized the individual's "social duties [in] the corporate life of a complex, yet united, society," the possession and conscientious performance of which were the best antidote to socially destructive "cupidity and ambition" (*RRC* 173–4). Religious belief, in other words, orients us toward *community*, toward *service* to it; it constrains us from, say, charging our fellows a usurious rate of interest or an unjust price for the things they need (*RRC* 174).[11]

According to Tawney, the decisive moment in the pivot away from service – toward (Lockean) individualism – is the Reformation: after Luther, he says, "God speaks to the soul, not through the mediation of the priesthood *or of social institutions built up by man,* but *solus cum solo,* as a voice in the heart and in the heart alone" (*RRC* 105; italics added). This theological innovation is the first step toward the dissolution of the once sacred social bonds: salvation is no longer a property of community, no longer the purpose of community, no longer attained through membership and performance of one's duties as member. Instead, it is a wholly private and domestic affair (*RCC* 19–20).[12]

This, says Tawney, is fertile soil for the capitalist spirit: because our spiritual well-being is no longer bound up with salutary, mutually beneficial relations with others, the ground is laid for our use of them *as means.*[13] We have already seen the high cost of such a view (in this and in the previous two chapters). How can we regain what has been lost? How can we excavate the twin pillars of community and service and, with them, a feeling of spiritual succor? Tawney's answer is a sectarian one, disappointing to many:[14] "The essence of all morality is this," he writes in his diary, "to believe that every human being is of infinite importance, and therefore that no considerations of expediency can justify the oppression of one by another" (*CPB* 67). So far, so good. "But to believe this," Tawney continues, "it is necessary to believe in God."[15] Little wonder, then, that *The Acquisitive Society* ends with a direct plea to the Church of England to promulgate a Christian "rule of life" in economic matters (*AS* 236–9).

# 10

## "Reflection, Brooding, Worry, Love, and Hatred": Nietzsche on a Higher Concept of Culture

R.H. Tawney's political philosophy is inextricable from his belief. "One of the things that strikes me as I grow older," he wrote, in 1912, at the age of thirty-two, "is the extraordinary truth and subtlety of religious dogmas at which, as an undergraduate, I used to laugh" (*CPB* 15). One such dogma is the Incarnation: if we believe that God entered the world in human form – and this we *must* believe if we believe in the life and divinity of Jesus Christ – then it follows that God is indeed interested in, and his law is applicable to, human affairs, including political and economic ones.[1] For example, in his 1937 address to the Conference on Christian Politics, Economics, and Citizenship, Tawney references the Incarnation twice: once, to dispel the (in his mind) mistaken assumption that Christianity is a wholly otherworldly faith, indifferent to the day's pressing questions of political and economic (in)justice; and, a second time, to outline his understanding of "humanity," of (what he elsewhere calls) the "human personality."[2] Tawney does not deny "man's [permanent, unchanging, lamentable] animal nature," but he emphasizes, as "the most important fact about human beings," their "humanity, which, in virtue of the Incarnation, they share with God."[3]

Tawney is adamant that there are no distinctions to be drawn here: the "higher law" of the Incarnation is an egalitarian one; it entails "the supreme value of *each* human personality *as such*" (*CPB* 65; italics added). And *this,* in turn, is the root of his "straightforward hatred" of capitalism: it is precisely because *every* person is of "infinite value" that the sort of "squalid" oppression to which workers are subject is prima facie unjust; no economic system that "stunts personality and corrupts human relations," as capitalism does and is structurally inclined to do, deserves our ongoing allegiance.[4] What is therefore necessary is the restoration of a specifically *Christian* morality – the *re*application of the Incarnationalist principle of "the [equal] sacredness of human personality" – to the domain of political economics.[5] In other words, Tawney's socialism is rooted in his egalitarianism, and his egalitarianism is rooted in his Christian theology; there is, in his mind, an inexorable path from Christ to equality to social democracy. That is why everything that R.H. Tawney stands for – Christianity and socialism, equality and democracy – is utterly detestable to Friedrich Nietzsche, to whom we now turn.


# 1


In *On the Genealogy of Morals,* Nietzsche gives us his history of Christianity: where, he asks, did Christianity come from?[6] And why did it conquer the world so thoroughly?[7] These questions matter to our inquiry, because, as we shall see, Nietzsche's condemnation of Christianity bears a striking resemblance to his condemnation of socialism: both Christianity and socialism, he says, are rooted in the *ressentiment*[8] of the weak; they are both a reaction to powerlessness, the attempt by the powerless to insulate themselves from the powerful (by redefining the demands of morality). And they are both ultimately nihilistic movements: they fundamentally misunderstand the nature of human life – what constitutes *real* human flourishing – and so accelerate the corruption and decay that (in Nietzsche's mind) characterizes modern life.

Of course, any history of Christianity must begin with the Jews. What, according to Nietzsche, is the essence of Judaism? Its priestly quality: the Jews, he says, more than any other people, "[embody] the most deeply repressed priestly vengefulness" (*GM* §7). What does it mean to be *priestly?* The priest, in Nietzsche's telling, is thoughtful, inward, anxious, and rule-bound, the complete antithesis of the warrior, who possesses "a powerful physicality, a flourishing, abundant, even overflowing health" and who delights in "war, adventure, hunting, dancing ... [in] vigorous, free, joyful activity" (*GM* §7).[9] Why are priests so vengeful? Precisely because they are weak, idle, passive, impotent; they live in a frightening and dangerous world, a world in which they are perpetually vulnerable to the strong, the vital, the spontaneous, the cruel. Doesn't this describe the Jewish (and early Christian) experience of persecution, slavery, and exile?

But priests are clever too: their weakness is matched by their depth, their creativity. And, in Nietzsche's mind, the Jews are the cleverest, deepest, most creative people of all: they are *so* creative, in fact, that they turn the moral universe upside down! Before Judaism's ascendance (via its appropriation by Christianity[10]), nobility, power, and mastery were celebrated above all. Now, in the new Jewish moral universe, "the wretched alone are good ... the suffering, deprived, sick, ugly alone are pious, alone are blessed by God," and the "powerful and noble are ... evil ... unblessed, accursed, and damned" (*GM* §7)! "One knows *who* inherited the Jewish valuation," Nietzsche adds, disdainfully (*GM* §7). This is the only sort of revenge available to the weak: without access to repelling physical force, priests must devalue their oppressors *at the level of ideas*, by creating a new moral universe. As we have seen, this new morality elevates the value of pity over power, altruism over strength, equality over nobility – not because pity, altruism, and equality are good in themselves; no, the new (Jewish priestly) values are a reaction to power, a self-interested attempt to domesticate the power of hated oppressors.

*This*, says Nietzsche, is the true origin of (our still dominant) Judeo-Christian morality: it is the historical by-product of physical weakness and of the psychology of *ressentiment* – the experience of a powerlessness that gives rise to an unpleasant and festering (but lucid and calculating) hate.[11] This is a radical and blasphemous view of morality, of course: in Nietzsche's telling, our conceptions of goodness and evil do not correspond to the world's (divinely ordained) moral fabric; there is no moral structure *out there*, the foundation and outlines of which are waiting to be intuited, and put into practice, by God's favored creation. Rather, our dominant assessments of goodness and evil are the contingent outcome of a self-interested struggle for power – a struggle between strong, doltish warriors and the clever, introspective priests who fear them, hate them, and who somehow manage to outwit them into submission.[12]

Why is it so hard for us to see this? Why does Nietzsche regard his own genealogy of morality as *so* novel, *so* shocking? Simply because "all *protracted* things are hard to see, to see whole" (*GM* §8). We have been living with Judeo-Christian morality for two thousand years; little wonder, then, that we have forgotten its origins, that we regard its assessments of goodness and evil – and its image of human flourishing – as *natural*.[13] But they are *not* natural, and Nietzsche needs us to see this; he *needs* us to see this, because, in his mind, the triumph of the new morality – the spectacularly successful "slave revolt in morality" (*GM* §8) – has had very destructive consequences for (real) human happiness and well-being: "What *if*," Nietzsche asks, "morality is the danger of dangers" (*GM* preface)? In fact, that *is* precisely the case: Christianity has made us "tame, easy to get along with, and useful to the herd"; it has made us moderate, sociable, prone to pity (*BGE* §199). But these are *not* the highest "*human values*"; they are the values of "herd-animals" desperate for safety (*BGE* §199). There is *more* to (human) life, says Nietzsche, than security and comfort, ease and tranquility: to live well, he says, we must *be* active, *court* responsibility, *vent* creativity.[14] In other words, Christianity's preaching of equality and justice for all *may* have eliminated *some* cruelty and suffering from the world; but it *also* blocked the path to genuine human greatness by dulling the craving for action, the will to independence, the drive to *stand out and be original*: it forced us to sacrifice not only our freedom and our pride, but "all self-confidence of the spirit" too (*BGE* §46; see also §§212 and 228; *D* §163; and *WP* §962). "One should not go to church," Nietzsche warns, "if one wants to breathe *pure* air" (*BGE* §30).

## 2

At socialist headquarters, the air isn't any cleaner. After all, socialists too are animated by the belief that cruelty and exploitation are incompatible with the demands of human dignity and equality; hence the pressing need to expropriate private property, socialize the means of production, democratize work, and thus transcend the disenfranchisement and alienation of the (vast) majority. "Everywhere," says Nietzsche, making obvious reference to Marx and his followers, "people are now raving, even under scientific disguises, about coming conditions of society in which 'the exploitative aspect' will be removed" (*BGE* §259). This, according to Nietzsche, is a familiar trope in human history – a new, modern (and yet still legible) slave revolt in morality. Indeed, for him, socialism is an extension of the deeply misled and gravely consequential Christian drive to restore our natural but forgotten equality, and to thus provide the "poor and lowly" a "gateway to happiness"; it is, in other words, an attempt by workers to name, sanctify, and then alleviate their suffering at the hands of the exploitive capitalists, just as the early Christians tried to alleviate their suffering at the hands of their cruel, rapacious Roman masters (*WP* §209; see also §765; and *TI* 69).[15]

Nietzsche draws our attention to this connection – the "common origin" of the socialist and the Christian impulses – often: in *The Will to Power*, for example, he characterizes socialists as "the envious," with "poisonous and desperate faces" – an allusion (conscious or not) to the Christian's "poisonous eye of *ressentiment*" described in the *Genealogy* (*WP* §125; and *GM* §11). It is therefore hardly surprising, he adds, that the things of this world that the Gospels pass judgment on – "property, gain, ... rank and status" – are also "all typical of the socialist doctrine" (*WP* §209; see also *WP* §762).[16] And in *The Antichrist*, Nietzsche professes his deep hatred of the "socialist rabble": its commitment to eliminate all inequality is, for Nietzsche, tantamount to the celebration of smallness and mediocrity (*AC* §57). Little wonder, then, that he calls the socialist ideal "the tyranny of the least and the dumbest": it validates and reflects the needs of the small-minded, weak, conformist rabble, which longs for nothing more than security against want, protection against danger, and the solid standing of an equal among like-minded equals (*WP* §125; see also *BGE* §§199–200).

According to Nietzsche, this emphasis on equality – and the accompanying drive to alleviate suffering – is the path to widespread mental stupefaction and, as a result, cultural torpor – "a will to the *denial* of life, a principle of disintegration and decay" (*BGE* §259; see also §203). Hence, his portrayal of socialism as nihilistic and life-denying – a trait it shares with Christianity. In opposition to this (in his mind) nightmarish "green-pasture happiness of the herd" – this association of stupid animals in permanent hibernation – Nietzsche substitutes the life of criticism, the life of thinking dangerously: novel forms of art, philosophy, and religion – *cultural regeneration* – can be produced, he says, only in the midst of concerted, violent struggle against the established assumptions and values of the flabby, unthinking majority. In other words, a well-lived life is incompatible with living safely and comfortably among equals – the dream of the socialists (and of the Christians too). Instead, genuine human flourishing requires "appropriation, injury, overpowering of what is alien and weaker" (*BGE* §259; see also §§13 and 201; and *WP* §§40, 125, and 132). Of course, such a life is unsuitable for the vast majority: it demands a calculated "hardness," conscientious self-discipline, a strange, earned comfort with the "imposition of one's own forms" despite the typically virulent opposition of those in possession of so-called common sense (ibid.); hence, only truly "free spirits" are capable of genuine creativity, and Nietzsche often gestures at his need to fish for, awaken, and even enlighten the innovators of the future (see, e.g., *BGE*, part 6, "We Scholars," esp. §§210–12).

Notice, here, the important implication of Nietzsche's view: he carves the world into a miniscule aristocracy of creators and a plebeian mass of weary, anxious cattle desperate for calm; and to consider these two classes equal, he adds, is simply absurd: creators tower over the herd – the latter group Nietzsche once called "so many blanks" (*N* 40) – and the world is a less interesting, less vibrant, less beautiful place when we fail to recognize the altogether natural distinctions between the creating and working classes.[17] In the end, though, it is the aristocrats who really suffer: the act of creation is hard labor, the pain of which is exacerbated by the hostility of those (always, inevitably) attached to the status quo. Who, after all, wants to be taught – as Nietzsche teaches – and can calmly accept – as Nietzsche believes truth-lovers must – that reason is powerless against the primal animal instincts; that genuine self-knowledge is an illusion and therefore impossible; *that God is dead because we killed him?* But such suffering *is* salutary: even if we *could* abolish it, we would not want to, for it is the source of art, knowledge, beauty, and truth – all those things without which human life is not worth living; hence the need for daring, hardness, and indifference to howls of blasphemy among the creative (see, e.g., *BGE* §188). "Every talent," says Nietzsche, in the posthumously published *Homer's Contest*, "must unfold itself in fighting" (*HC* 37; see also *BGE* §188).


## 3


Given his overwhelming hatred of socialism, perhaps the "free spirits" that Nietzsche summons are ... *capitalists?* Some have supposed so, and there is a superficial plausibility to such a view.[18] After all, Nietzsche celebrates energy, striving, relentless *growth*; he hates socialism because of its promise of *peace* on earth: peace and quiet is the cow's dream (*WP* §125). But such an interpretation – Nietzsche as bourgeois apologist, the Übermensch as businessman – is not tenable. Indeed, a deep hatred of capitalism is a characteristic and recurring theme throughout his writings: in Nietzsche's second major publication, *Untimely Meditations*, he describes the "money economy" as "hugely contemptible," and he laments the ascendance and dominance of "the crudest and most evil ... egoism of the money makers," which now "hold[s] sway over almost everything on earth" (*UM* 148 and 150). Indeed, "the economic principle of *laissez-faire*" has become "the [whole of] morality of whole nations" (*UM* 132). That is why Nietzsche believed that the (fairly recently industrialized) Germany of his day was such a depressing wasteland: concern for the bank account dominated the concern for the soul. It is striking that Nietzsche says much the same thing in his penultimate major work, *Ecce Homo*. There, he reflects on the *Untimely Meditations* and comes to much the same conclusion: the early work does not give voice to some youthful, naive, and superficial "Jack the Dreamer" looking for a fight; it remains in Nietzsche's mind a powerful, compelling, and appropriately "ruthless" critique of the German "culture" of the late nineteenth century – a public culture characterized by its single-minded obsession with work, the economy, the "mechanical grinding of [industrial] gears," and its concomitant neglect of "a higher concept of culture" (*EH* 3:732–3).

*This* is the heart of Nietzsche's critique of capitalism: the single-minded pursuit of wealth, he says, is a "disease" that produces devastating intellectual, aesthetic, and spiritual symptoms (*EH* 3:732–3). For example, under capitalism, the purpose of education is no longer "the production of the philosopher, the artist and the saint," as it *should* be; instead, education is thought of as nothing more than a means to the acquisition of the skills and knowledge necessary for the "speedy" accumulation of "a very great deal of money" (*UM* 160 and 165). In fact, modern education (under capitalism) is characterized by its "hatred of [anything] that makes one solitary, that proposes goals that transcend money and money-making" (*UM* 160 and 165). But, for Nietzsche, the production of "genuine culture" – art, philosophy, religion – explicitly requires such isolation: meaningful cultural achievements, he says, *always* begin with "the *feeling of distance*" from the paradigmatic assumptions and values of the dominant culture (*EH* 737).[19] In fact, Nietzsche believes that his own (in his mind revolutionary) achievement in philosophy was made possible by a thoroughgoing indifference to all those things highly valued by his contemporaries: "*honor ... women ...* [and most of all] *money!*" (*EH* 2:711 and 3:737).

But such indifference does not come easily: the "sovereign contempt for everything" conventional – the keen sense of one's own difference and separateness, one's need to preserve one's independence at all costs – must be nursed and nurtured through "self-discipline, self-defence to the point of hardness" (*EH* 3:733 and 3:736; see also *BGE* §§212 and 257). And this requires, in large part, immunization from market pressures. After all, the world of work is the realm of thoughtless conformity, mind-numbing routinization, and energy-dissipating physical exertion: "What is invariably meant [by work]," says Nietzsche, "is relentless industry from early till late ... [work] keeps everybody in harness and powerfully obstructs the development of reason, of the desire for independence ... [work] takes away reflection, brooding, worry, love, and hatred; it always sets a small goal before one's eyes and permits easy and regular satisfaction" (*D* 82). Such "easy and regular satisfaction" is for Nietzsche the hallmark of the modern economic machine: "Security," he adds, "is now adored as the supreme goddess," achievable by an ever-growing majority (ibid.). But such comfort is not without costs – pervasive intellectual stagnation chief among them. Capitalism, after all, is constitutionally suspicious of all nonmonetized dimensions of human life – abstract thought, critical reflection, risky experimentation. And the malaise this fosters in turn negates the possibility of the sort of "world-historical ... lightning bolts" that promote spiritual renewal and cultural innovation (*EH* 3:736–7). Hence, "all great things," says Nietzsche, pithily encapsulating his view, "occur away from ... the marketplace" (*Z* 79).

## 4

Nietzsche's intellectual odyssey is deeply unfortunate and probably without parallel in the history of ideas: he was a relentless critic of (specifically German[20]) nationalism, militarism, and anti-Semitism. That is why the Nazi appropriation of Nietzsche's thought is both ironic and chilling: in place of Nietzsche's plea for cultural innovation, Hitler substitutes the *Reichskulturkammer*; in place of Nietzsche's impersonal hatred of money and money-making, a venomous and deeply personal hatred of Jews. What interests Nietzsche most, of course, is the combat *of the mind*, not the violent conflict of armies; he celebrates the battlefield *of ideas*, not the battlefield of bombs and guns and tanks. Nazism – and fascism more generally – can therefore represent only a deranged, despicable, dishonest mirror of Nietzsche's thought.[21]

And yet even the most sympathetic reader will struggle with Nietzsche's oft-irresponsible vocabulary: he speaks too frequently – and perhaps at times a bit too gleefully – of "injury, violation, exploitation, and destruction" as permanent and characteristic features of the fabric of human life (*GM*, Second Essay, §11; see also *GM*, Second Essay, §6; and *BGE* §259); he rejoices in dispelling the illusion that the world can be made pacific (*BGE* §13); and he even gestures – briefly but evocatively – at the catalytic role of a "menacing ... large-scale politics" to initiate his longed-for cultural renaissance (*BGE* §208).[22] In other words, it *can* fairly be said that Nietzsche unwittingly stirs the subterranean fascist unconscious into full daylight consciousness: his hatred of capital, his longing for spiritual purgation and cultural renaissance, his division of society into (master and slave) classes, and, most damningly, his admission that violence is necessary to purify and remake the world – all these beliefs reemerge, in a demented and dangerous form, in the fascist imagination.[23]

This tendency is perhaps easiest to trace in Italian political thought.[24] In his canonical "Futurist Manifesto," published less than a decade after Nietzsche's death, the poet F.T. Marinetti laments the culture's prevailing "contemplative stillness" – the kind of widespread passive stupefaction that Nietzsche diagnoses as the main sickness of modern life under capitalism.[25] According to Marinetti, this cultural, spiritual, and aesthetic malaise – no, *crisis* – is particularly acute among the Italians: Italy, he says, is suffering from "the stinking canker of its professors, archaeologists, tour guides and antiquarians," all of whom have reduced it to "a marketplace for junk dealers." This will to relive, deify, and (perhaps most importantly) commodify the ancient past is apparent everywhere: the peninsula, after all, is littered with an "endless number of museums," all designed to nurture the people's nostalgia for Italy's lost imperial glory, and to boost the value of all those antiquities trafficked by the "materialistic, self-serving" bourgeoisie. But again, for Marinetti, this is a sign of intellectual death and decay, not mass enlightenment:

museums are actually mausoleums filled with a "grim profusion of corpses that no one remembers"; they are ghostly places "where things sleep on forever, alongside other loathsome or nameless things." He therefore gleefully imagines all those "revered old canvases, washed out and tattered, drifting away" in a catastrophic flood.

A revolution – or, to use a Nietzschean idiom, *a cultural renaissance* – is therefore necessary: hence Marinetti's unreserved celebration of "courage, boldness and rebellion," all to the point of "recklessness." Indeed, for Marinetti, the good life is the creative, energetic life – a life of "aggressive action" animated by the "beauty [of] struggle" against the established – *now dead* – canons of art, poetry, and literature. And this struggle is not a half-hearted one: "We wish to *destroy* museums, libraries, academies of any sort," says Marinetti, and in doing so redirect all the creative energy now wasted in the "unending, futile veneration [of] the past." Such veneration, however futile and fruitless, remains deeply entrenched; and so Marinetti makes frequent use of violent tropes: the new poets – his fellow artists of the future – must "love ... danger," they must "glorify" aggression, they must make frequent use of "the slap and the punching fist," and must think of their intellectual activity as a form of "violent assault" – all in the service of waking the culture from its slumbering "reverie." With all of this, Nietzsche can surely agree: cultural vitality and (by extension) spiritual health demand constant renewal through struggle and innovation; the more deeply entrenched the status quo, the more stagnant and impoverished the lives of those living under its dominating sway. And that is why those who "fight" against such stagnation are the heroes of both the Nietzschean and futurist imaginations.

In the "Futurist Manifesto," though, the language of cleansing violence quickly exceeds the (relatively low-stakes) bounds of the intellectual and the aesthetic: Marinetti not only celebrates, and tries to nurture, the "aggressive action" necessary to disassemble and then replace the values and assumptions of the dominant culture; he also valorizes war itself, "the sole cleanser of the world." "We wish to glorify war, militarism, [and] patriotism," he says, all "beautiful ideas worth dying for." Here, we confront Marinetti's casual – shockingly casual – conflation of two distinct realms of human existence: for him, unlike for Nietzsche, the battlefield of ideas leads inevitably to the battlefield of arms; those engaged in the former cannot dissociate themselves from the latter without forfeiting their credentials as genuine intellectuals, poets, and artists. And so, for Marinetti, there is nothing peculiar or dissonant about calling, first, for the destruction of museums, art galleries, and libraries, and second, inexorably, for the "pitiless demolition [of] all venerated cities!" In the pages of the "Futurist Manifesto," the will to remake men's minds develops into the will to remake the physical world – it leads, in other words, to politics and to war.

How, then, to explain the massive distance – intellectually, not temporally – between Nietzsche's disdain for militarism and Italian futurism's wholesale embrace of it? The answer lies, at least in part, in the attitude that each possesses toward technology: for Nietzsche, technology is inextricably linked to the capitalist-industrial machine and is therefore the object of reproach; there isn't the slightest sense anywhere in Nietzsche's oeuvre that modern technology enhances or improves human life. After all, the meaningful activities in human life – thinking, dreaming, *creating* – transcend the movement of time and so do not and cannot benefit from, say, superficial improvements in society's productive efficiency or infrastructure. For the futurists, by contrast – and this is really no surprise given the movement's self-chosen name – the reverence for technology is intense, quasi-religious: Marinetti proclaims that the world has been "enriched by a new beauty, the beauty of speed"; he paints a vivid image of "our modern capitals ... pulsating" with a new energy, overrun with "railway stations devouring ... smoke-belching locomotives ... workshops hanging from the clouds by their twisted threads of smoke ... the lissome flight of the airplane." And, for Marinetti, technology and war waging are indissolubly linked, both in the imagination and in practice: he describes a "roaring motorcar, which seems to race on like machine-gun fire"; "bridges ... flashing in the sunlight like gleaming knives"; "locomotives champing down on their wheels like enormous steel horses"; and, most ominously, the "nightly ardor of ... arsenals and shipyards, ablaze with their violent electric moons."

The beauty of these images, while undeniable, is also undeniably marred by Marinetti's totally unreserved celebration of violence; while this surely grates on our modern, pacifist sensibilities, it is nevertheless the hallmark of fascist thought – the staunch belief in the salutary, spiritual, *cleansing* power of war, the only effective antidote to the evils of acquisitive modernity.[26] Hence Marinetti's staunch support for Italy's entrance into the First World War: in his 1914 pamphlet, "Manifesto to

Students," he acknowledges the "glorious future [seething] in [Italy's] breast," but warns that that future can only be "fully realized in the great world war."[27] War, in other words, is not *only* the antidote to the present crisis; it is *also* the cathartic means by which the desired, new, "*glorious*" epoch comes into being. "The War," says Marinetti, in precisely this vein, "will rejuvenate Italy, will enrich her with men of action, will force her to no longer live off the past, ... but off her own national forces."

# 11

# "The Nobler Exercise of the Faculties": Keynes on the Art of Enjoyment

To coax his fellow free spirits out of hibernation – *that* is *the* main aim of Nietzsche's philosophy. The economic and political forces of modern life – socialism, capitalism, democracy – lead to thoughtlessness and pointlessness, the lowering and narrowing of horizons, boredom and mediocrity. And so the possibility of a much-needed cultural and intellectual revival depends on nourishing the "pathos of distance" in those rare great minds – that feeling of distinction and superiority, the need for distance and isolation, the confidence to vent their will to power, to destroy and remake the world (*BGE* §257). In part 4 of *Beyond Good and Evil*, for example, Nietzsche gives us some hints about what real creativity looks like in practice: a true "genius" (*BGE* §206), he says, thinks at a "presto" pace (*BGE* §213), embarks on dangerous experiments and advances risky hypotheses (*BGE* §§205 and 210), creates and legislates new (moral) values and new ways of looking at the world (*BGE* §§203 and 211).[1] The rising to consciousness and cultivation of this sort of philosopher – the "man of tomorrow and the day after tomorrow" (*BGE* §212) – is the purpose of, and the only redemption for, human existence; hence, the (in Nietzsche's mind) pressing need to fish for and to hook "spirits strong and original enough to ... revalue and invert 'eternal values'" (*BGE* §202).[2]

Of course, such an endeavor is not without its obstacles. One obvious source of trouble is Nietzsche's admission that this way of thinking cannot be taught (or learned): genius, he says, is a *state of being*; one *is* a (real) philosopher (not a philosophy professor), *or one is not* (*BGE* §213). There is, as a result, no way to routinize or institutionalize the philosophy of the future: how can we legislate the depth and profundity of the soul? This explains (in large part) the absence of any (political) programmatic component in Nietzsche's philosophy: there are, as we have seen, occasional, fleeting references to the instrumental value of "large-scale politics" in bringing about an intellectual renaissance.[3] But, for the most part, Nietzsche turns away from politics; for him – unlike for, say, Aristotle – meaningful self-realization *must* occur *away* from (forced compromise with) others.[4]

Fishing for free spirits poses (*grave*) risks too: we may accidentally catch a shark! Nietzsche *did* see this risk clearly: in June 1884, in a letter written to Malwida von Meysenbug, he writes, "The sort of unqualified and utterly unsuitable people who may one day come to invoke my authority is a thought that fills me with dread."[5] As we have seen, Nietzsche was right to be concerned.[6] Marinetti, for one, was thrilled by Nietzsche in his youth.[7] And the Nietzschean echoes in the "Futurist Manifesto" – and in the political activities of the movement it founded – are undeniable.[8] And later, Nietzsche provides intellectual sustenance and legitimacy to the leaders of Europe's two most powerful fascist governments: it was Mussolini's claim to have carefully studied Nietzsche – his impressive erudition – that gave him the air of scholarly respectability so desperately craved by his bourgeois contemporaries.[9] And who, having seen it, can forget Heinrich Hoffman's chilling photograph of a pensive Hitler before the bust of Nietzsche at Weimar?[10]

This is not the place to debate the fascist appropriations – perversions, perhaps – of Nietzsche's thought.[11] Instead, we turn to Keynes. At first glance, this seems like an awkward transition and, in some ways, it is: Nietzsche had nothing but disdain for politics and for politicians, while Keynes was the public intellectual par excellence.[12] More fundamentally, Nietzsche's conception of power as the exclusive preserve and privilege of the aristocracy (of the soul) is *totally incompatible* with Keynes's unambiguously liberal commitments. And yet, there *is* a (to many) surprising thematic overlap at work here: like Nietzsche, Keynes believes that modernity is almost wholly devoid of *real* culture. And, also like

Nietzsche, Keynes lays much of the blame for this sorry state at the feet of the bourgeoisie whose unrelenting obsession with the accumulation of wealth blinds them to the possibility, and value, of aesthetic pleasure. This is (to most) an unfamiliar side of Keynes.[13] But the starting assumption here is that Keynes's economic prescriptions, while surely more famous, are less fundamental to his thought than his ethics: production and distribution, competition and consumption – to Keynes, these things are less interesting, and less important, than art and literature, the free play of the imagination, the pursuit of a life filled with beauty.

# 1

Keynes began his university career as a student of philosophy, and his encounter with Edmund Burke was an important – indeed, formative – intellectual experience. In an unpublished 1904 essay, entitled "The Political Doctrine of Edmund Burke," Keynes celebrates Burke's political "timidity" – his principled unwillingness to "[introduce] present evil for the sake of future benefits."[14] This, of course, is the central insight of Burke's canonical *Reflections on the Revolution in France*: that it is the height of foolish impetuosity to tear down a set of functional political institutions – a hereditary monarchy, as in the case of France – in order to replace them with something experimental and untested – say, the comparatively novel institutions of representative constitutional democracy.[15] Social life is simply not fluid in this way: institutions demand a certain kind of culture for support and actually nurture that culture over the course of their history. The French therefore understand what it is like to live under a king, having done so for more than a millennium; but they do *not* understand the sorts of practices and virtues – or possess the long, complicated experience, the history of errors – necessary to sustain functional constitutionalism. And so, when it comes to democracy, French soil is arid, and hasty implantation is sure to produce unwanted – and potentially quite catastrophic – consequences. While the present regime may be far from perfect – this Burke repeatedly acknowledges – fear of the unknown always ought to trump the revolutionary zeal nursed by dissatisfaction with the present; hence the always pressing need for "prudence, reverence and calculation" among the political classes.

The power of Burke's critique – and the appeal of his philosophy more generally – is surely amplified by the fact that he was wholly correct: the French Revolution leads to the Reign of Terror, which, in turn, leads to military dictatorship under Napoleon.[16] For many, Keynes included, this cataclysmic chain of events stands as a vindication of Burke's essential view: that our powers of prediction are ever so "slight," and our understanding of the range of consequences of our actions is always "uncertain." Hence, the willingness to sacrifice present happiness for the possibility of greater happiness in the (potentially very) distant future – *this* is the permanent cry of all revolutionary movements – is simply folly. This belief leaves a distinct impression on Keynes: "there is no small element of truth" in Burke's conservatism, he says, "and no small tendency in revolutionary reformers to overlook it." It is therefore no surprise that there runs throughout Keynes's writings – beginning in 1904 and lasting to the end of his life – a permanent disdain for those willing to accept painful sacrifices in the present in order to obtain some future gain, however remote and uncertain, for themselves or (even worse) for posterity.

For example, in his *The Economic Consequences of the Peace*, which was published in 1919 and brought Keynes his first taste of world fame, he describes, with palpable disdain, the "new rich of the nineteenth century" – how they "were not brought up to large expenditures, and preferred ... to save ... [rather than indulge in] the pleasures of immediate consumption" (2.10).[17] For this nascent European bourgeoisie, adds Keynes, "the duty of 'saving' became nine-tenths of virtue"; the purpose of human life was to contribute to "progress ... [and to] the future security and improvement of the race" (2.11). It is therefore no surprise that, in his (perhaps most famous work) *The General Theory of Employment, Interest and Money*, Keynes blames the widespread inclination toward delayed gratification as the cause of the Great Depression: throughout the 1920s and into the 1930s, he says, the holders of money possessed a strong – indeed, immovable – "liquidity preference"; they desired, that is, to keep their capital saved in (liquid) cash as opposed to (illiquid) investments (14.115). Why, according to Keynes, is this a problem? Because the "liquidity preference" *also* leads to high interest rates and (by extension) high unemployment; after all, if those with vision and ambition are reticent to borrow, the potential job-creating power of their economic activity remains unrealized. In other words, the desire to save – to renounce today, for the sake of tomorrow – leads, somewhat counterintuitively, to negative social consequences – in this case, less investment and fewer jobs.[18]

For Keynes, this was emblematic of a deeper – and deeply problematic – cultural and psychological attitude: the widespread belief that delayed gratification is a form of virtue and, by extension, that the maximal delay of pleasure is the essential path to "immortality" (9.329). Such a view of life canonizes the act of saving more than anything else, and those who practice it are "more concerned with the remote future results of [their] actions than with their own quality or their immediate effects on our own environment" (9.329). Keynes regards this obsession with immortality as "spurious and delusive," and it is hardly an overstatement to say that the main purpose of his writing is to dislodge it from its ascendant position in the culture (9.329). After all, this obsession not only impoverishes the lives of those under its sway – a novel argument of Keynes's to which we turn in detail below; it *also* produces damning social consequences. We have already seen these dynamics at work: the more individuals save – and, by extension, the less they invest and consume – the worse off, economically speaking, the wider society tends to be.

Keynes acknowledges that this argument is, on the surface, somewhat counterintuitive: after all, saving is widely – though, as we shall see, wrongly – held to be good for the individual; and so, must it not also be good for the community? Better, so this (faulty) line of thinking goes, to abstain from using our money *today* so that it may grow into even more money *tomorrow*, thanks to the alchemical power of compound interest. Surely *everyone* benefits when a *small* sum of money is transformed into something much *larger*? According to Keynes, this is, simply, wrong: "In contemporary conditions," he says, "the growth of wealth, so far from being dependent on the abstinence of the rich, as is commonly supposed, is more likely to be impeded by it" (7.372). After all, the abstinence of the rich, nurtured by a (typically religious, immortality desirous) culture of thrift, leads to less investment, less consumption, and less employment.

Keynes does not take full credit for this insight. In *The General Theory*, he traces his own views on savings and consumption to the eighteenth century, to the poet and philosopher Bernard Mandeville, whose short poem the "Grumbling Hive," was met with howls of execration when it was published in 1705 (7.358). What, exactly, was so offensive about

Mandeville's work to his contemporaries? His unabashed endorsement of the social benefits of commerce in luxury! Indeed, in his poem, Mandeville excoriates the "virtues" of an austere, frugal society – a society that thinks of self-abnegation and abstinence as forms of virtue – arguing instead for the wholesale embrace of conspicuous consumption; *this*, he argues, is the path to fuller employment and prosperity, happiness and well-being. How, then, to bring about this much needed increase in the circulation of capital in society, an increase that runs so fundamentally counter to prevailing cultural expectations and (by extension) the psychological inclinations of consumers? For Mandeville, the answer is "the great art ... [of] Government": it is the responsibility of the state, he says, "to promote as great a variety in Manufactures, Arts and Handicrafts as human wit can invent ... and to encourage Agriculture and Fishery in all their branches" (quoted at 7.361).

Clearly, this argument makes a deep impression on Keynes: what is needed, he says, in wholehearted agreement with Mandeville's prescription, is the creation of "central [i.e., state] controls to bring about an adjustment between the propensity to consume and the inducement to invest" (7.379). Of course, this is the heart of the economic philosophy known as Keynesianism: the belief that the economy is not a self-regulating mechanism best left to its own devices and that its proper functioning – which is to say, the maintenance of a self-reinforcing cycle of high employment, high wages, high demand, and high consumption – requires the keen interventionist hand of the state. For example, it is the responsibility of the state to properly manage its currency to avoid both inflation and deflation: when there is too much money circulating in the economy, the purchasing power of those who possess it decreases; this inflation impoverishes the vast majority of consumers – though there is always a small, despised class of "profiteers" – and also creates a general atmosphere of insecurity and class resentment (2.148). When, conversely, the price of goods falls – on account of an excessive decrease in the supply of money – this is a disincentive for entrepreneurship and, by extension, employment (4.34). That is why Keynes speaks of both inflation and deflation as evils to be avoided. And this avoidance requires the careful planning and executive powers – the "*deliberate decision*" and, more specifically, the "moderation" – of the state. The state, adds Keynes, "must revise what has become intolerable," including the irresponsible expansion (or contraction) of the money supply, as well as the (often grossly) inequitable distribution of income (4.55–6).[19]

According to Keynes, such a view runs fundamentally counter to "the individualistic capitalism of today," and to the "rivulets of thought" of all those "philosophers" and "economists" whose main intellectual purpose is to justify and thus enhance its stability (9.271). Indeed, the prevailing system – and the dominant philosophy that supports it – is characterized by its "deep distrust" of all forms of government "regulation" (4.35). Economic decisions, so this line of thinking goes, are best left to individual producers and consumers, both of whom are able to effectively communicate through price signals and patterns of consumption (4.35). And what is more – what is *better*, divine maybe[20] – is that all this self-seeking – individuals in hot pursuit of "private profit," animated by "the love of money" – "promote[s] the general interest [of the public] at the same time" (9.273)! The germ of such a doctrine is "*just* discoverable in Adam Smith," says Keynes, though full-blown laissez-faire was "not fully and self-consciously developed until the nineteenth century" (9.274; italics added). It emerges fully – can *only* emerge fully – *after* Darwin, when ideas about "ruthless struggle," "free competition," and (most importantly) "the survival of the fittest" became dominant among "our erstwhile 'heroes,' the great business men" (9.274–5). The path to prosperity, in such a view, requires the maximal scope of (economic) liberty, so that the dynamism – the "skill and good sense" – of all those "great captain[s] of industry" is not extinguished by the excessive regulatory constraints of the state; it follows that *any* form of central control – taxation, regulation, redistribution, and the like – is "not merely inexpedient, but impious ... [likely to] retard the onward movement of the mighty [capitalist] process" (9.288).

Keynes disagrees, of course, and vehemently so: there is no natural harmony between private profit and public good – rampant "egoism" does not inevitably lead to "the greatest good of the greatest number" – and the belief in such an illusory union is merely a reflection of the intellectual sway of a miniscule class, a class in secure possession of society's "educational machine" (9.274 and 9.279). Indeed, in Keynes's mind, the appeal of laissez-faire is not its truthful account of human nature, or its accurate depiction of economic life; its appeal is, first and foremost, its (admittedly "beautiful") *simplicity*. But this simplicity, however stunning, cannot withstand the scrutiny of facts: the argument for laissez-faire, says Keynes, ultimately depends on a "variety of unreal assumptions," the most misleading and destructive of which is that "enlightened self-interest always operates in the public interest" (9.283).

This simply is not so: when markets operate freely, as per the demands of laissez-faire, "great inequalities of wealth come about," that "wealth [gets] distributed where it is not appreciated most," and those "trampled underfoot ... [by] the [anxious, greedy] herd" experience real, undeniable "suffering" (9.284). No sane, compassionate society can accept this: it is therefore *essential* that the state undertake concerted "social action for the public good"; such measures might include, for example, control of the currency and of credit by a central institution, the implementation of legislation to ensure the correct level of saving and that such savings are directed to appropriate channels, and a national population policy – including matters related to birth control and the use of contraceptives, as well as the economic rights and standing of women – to prevent overpopulation (9.290–2). Of course, such a Keynesian policy regime will also include much more state (infrastructural) spending in order to create employment, robust economic redistribution through progressive schemes of taxation, as well as generous schemes of unemployment, health, and housing insurance. This is not the place for a detailed catalog of the macroeconomic tools and policies endorsed by Keynes.[21] Instead, the remainder of this chapter focuses on the moral philosophical argument that Keynes advances in support of state-directed capitalism: compared to Keynes's technical economic contribution, there is little understanding or appreciation of the image of human flourishing that undergirds his argument against laissez-faire capitalism.

## 2

Why, exactly, is Keynes so hostile to the (in his mind) cultish obsession with saving among the European bourgeoisie? Precisely because, compared to the vast bulk of human history, his contemporaries live in an "economic Eldorado, ... [an] economic Utopia"; they have slayed the "devil ... Malthus disclosed" (2.5). Indeed, before the eighteenth century, this was no sure thing: "the founders of political economy," says Keynes, were filled with a "deep-seated melancholy," always fighting "false hope" that food supply would reliably outpace population growth (2.5). But, by the twentieth century, this is no longer in doubt: food has become "easier to secure" – partly as a result of technological innovation and the increasing scale of production it enables, but also because of American and African colonization – and this has in turn led to the availability of "more workmen ... to prepare industrial products and capital goods" (2.5). In other words, after 1900, a condition of general, though admittedly unequal, prosperity was "normal, certain, and permanent, except in the direction of further improvement" (2.6). There was, and was going to be, in perpetuity, "enough to go around," enough so that "overwork, overcrowding and underfeeding" would become relics of the not so distant but still unrecognizable past (2.11).

Of course, the wars shattered all this momentum: "The politics of militarism and imperialism, of racial and cultural rivalries ... play[ed] the serpent to this paradise" (2.6). But, in a strange and unpredictable way, Keynes sees a silver lining: "The war," he says, "has disclosed the possibility of consumption to all and the vanity of abstinence to many ... the capitalist classes, no longer confident of the future, may seek to enjoy more fully their liberties of consumption" (2.12). In other words, the calamity of war forces Europe's bourgeoisie to ask a question that hadn't yet occurred to them (given the relative historical novelty of their elevated social position): What, exactly, is all this feverish accumulation *for*? Once we have secured the "comforts and necessities of the body" – through the familiar practices of capitalist accumulation – to what do we turn next? Perhaps to the "nobler exercise of the faculties" (2.11)? But, again, in Keynes's view, the contemporary bourgeoisie has no meaningful answer to what such nobility actually means or requires in daily practice: "The cake increased," he says, "but to what end was not clearly contemplated ... the virtue of the cake was that it was never to be consumed" (2.11). Thus were human beings reduced to insects: "like bees they saved and accumulated," without any overarching sense of the purpose of their sacrifice (2.7).

*This* is what Keynes hopes to restore; he wants to replace the present worship of "compound interest" with a new (undeniably highbrow) devotion to leisure and pleasure – what he typically calls the "arts of enjoyment" (2.11). After all, compared to the vast majority of human history, there is very little labor to be performed today – there is a kind of automaticity and thus a certainty to the satisfaction of our most basic needs; *this* is what Keynes means when he speaks of our having solved our "economic problem," all thanks to technical innovation in both agriculture and industry and (perhaps more decisively) to "the power of compound interest," a power that "staggers[s] the imagination" (9.xvii; see also 9.320–4). But, again, this gives rise to a *new* quandary: how to make effective use of our hard-fought free time! This is, in many ways, "the moral problem of our age": to somehow replace "the universal individual striving after economic security as the prime object of endeavour" (9.267). But replace with *what,* exactly? Now that we are able to "perform all the operations of agriculture, mining, and manufacture with a quarter of the human effort to which we have been accustomed," what are we going to do with the rest of our time?

First, we must learn to recognize the existence of such leisure in the first place – no easy feat, given psychological make-up of capitalist society, a society whose members dedicate all their energy to exclusively economic purposes. "How few of us," Keynes laments, "can sing" (9.327)! This is hardly surprising; after all, for the vast majority of human history, "the economic problem, the struggle for subsistence, ... has been the primary, most pressing problem of the human race.... We have been trained too long to strive and not to enjoy" (9.326–7). But, as it turns out, the economic problem is not insuperable; it is *not "the permanent problem of the human race"* (9.325). The permanent question is therefore not, *how to live,* but rather, how to live "wisely and agreeably and *well*" (9.327; italics added). And the answer to this second more pressing (because permanent) question requires, in Keynes's view, nothing less than "a revolution in our ways of thinking and feeling about money" (9.270). Indeed, what is required is an entirely new conception of wealth, one that regards money as nothing more than "a *means* to the enjoyment of life," not exclusively "as a possession" to hoard up to the fullest (9.328; italics added).

Keynes understands the depth of this sea change, and he also recognizes the moral vertigo that such a reorientation is likely to induce: he imagines a very different world, culturally and psychologically speaking, one in which "the accumulation of wealth is no longer of high social importance" and "the love of money ... will be recognized ... [as] a somewhat disgusting morbidity ... a semi-pathological propensity [best handed over to] the specialists in mental disease" (9.328).[22] But this unfamiliar world is sure to be a better and happier one: much less prone to delayed gratification and its attendant miseries and frustrations, and much more susceptible to joy, pleasure, and present fulfillment. In precisely this context, Keynes describes a new breed of hero, one to displace those bourgeois titans of industry currently worshipped: we must learn to cherish and emulate "those who can teach us how to pluck the hour and the day virtuously and well, the delightful people who are capable of taking direct enjoyment in things," not those willing to sacrifice pleasure today for some dimly outlined future (9.330). After all, "those [who] walk most truly in the paths of virtue and sane wisdom," he adds, "take least thought for tomorrow"; only *these* sorts of people "can keep alive, and cultivate into a fuller perfection, the art of life itself" (9.327).

*The art of life*: this, perhaps more than anything, is the heart of the Keynesian moral enterprise; the economic dimensions of this thought – his emphasis on the need for a sensible population policy, the competent stewardship of the economy by the state in the hopes of striking a proper balance between saving and consumption, and so on – must therefore be thought of as (nothing more than) a means to this account of human flourishing, however idiosyncratic. And such flourishing always requires the active support and encouragement of the state. For example, the government must enable and promote – through the financial generosity of the "public exchequer" – "the civilising arts of life *as part of their duty*"; it must provide all persons, regardless of occupation or class or place of residence, with the "opportunity for contact with traditional and contemporary arts in their noblest forms" (28.367; italics added). When such contact is prioritized and guaranteed by the state, "new work will spring more abundantly in unexpected quarters and in unforeseen shapes," enriching the lives of all citizens, both refined aesthetes and relative novices (28.368). The "first aim" of such exposure, adds Keynes, is "enjoyment," not instruction – to nurture the (too easily forgotten) feeling that there is more to life than the pursuit of money, and to promote the (too rarely stated) tenet that our natural susceptibility to beauty and pleasure ought to be embraced and cultivated, not dulled by mind-numbing labor and the pressure of mere survival (28.368).

## 3

What is the ultimate purpose of Keynesianism? Many critics allege, and deeply believe, that here lurks Bolshevism: creeping centralization, state overreach, dogma, and, inevitably, terror.[23] But Keynes is no friend to Marx or to Marx's twentieth-century followers: he is always careful to emphasize that his theory is not, at bottom, socialist. In fact, he is befuddled and dismayed by the hold that Marxism and socialism continue to have on Europe's intellectual and political culture: how such an "illogical and dull" doctrine can exercise "so powerful and enduring an influence over the minds of men and, through them, the events of history," Keynes cannot fathom (9.284). There is simply "no case," he says, for a "system of state socialism [that] embrace[s] most of the economic life of the community"; all that is necessary is a set of state controls to "augment" the workings – and correct the defects – of the familiar capitalist economy based on the institution of private property (7.377). In other words, it is best if the vast majority of society's firms remain financed by private capital – and operated privately too, according to the laws of supply and demand – and the state lurks in the background "curbing" all those undesirable outcomes produced by unfettered economies – too much saving and too little employment, too much inequality and too little investment (7.379). In Keynes's mind, this amounts to (nothing more than) smoothing the sharp edges of the capitalist system; hence, he regards his economic theory as "moderately conservative in its implications," whereas the socialist takeover of the whole economy – including the productive equipment of private firms – is both excessively radical and ultimately unnecessary (7.376).

But even more than its economic doctrinal shortcomings, Keynes is hostile toward state socialism for its deleterious *moral* effects. A trip to Soviet Russia in 1925 drove this lesson home: Keynes writes of the way that Leninism – a "new religion" – "take[s] the colour and gaiety and freedom out of everyday life and offer[s] a drab substitute in the square wooden faces of its devotees"; and, "like all new religions, it persecutes without justice or pity those who actively resist it" (9.255–6). Keynes cannot accept either – the joylessness induced by total state control or the intellectual conformity created by strict doctrinal orthodoxy. Unfortunately, adds Keynes, such a predicament is inevitable: once "a small minority of enthusiastic converts" captures the instruments of state power – as in the case of the Bolshevik Revolution – the destruction of "the liberty and security of daily life" cannot be far behind; better, then, to breathe in "free air undarkened by the horrors of religion," including those uniquely modern mass religions that disingenuously masquerade as political philosophy (9.257).

*This*, in Keynes's mind, is the decisive argument against state socialism: its economic inefficiency is regrettable – a death knell, most likely[24] – but its disdain for individualism is wholly unacceptable and the most compelling argument for its abandonment. Life, under socialism, is "a life without security or joy," both of which are sacrificed in the hopes of achieving some uncertain future good (9.258). We have already encountered – repeatedly, and in various instantiations – Keynes's hostility to such a view of life: for him, living well means being *present*; sacrificial lambs do not have happy, rewarding, fulfilling lives. *That* sort of happiness is accessible *only* to those who possess secure "personal liberty" *now* (7.379). And this sort of freedom is available only in a *reasonably* decentralized society, a society that gives generous space for the pursuit of individual self-interest but that *also* carefully, though not excessively, regulates that pursuit; after all, the absence of such regulation – thoroughgoing laissez-faire – leads to the loss of freedom for most, a freedom that can be restored only by concerted state action (7.379).

Of course, this raises two obvious and important questions: Why is freedom valuable? And why does its absence constitute a loss? According to Keynes, every society must "safeguard ... personal liberty" – by, say, promoting full employment and putting in place a generous and accessible society safety net – because the widest possible "field for the exercise of personal choice" leads, in turn, to the greatest "variety of life" (7.379). And such "variety" is an intrinsically valuable good: it preserves familiar traditions without letting them ossify; it produces novel and surprising experiments in living, experiments that give us a sense of the immense, pleasing array of human ends; and it also produces a comfort with, and appetite for, innovation and improvement.[25] The absence of such freedom – and, by extension, such variety – is "greatest of all the losses of the homogeneous or totalitarian state" (7.379). As an example, here, Keynes discusses artists, who, by their very nature, are "individual and free, undisciplined, unregimented, uncontrolled";

the loss of such people – on account, say, of the crushing burden of (lowly, dehumanizing) economic imperatives or the intellectually stultifying demands of orthodoxy – should be a loss that no civilized society should accept or permit (28.367). After all, it is the artist who "leads the rest of us into fresh pastures ... enlarging our sensibility and purifying our instincts"; without such persons, there is no prospect for "a communal *civilized* life" (28.372; italics added).

# 12

# "A Narrow Field of Vision": Hayek on the Limits of Knowledge

The period between 1945 and 1970 is often referred to as the "Golden Age" of *state-directed* capitalism in the West: the output of manufactures there quadrupled between the early 1950s and the early 1970s and, even more impressively, international trade in manufactured products grew *tenfold*.[1] Indeed, by the early 1960s, the majority of the capitalist world had reached a condition of (nearly) full employment, with Western European unemployment averaging a mere 1.5 per cent – the best defense against recidivist militarism, according to the conventional wisdom of the day.[2] *This* was the economic "Eldorado" Keynesian macroeconomics had promised before and after the war: explosive economic growth *facilitated by the state*, leading to full employment and to mass consumption by a well-paid labor force.[3] Indeed, none of this would have been possible without the careful guidance of state actors: throughout the West, industrialization was "backed, supervised, steered, and sometimes planned and managed by governments," from France and Spain in Europe to Japan, Singapore, and South Korea.[4] And, at the same time, those governments were committed to full employment – achieved primarily through generous public spending and (occasionally) outright nationalization in large-scale industry, such as electricity, coal, and rail transportation – and to the economic and social welfare of those (relative few) unable to find work in such times of plenty. This safety net required a vast and dense network of programs, including unemployment insurance, old age pensions, universal health care, as well as subsidized housing and education.[5]

Of course, this "Golden Age" did not last: rising wages set in motion, and sustained for more than two decades, a booming, buoyant consumer market, which in turn made possible long-term full employment; but the high (and ever-rising) prices generated by such rabid demand eventually grew beyond the bounds of workers' purchasing power. In other words, by the late 1960s, (increasingly exorbitant) inflation enters the scene: the age of prosperity created an army of willing consumers – with access to automobiles, televisions, refrigerators, foreign travel, and the like – but wages simply could not keep pace with prices. As Hobsbawm memorably puts it, "The regular and welcome rises [in wages] so long negotiated by their unions were actually much less than could be screwed out of the market [by workers]."[6] For the common Keynesian this constituted a somewhat perplexing riddle: inflation was thought to be a worthwhile consequence of full employment; after all, increasingly well-compensated workers could happily afford a gradual rise in the price of typical consumer goods. But a *sharp* rise in the cost of those goods – a rise that outpaced the growth in wages – was simply not acceptable. Many states therefore tried to avert a crisis, first, by reducing the supply of money – a typical Keynesian response to inflation, as we saw in the previous chapter. Eventually, though, more aggressive and radical solutions became necessary, including the temporary freezing of prices altogether, which produced a narrowing of profit margins and, in turn, a predictable upswing in unemployment.[7]

For a generous (and expensive to maintain) welfare state, this is a dangerous confluence of events: private firms are less profitable, thus reducing corporate taxation revenues, just as workers become more vulnerable, thus increasing welfare-related expenditures; the potentially quite extraordinary burden of closing this gap then falls on private citizens, which is sure to provoke socially and politically destabilizing resentment. This was precisely the case throughout much of the developed world: a generation accustomed – and thus feeling entitled, in perpetuity – to full and secure employment, reliably rising wages, and generous support from the state was unlikely to forfeit such benefits without a fight.[8] But the intellectual tide had turned, and decisively so amongst the influential political classes of the United States and Great Britain: after nearly three decades of high government spending – and with it, unsustainable deficits and disincentivizing rates of corporate and income taxation – there was very little to show for it – other than crippling inflation, dangerously high unemployment, and sluggish economic growth.[9]

## 1

Friedrich Hayek had seen all of this before – *twice*, in fact – first in his native Vienna in the years during and following the First World War and then in Germany in the years leading up to the Second (see section 2 below). Indeed, the Viennese case made such a deep and enduring impression on the young Hayek that he returned to it thirty years later, in *The Constitution of Liberty*, as a typical example of wrongheaded, socially destructive state interference with the laws of supply and demand (*CL* chap. 22). Here, the intervention took the form of rent control, which began in 1917 (and still continues today): as industrialization accelerated, and (later) as displaced persons streamed into Vienna from the east, the city's housing crisis became more and more acute; the government therefore tried to prevent landlords from exploiting those in search of housing through the imposition of "rent restriction[s] or the placing of ceilings on the rent of dwellings" (*CL* 468). This was an ideological gambit, in many ways: the government – populated by members of the Austrian Social Democratic party – had come to see itself as the protector of the working class; and so, concerted state action, *for* the exploited masses, and *against* the interests of exploitive property-owners, was required by *the demands of social justice*, a force for which the state was the most important and effective agent.[10]

The results, however, were socially and economically destructive: government action rendered the ownership of rental property a money-losing enterprise and, as a result, landlords lost interest in the upkeep of the buildings they already owned, as well as in acquisition and construction of new ones; there was also a conspicuous drop in the circulation of capital in the economy, as owners were no longer able to spend the proceeds collected in rent or borrow by using their (now essentially worthless) rental properties as collateral.[11] In other words, the housing crisis had been *intensified*, not alleviated; and what is more, the vitality of the other sectors of the economy had also been compromised by the general lack of entrepreneurship, innovation, and risk-taking among the property-owning classes. There were fewer and worse places to live, as well as more dismal economic prospects for both workers and owners.

For Hayek, the lesson of this episode was clear: state intervention *may* provide *temporary* relief *for some,* but such action is also sure to produce unintended and yet still potentially very grave consequences for society as a whole. Such was the case in Vienna, and in all those European cities plagued by rent control: dilapidation and homelessness, the diversion of public funds to needs better satisfied with private capital, and general economic stagnation with all its attendant miseries. "Whoever has seen the progressive decay of housing conditions and the effects on the general manner of life of the people of Paris, of Vienna, or even of London," says Hayek, "will appreciate the deadly effect that this one measure can have on the whole character of an economy – and even of a people" (*CL* 469). Indeed, in the case of Viennese rent control, the negative consequences of intervention extended beyond the bounds of the economic; these measures *also* led to intense *political* polarization and to more keenly felt class conflict: property-owners regarded rent control as, at bottom, a form of state expropriation of private property – *the* cardinal sin of political life – and so threw their support toward the right-wing, nationalist, anti-parliamentary – which is to say, *proto-fascist* – Home Front (*Heimwehr*) party.[12]

According to Hayek, rent control – and interventionist policies like it, up to and including the most radical step of total state ownership of large-scale industry – is emblematic of a specifically governmental, *and wholly deluded,* attitude toward the economy: namely, the belief that such a thing can be planned, and then controlled, from the top – that prices, wages, targets, quotas, and rents too can be determined in advance of actual processes of production and exchange. Throughout the 1920s and 1930s – as the result, no doubt in part, of the intellectual influence of Keynes, but also of the rapid, impressive industrialization achieved in Russia through short-term Soviet planning – there was a widespread belief that state action was the antidote to unfettered market competition. Laissez-faire had caused the Great Depression, after all, and so policy-makers and intellectuals regarded state ownership, direction, regulation, and redistribution as the path to stability and to greater equality.[13] It was necessary, in other words, to make society *rational* through concerted state action in order to avoid the irrationalities – the unpredictable booms and busts, with the concomitant effects on prices, production, and employment – of a purer capitalism. For example, in 1942, the British Labour Party issued a pamphlet, "The Old World and the New Society," that laid out the principles for the reconstruction of postwar society, including the belief that "there must be no return to unplanned competitive world of the inter-War years," that "the basis of our democracy must be planned production for community use," and that the state "controls" established in wartime "in industry and agriculture should be maintained."[14] Indeed, wartime socialism – during which the state commandeered society's productive infrastructure, operating them at full capacity, according to the dictates of military necessity – led to a massive economic boom, furnishing those in favor of planning with even more encouragement and hope for a postcapitalist, state-led future.[15]

It is hardly an overstatement to say that debunking this collection of principles, however vague and therefore permissive they may be, is *the* central purpose of Hayek's intellectual oeuvre: he was horrified to see the British walking down the same road in 1942 that, in his mind, had led the Germans to Nazism, the Russians to Stalinism, and the Italians to fascism (*RS* 58 and 66). This is precisely the theme of Hayek's perhaps most famous work, *The Road to Serfdom*: that socialism *creeps*, and that the increasing concentration of state power it entails leads inexorably to the loss of freedom for the individuals it was meant to liberate – from uncertainty and want, from exploitation and oppression. With the clarity of hindsight, such fears seem overwrought: the British – too firmly in possession of solid common sense and too keenly aware of their status as the inventors (and therefore protectors) of modern (constitutional) political liberty – never flirted with dictatorship, not even for an instant. But Hayek still thought it was necessary to sound the alarm, particularly so given the volatile political climate of the middle decades of the century; and, again, this volatility – the stunning descent to dictatorship – was the by-product of processes of socialist centralization: "We have progressively abandoned that freedom in economic affairs," says Hayek, "without which personal and political freedom has never existed in the past" (*RS* 67).

Notice, here, the emphasis on freedom, not merely economic but "personal and political" too: Hayek is animated not by the bourgeois desire to accumulate fantastic wealth, but by the liberal desire to preserve hard-won liberty; indeed, he carefully places his own thought in the tradition of British liberalism – the liberalism of "Cobden and Bright, Smith and Hume, Locke and Milton" – emphasizing that "individualism," while discredited *today* by Keynes's equation of it with "egotism and selfishness," remains the only compelling political philosophy available to us (*RS* 68). And the only way to protect the individualist milieu entailed by such a philosophy is to vigilantly restrain the state's encroachment upon it. *This* is Hayek's mission in *The Road to Serfdom*: to show that "the leading [socialist] ideas which during the last generation have become common to most people and [which] have determined the major changes in our social life" actually lead us to "bondage and misery," not "freedom and prosperity" (*RS* 65). The gravest threat to that freedom and prosperity is not (as Keynes teaches) unrestrained, manic competition; it is, rather, state ambition and overreach.

## 2

The case of interwar Germany looms large in *The Road to Serfdom*. Chapter 12, for example, is entitled (somewhat predictably, but still very powerfully), "The Socialist Roots of Naziism"; there, Hayek traces the origins of the "Hitlerian doctrine," which he ultimately finds in the "anti-capitalist resentment" characteristic of German thought after 1914 (*RS* 183). Indeed, in Hayek's mind, it was the German intelligentsia's venomous detestation of the (pacifist, internationalist, democratic) bourgeoisie – their relentless discrediting of a countervailing liberal force – that made Hitler's rise to power possible: under the sway and stewardship of the Marxist professors, the people were gradually made to feel comfortable with the sorts of political tendencies and practices once thought unimaginable in the land of (the canonical liberals) Kant and Hegel – concentration of state power, expropriation of private property, gradual loss of personal liberty, eventual total control; thus leads "totalitarian economics" to the totalitarian state (*RS* 186).

As his scapegoat, here, Hayek selects Werner Sombart: Sombart's 1915 book, *Merchants and Heroes*, disparages the (quintessentially English) "commercial" view of life and laments the dulling of the "heroic" warrior instincts that occurs in modern capitalist society (*RS*

186). The purpose of human life, continues Sombart, is not the pursuit of individual (i.e., commercial) initiatives; instead, human life is meaningful only insofar as one advances the aims and interests of the community. To Hayek, the danger in this line of reasoning is painfully obvious: the kind of collectivist immersion Sombart desires typically – no, *necessarily* – takes place in the pursuit of "military ends"; indeed, for Sombart, war is "the *consummation* of the heroic view of life" and the exclusive path to personal fulfillment (*RS* 184; italics added). And war, as we have already seen, demands centralized coordination: scarce resources necessary for victory cannot be wasted in fruitless competition for private profit; instead, those resources must be marshaled and then carefully directed according to the dictates of war planning. The war economy is a thus a socialist economy – an inevitable outcome of Sombart's bellicose view of human life.

*These* are the first steps on the road to serfdom: the veneration of warrior heroism and the disdain for individuality and for liberty; the suspicion of the market and the substitution of planning for competition; the obsession with unchecked power, monopoly, and cartelization; the call for unquestioned obedience to expertise; and, finally, the deification of the state. All of these trends are present in Germany between the wars, says Hayek, which makes the German case worthy of careful study for those looking to avoid a similar outcome elsewhere. Chapter 12 is thus a pithy intellectual history of the intense and widespread fervor that German intellectuals and politicians felt for "the ideal of organization": their belief that socialism is "a higher and more advanced economic system" than capitalism, and their concomitant zeal for the "central planning of all aspects of life" (*RS* 184).

As an example, here, Hayek quotes the Nobel Prize–winning chemist Wilhelm Ostwald: "I will explain to you now Germany's great secret: we, *or perhaps the German race*, have discovered the significance of organization.... Germany wants to organize Europe which up to now still lacks organization" (*RS* 186; italics added). For Hayek, this quote is highly evocative: it gives powerful expression, however subtly, to the happy marriage of socialism with nationalism and with militarism too. But this marriage, however happy, is also calamitous for those outside its bonds, as history unambiguously attests: it was, according to Hayek, the eventual "drawing together" of the socialist left and the conservative right – an intellectual and political union made possible by each side's deep well of hatred for liberalism, a well no doubt deepened by the shame of having lost the war to the ultra-bourgeois English – that paved the way for Hitler (*RS* 192).

Hayek dubs this movement "Conservative Socialism" – an attempt to capture its ideological peculiarity, the mild schizophrenia traceable at its origins (*RS* 192). But there is another binding element that makes this unexpected left-right merger possible and then strong: the shared reverence for, and unshakeable faith in, science and technology. Indeed, between 1840 and 1940, says Hayek, Germans – more than any other Europeans – become obsessed by the alluring possibility of the total "scientific organization of society": its leading intellectuals – from both sides of the ideological spectrum, socialist and conservative – were chemists and engineers, all animated by "contempt for anything which was not consciously organized by superior minds according to a scientific blueprint" (*RS* 200). Of course, such a vision of society requires near total state control; hence the allure of the political strongman capable of producing it (*RS* 204). Hayek pulls no punches here: the willingness with which Germany's "scholars and scientists put themselves readily at the service of the new rulers," he says, "is one of the most depressing and shameful spectacles in the whole history of the rise of National Socialism"; it puts on full display scientists' destructive single-mindedness, their susceptibility to moral blindness, their indifference to the human costs of practically realizing the demands of theoretical reason (*RS* 204).

The open ire with which Hayek treats these intellectuals is very telling: there runs throughout *The Road to Serfdom* a recurring and unsubtle disdain for all those who believe that the path to salvation – to lasting freedom, genuine equality, and sustainable prosperity – runs through science; specifically, through the scientific attitude that the world is wholly knowable, and that its problems are solvable through the collection, and correct interpretation, of all the relevant facts of the matter. Of course, this is precisely the intuition that undergirds all attempts at central planning: the demand that "all economic activity [proceed] according to a single plan" – the belief that all of society's economic resources can be "consciously directed to serve particular ends in a definite way" – implies accurate knowledge of society's most pressing needs, as well as the means to efficiently and effectively satisfy them (*RS* 85). Indeed, socialists *must* believe that it is possible to obtain "a coherent picture of the complete economic process," without which centralized coordination cannot be effective (*RS* 95).

According to Hayek, though, *no such picture exists*: "The factors which have to be taken into account [for it are] so numerous that it is impossible to gain a synoptic view of them" (*RS* 95). *This* is the epistemological argument against state socialism – not only its desirability, but also its very possibility! After all, the information upon which socialism depends cannot be possessed – it is too diffuse, too dynamic, too uncertain. The sort of central planning at socialism's heart is therefore "stupendously" difficult and, ultimately, impossible (*RS* 89). "Nobody," adds Hayek, "not any one centre ... can consciously balance all the considerations bearing on the decisions of so many individuals" (*RS* 95). There is a resemblance, here, to the earlier argument against Viennese rent control, but also a not insignificant expansion of it: not only do we possess too little knowledge about the future consequences of our large-scale macroeconomic actions, such as the deliberate fixing of the price of housing or the nationalization of industry; we *also* possess too little knowledge about our *present* needs, as well as the path to their effective fulfillment. The "whole" is simply too "complicated," says Hayek, and so the reliance on "conscious central planning for the growth of our industrial system" is sure to produce results that are "clumsy, primitive, and limited in scope" (*RS* 96). Better, then, to rely on "the price system," which "enables entrepreneurs, by watching the movement of comparatively few prices, ... to adjust their activities to those of their fellows"; the result of such open competition is an industrial system that, by comparison, achieves a much more advanced degree of "differentiation, complexity and flexibility" (*RS* 96).

This is (to put it mildly) a recurring theme throughout Hayek's writings: a decade before *The Road to Serfdom*, he published a commentary on Soviet five-year planning; and, unsurprisingly, in Hayek's mind, that experiment was a catastrophic failure: while central planning did produce "colossal instruments of production" – this is the basis of much (misled) admiration in the West – it *also* produced "over-development" in inessential industries, and "under-development" in essential ones (*CEP* 204). Indeed, for Hayek, the "Russian Experiment" is characterized by the predictable and grievous "misuse of resources": tractor factories possessed state of the art equipment, to be sure, but "the position of the great masses deteriorated" as a result of the decline in the availability of consumer goods; breakthroughs in military engineering occurred with breakneck speed, but this also led to a damaging shortage of capital for more even, sensible investment in industry (*CEP* 205). For Hayek, this confluence of pathologies – the systematic misallocation of resources, the uneven development of industry, the ever-worsening position of ordinary consumers – is an irrefutable testament to the "inherent difficulties of any central planning" (*CEP* 206). It also worth noting, Hayek adds, that the power of the state – always so keen to persecute those guilty of "obstructing the plan by not obeying the orders of the central authority" – increased by irrevocable degrees (*CEP* 206).

Of course, the Soviet endeavor was doomed from the start: the possession of the knowledge required for its genuine success – so diffuse, so uncertain – would require a level of God-like omnipotence; no such power – and therefore no such access to "perfect knowledge" – exists for mere mortals, who can only acquire, and then communicate, economic data in (comparatively miniscule) bits and pieces (*UKS* 527). "The 'data' from which the economic calculus starts," says Hayek, "are never for the whole society 'given' to a single mind which could work out the implications"; such data "can never be so given" precisely because they exist "solely as the dispersed bits of incomplete and frequently contradictory knowledge" (*UKS* 519). The only reasonable response to such a predicament – to the necessary diffusion of knowledge, and the insuperable limits to central planning posed by this fact – is thoroughgoing "decentralization," *not* the (desperate) ramping *up* of centralization; what is required, in other words, is *competition,* not planning: "The very complexity of the division of labour under modern conditions," says Hayek, "makes competition the only method by which coordination can be adequately brought about" (*RS* 95).

This is part of Hayek's attempt to reframe "the economic problem of society": the problem, he says, is not the proper allocation of resources, as the planners assume; it is the effective "utilization of knowledge which is not given to anyone in its totality" (*UKS* 520). And, for Hayek, economic knowledge is collected and applied most effectively by individual entrepreneurs, not bureaucrats. After all, it is individuals who possess knowledge "of people, of local conditions, of [those] special circumstances ... of the moment not known to others" (*UKS* 522). This is precisely the sort of knowledge to which state planners, surveying society from such great heights, are constitutionally blind; but this *also* happens to be the sort of information that leads to the effective and predictable satisfaction of people's actual, fleeting needs! This is precisely Hayek's point, of course: the planners have an aura of scientific respectability, very much in vogue; sadly for them, though, the information they need for effective action can never be fully possessed. For individual entrepreneurs, by contrast, the information they need for success are the familiar and tangible data of daily life. As examples, here, Hayek mentions the "shipper who earns his living from using otherwise empty or half-filled journeys of tramp-steamers, the estate agent whose whole knowledge is almost exclusively one of temporary opportunities, or the *arbitrageur* who gains from local differences of commodity prices" (*UKS* 522).

Such ingenuity, foresight, adaptability, and risk-taking ought to be celebrated, not shunned; these salutary forces must be unleashed and nurtured by competition, not restrained by a rigid plan or by the demands of ideological orthodoxy. Hence, the need for decentralization: "Only [then] can we insure that the knowledge of the particular circumstances of time and place will be used promptly," and (by extension) that the present needs of consumers are effectively, and cheaply, satisfied (*UKS* 524). Why *cheaply*? Because demand creates an influx of competition, increasing the supply of the desired good and lowering its price; this, in turn, sets in motion the entrepreneurial spirit of producers eager to lower the cost of resource inputs or production processes or (ideally) both. This requires a lot of information, to be sure, but significantly less than the complete information set desired by planners; and such (comparatively limited) knowledge is easily obtainable through the price mechanism for resource inputs and equipment. Here, Hayek describes a harmonious, productive universe in spontaneous motion: consumers sending signals to responsive producers sending signals to responsive suppliers and on and on – all the happy and unconscious outcome of individuals acting according to a narrow "field of vision," and all made possible by the flexibility of "the price system" (*UKS* 525). This no plan can ever accomplish: the profitable allocation of resources is always much too fluid, given their unpredictable scarcity and the fleeting whims of those who want them; that is why the adaptability of the price mechanism is superior to the rigidities of a central plan: it produces the best possible goods at the lowest possible price by harnessing the spontaneity, ambition, and information advantage of entrepreneurs. "Where effective competition can be created," Hayek proclaims, decisively, "it is a better way of guiding individual efforts than any other" (*RS* 86).

Notice, here, the assumption that "*effective* competition" must be "created": Hayek is *not* an anarchist, by any means, and he frequently emphasizes the need to avoid a "dogmatic laissez-faire attitude" (*RS* 85). Indeed, the state has a necessary and important role to play in "making the best possible use of the forces of competition" (*RS* 85). For example, without the "adequate organization [by the state] of certain institutions like money, markets, channels of information," competition will be "ineffective" (*RS* 87). A "carefully thought out legal framework" is also required, one that "recognize[s] the principle of private property and freedom of contract"; so too are regulations on production and employment, all accessible to common sense (though obviously more complicated in design and enforcement), such as prohibitions against "the use of certain poisonous substances" and strict control of "working hours" and conditions (*RS* 86).[16] Hayek also emphasizes the state's provision of safe, comprehensive transit infrastructure, "which can never be adequately provided by private enterprise" (*RS* 87). But, again, states ought not do more than that: the *only* effective link between supply and demand – the only mechanism of effective coordination between producers and consumers – is *price set by free – which is to say, competitive – exchange.* States must therefore permanently resist the temptation to set those prices (or quantities) through the exercise of its "coercive or arbitrary authority" (*RS* 86).

## 3

Hayek's epistemology is not the entirety of his argument against state socialism: there is also an important *moral* dimension to that view. Indeed, at bottom, Hayek's opposition to socialism and to state planning rests on a particular image of human freedom: even *if* central planning is *possible,* he says – which, as we have seen in detail, it is decidedly *not* – it would not be *desirable,* for such planning violates the freedom of those forced to submit to it. This is so, says Hayek, because our economic concerns are inextricably bound up with – actually, they are (in most cases) subservient to – our more fundamental interests; we participate in the market and in work, that is, in the hopes of achieving – of accumulating the means necessary to realize – our more basic aims, whatever they happen to be.

In some cases, certainly, the accumulation of wealth may be that basic aim; that is what Keynes and his followers would have us believe about life under capitalism – that it leads to feverish accumulation without purpose. But such a view ignores the fact that human aims are endlessly plural – that economic means are utilized in the pursuit of an end-lessly heterogeneous catalog of aims and purposes, from the hopelessly selfish (as Keynes emphasizes) to the pleasingly altruistic (a possibility that Keynes systematically ignores). This is precisely what Hayek means when he says that "economic control is not merely control of a sector of human life which can be separated from the rest"; the economic realm is inextricable from the "higher values" of human life – it does not, and cannot, occupy some separate psychic space, for no such separation (between the economic and moral) is possible (*RS* 127).

The implication of such a view is obvious: the economic control to which the planners aspire is "the control of the means for all our ends" – control, that is, over where, when, and how to work (*RS* 127). But such control *never* ends there: "Whoever has sole control of the means must also determine the ends which are to be served" – what we should produce, how we ought to expend our energy, "in short, what [we] should believe and strive for" (*RS* 127). Hence, Hayek's equation of "economic control" with "totalitarianism" in the title of chapter 7 of *The Road to Serf-dom*: when we are deprived of the opportunity to choose how, and in the service of what ends, to work, so too are we deprived of our individuality and, at bottom, our freedom. "To be controlled in our economic pur-suits," adds Hayek, "means to be always controlled" (*RS* 126). This is yet *another* decisive argument against socialism – the way it saps the world of color and character, vitality and diversity, meaning and purpose. This stands as a rare point of agreement between Keynes and Hayek.[17] But Hayek draws a different conclusion, of course: for him, the only way to preserve our freedom – and with it, vibrant individuality – is through the dilution of state power wrought by capitalism, without which individuals cannot achieve what Hayek desires most – "the fullest development of individual personality" (*RS* 115).

*This* is where Hayek's immersion in – and self-conscious identifica-tion with – British liberalism is most apparent: in *The Road to Serfdom*, he describes the state as "a piece of utilitarian machinery," the purpose of which is to facilitate, but not dictate (or direct) the course of, individual self-development (*RS* 115). Whereas the socialist state "take[s] sides, impose[s] its values upon people, ... choose[s] the ends for them," the liberal state preserves a generous sphere of noninterference guaranteed by law – a clearly demarcated private space where our "own views and tastes [reign] supreme," and within which we are free to "develop of our own gifts and bents" (*RS* 68 and 115; see also *CL* 207–9). Of course, individuals are *also* free to put their (often hard-earned) knowledge to the best possible – which is to say, most profitable – use on the market, confident that the state will always refrain from, say, expropriating machinery, barring certain persons from certain occupations, or arbitrarily changing the rules surrounding taxation (*RS* 118; see also *CL* 224). Indeed, for Hayek, our freedom as producers is perhaps the most important instantiation of "the will to shape and guide our daily lives" (*RS* 128). After all, for the vast majority, "the time we spend at our work is a large part of our whole lives"; our occupation thus "determines the place where and the people among whom we live," making the freedom to choose occupations "more important for our happiness than freedom to spend our income during hours of leisure," though of course we ought to securely possess the latter freedom as well (*RS* 128).[18]

## 4

If the 1950s and 1960s belonged to Keynes, then the 1970s and 1980s belonged to Hayek – *decisively so.*[19] This was especially the case in the United States, where Hayek taught from 1950 to 1962 (at the University of Chicago). One of Hayek's most influential acolytes is James M. Buchanan whose famous essay "Classical Liberalism as an Organizing Ideal" gives expression to some quintessential Hayekian themes and ideas: that there is a certain "uniformity in human nature" – one that compels all persons to "seek their own interests" – and that this "simple behavioural rule" in turn produces a "complex [social] order" – namely, the modern market economy of producers and consumers, for whom interaction is both freely undertaken and "mutually beneficial" (*NAC* 67). Of course, the political implication of such a view is obvious: that there is simply no need for "some all-powerful authority, some sovereign, to orchestrate the productive, allocative, distributive and evaluative processes summarized as 'the economy'" (*NAC* 66). The purpose of the state, in other words, is (merely) to "enforce property and contracts," and to thus facilitate the natural and salutary acquisitiveness of society's "separated but interdependent" members (*NAC* 66). "Mutually satisfactory outcomes" are inevitable, adds Buchanan, "without the necessary services of a choice maker, as such" (*NAC* 66).

So far, we are on familiar ground: when it comes to the production of wealth, the savvy and spontaneity of individuals is always more effective than the (comparatively rigid and therefore inefficient) planning, coordination, and direction of central institutions. And, like Hayek, Buchanan too goes beyond this exclusively utilitarian logic; the argument *for* markets *also* has an essential *moral* dimension – it is in an outgrowth of the even more fundamental commitment to equality. "All persons in the trading nexus are to be considered as natural equals," says Buchanan, "each one of whom is assumed to be equally capable of making exchanges and living with the consequences" (*NAC* 67). This is a very powerful move, to be sure: in Buchanan's view, the market is the only coordinating mechanism compatible with the fact of our natural equality: it is only as participants in market processes – when we are free to choose what to make and buy, and to live with the consequences of those decisions, good and bad – that we give expression to – and acquire recognition of – our (equal) autonomy. It follows, of course, that any *deviation* from the market – in the form, say, of industrial planning, income redistribution, mandated wage hikes, rent control, and the like – is *also* a deviation from natural equality and thus a tacit acceptance of hierarchy. After all, the underlying premise of all (socialist) economic intervention, however subtle, is that some are "natural masters" and the rest "natural slaves," and that the latter are rightly subject to the wisdom and good sense of the former. This, adds Buchanan, is a now obsolete "Platonic" worldview – a world of mastery and slavery, authority and obedience – rightly and decisively debunked by the "followers of Adam Smith" (*NAC* 67).

# 13

## "The Curse of Money": Rawls on Plutocracy and the Demands of Economic Justice

*The Road to Serfdom* begins with a discussion of the "supreme tragedy" now threatening England and the United States: both countries were once rock-solid bastions of (economic) freedom, but they are quickly falling under the intellectual sway of the socialists, all of whom possess a deep and virulent "contempt for nineteenth-century liberalism" (*RS* 58). Of course, Hayek is opposed to all socialist modes of economic organization: the concentration of state power entailed by central planning leads, slowly but surely, to totalitarian control – *this* is the main lesson of *The Road to Serfdom*, and of Hayek's oeuvre more generally. As we saw in the previous chapter, the German case is the most important (because most consequential) example: her socialist wave of the 1920s and 1930s, says Hayek, "prepared the way [for] the Nazi system" (*RS* 58).

It is important to be clear on Hayek's meaning here: the interwar socialists were *not* Nazis; in fact, they were "people of good will, men who were admired and held up as models in the democratic countries" (*RS* 59). Instead, Hayek's point is about the fluid and unpredictable nature of our ascendant ideas: they are human creations, of course, but they also take on an independent life once they have been released into the world and made subject to interpretation, appropriation, and reformulation. And sometimes they undergo impossibly grotesque

mutations! However misled socialism may be in questions of practice –
in Hayek's opinion, at least – its essential goal is rooted in (universal)
human emancipation; that such a doctrine can be distorted into a racist
and bellicose ideology is both deeply disturbing and a stern warning.

After all, our ideas – even grotesque ones like Nazism – have *power*:
they inevitably enter the realm of practical application; they have consequences that no one anticipates and, in some cases, no one wants. In
other words, we become "*captives* of the ideas we have created," even
though those ideas rarely – no, never – remain fully *ours* (*RS* 58; italics
added). Such was the case in Germany, where the socialist centralization
of power – undertaken in the noble and worthwhile interest of workers'
equality, fairly distributed prosperity and leisure, and the like – laid
the institutional and (perhaps more importantly) psychological foundation for a deranged strongman. Again, Hayek's main intellectual
purpose is to draw attention to this unfortunate causal link and, more
importantly, to avoid a similar fate elsewhere; he was indeed tireless
in his efforts to spread his own ideas and thus retard the socialist wave
sweeping (at least in his mind) the West.[1] But there is a sad irony at
work here: the solution proposed by Hayek – an immovable commitment to *near*-total economic liberty – also initiates its own history of
uncharitable, and politically influential, interpreters. Indeed, in the
minds of his disciples, Hayek's sensible liberalism gets distorted into a
quasi-religious, world-remaking zeal for *total* market purity.

We can see this clearly in the work of James M. Buchanan, who is
open and frank about the depth of his debt to Hayek. It was Hayek, after
all, who exposed the "fatal conceit" of all those committed socialists
who stubbornly believed that stable and productive economies would
somehow "emerge omnisciently from the planning boards" (*NAC* 62).
Unfortunately, for the socialists, such a view runs counter to "the
basic elements of [sound] economic science": "mutually satisfactory
outcomes" are produced by the "interactions of separated but interdependent choosers," not by a sovereign "choice maker" (*NAC* 65–6).
*This* is the intellectual and moral heart of classical liberalism (or, as its
twentieth-century manifestation is typically referred to, neoliberalism).
And, as we have already seen, this is not *just* an argument about the
correct path to prosperity – though it was surely that, first and foremost.
Buchanan *also* celebrates the secure *normative* grounding of market
society: when the state interferes with the activity of producers and consumers – when it sets production targets, prices, wages, rents and so

on – it undermines the freedom and equality of those subject to such measures. After all, under the (legal, state-sanctioned) imperatives of central planning, individuals are reduced to the instruments of those who occupy the higher echelons of the (supposed) "natural hierarchy," and who therefore possess the right to command others, and to direct the expenditure of their time and energy, from on high (*NAC* 67).

No one who genuinely believes in equality can accept this hierarchical mode of organization. And who among us can reject equality without shame and public censure? Thus, we arrive at the classical liberal view that "catallaxy" *is* morality – that a maximally free market society is the highest and fullest expression of the demands of morality (*NAC* 66). As already noted, this is a powerful and important move: Buchanan here asks us to commit to a moral value about which we ought not have any reservations – the value of equality – and in doing so also forces us to commit to an institution – the free market – about which we cannot help but have serious reservations. Quite the ideological sleight of hand! Reasonable reservations about central planning – its efficacy, as well as its implications for citizens' ends-status – have been subtly transformed into unreasonable reservations about the legitimacy of state action altogether. Certainly the state is responsible for the provision of law and order – this no one can sensibly deny. But the state ought not do much more that that; and the further it strays beyond this basic minimum, the more it compromises its own moral standing and, by extension, its legitimacy. "Markets," says Buchanan, "allow the role of politics to be minimized and limited to the construction and maintenance of the parametric framework for exchange processes" (*NAC* 69).

As it turns out, Hayek disagrees – a fact sure to surprise, and dismay, many of those inspired by him, Buchanan chief among them.[2] Indeed, in *The Constitution of Liberty* – a late work – Hayek *rejects* the view that the "the activities of government should be limited [*exclusively*] to the maintenance of law and order" (*CL* 374). The state *does* have an important role to play in protecting the liberty and promoting the welfare of its subjects. For example, the state is responsible for the provision of important public goods, financed by taxation: it must act in the service of workplace safety, environmental sustainability, and general social well-being, none of which can be reliably secured without "legislative activity" and "direct regulation by authority" (*RS* 87). Hayek *also* emphasizes – evocatively so – the eventual need for a not insignificant amount of economic redistribution: "As we grow richer," he says, in an uncharacteristic vernacular, "that minimum of sustenance which the community has always provided for those not able to look after themselves, and which can be provided *outside the market*, will gradually rise ... government may, usefully and without doing any harm, assist or even lead in such endeavors" (*CL* 374; italics added; see also *RS* 148; and *LLL* 3.395). And yet further still, "There is [also] little reason," Hayek adds, "why the government should not play some role, or even take the initiative, in such areas as social insurance and education, or temporarily subsidize certain experimental developments" (*CL* 374).

It is naive and unrealistic to deny this: states have *always* "made provision for the indigent, unfortunate, and disabled," and rightly so; such service measures are "legitimate and unobjectionable" (*CL* 374). But there must *also* be well-articulated, insuperable limits to such programs: one of Hayek's greatest fears is the zeal with which special interests – labor unions chief among them – attempt to coopt the redistributive instruments of state, reducing their fellow citizens to mere instruments of sectarian (socialist) pursuits (*CL* 376; see also *CL*, chap. 18; and *LLL* 2, chap. 9, esp. 80–4). It would be wrong to deny Hayek's deep concern with – and frequent warnings against – the misuse of state resources under the banner of "social justice" (*CL* 376). But Hayek *was* also keenly aware of the pathological tendency of markets to create stark economic inequality, and he accepted – indeed, promoted – the role of government in alleviating it.[3] The challenge, here, is to strike the appropriate balance between public care and individual responsibility: states must never possess a monopoly in social, medical, and educational services, for this negates the possibility of developing better ways to satisfy those needs through competition and experimentation; but neither can the state wholly abdicate its responsibility for the provision of welfare for its most marginalized and destitute citizens (*CL* 377). "There is no incompatibility," says Hayek, "between the state's providing greater security ... and the preservation of individual freedom" (*RS* 148).

Unfortunately, many of Hayek's followers have been rendered blind to the need for, and utility of, such endeavors: for them, the state is an object of permanent suspicion and hostility – a relic of the hard-fought ideological battle with those who favor socialist planning. Once again, Buchanan provides a representative example: he calls attention to the way that "ideas in political theory" have fallen behind "the understandings developed in classical [i.e., Smithian] economics" (*NAC* 66). Only the economists understand that there is no longer any need for "hands-on politicized intrusions in market processes"; meanwhile, the philosophers continue to expend – no, *waste* – "much time and energy" contemplating, and trying to find normative justification for, the requisite "social welfare functions" of the state (*NAC* 66). In Buchanan's view, such functions are obsolete: the market satisfies the (welfare) needs of all; rather, the market gives all participants the *opportunity* to satisfy such needs, and an essential part of autonomy is bearing the responsibility for failing to do so. Redistribution *also* contravenes the equal freedom of the successful: it forces them to subsidize the poor decision-making and bad luck of others.

## 1

This is the right moment to turn to John Rawls, according to whom the sort of "hands-on politicized intrusions in market processes" that Buchanan consigns to obsolescence are *an essential precondition of justice.* Indeed, the "ideas in political theory" to which Buchanan alludes in the previous paragraph might as well be – and probably *are*[4] – Rawls's ideas! After all, in *A Theory of Justice,* Rawls explicitly *includes* the market as part of the "basic structure" of society – for him, the "primary subject" of justice (*TJ* 6). This is an important and consequential move: the "basic structure" is society's integrated network of "major social institutions" – its "political constitution," for example, as well as its "principal economic and social arrangements," including the market, the rights of private property, levels of saving, taxation, redistribution, and so on (*TJ* 6). These institutions matter *deeply* to those living under them: they "distribute fundamental rights and duties," and they also "influence," *profoundly* so, citizens' "life prospects, what they can expect to be and how well they can hope to do" (*TJ* 6). What is not equally obvious, though, is whether (and why) our basic *economic* institutions – and, by extension, the distributive outcomes produced by them – fall within the purview of *justice.* As we have seen, Buchanan says they do not: what is required is simply that prices (not state planning) determine the allocation of resources and the production and consumption of goods, and that workers are mobile and possess total freedom of occupation. When these conditions are met, the resultant distribution of income and wealth is a morally neutral fact and so does not give rise to the need for (demanding redistributive) action by the state.[5]

Rawls disagrees: there is, he says, an important difference between the allocative and distributive domains of economic life. The former should indeed be market-directed: this is necessary for both efficiency and (more decisively) for the preservation of individual liberty (*TJ* 240–1).[6] But the latter – the distribution of income and wealth – should *not* be market-directed, because (massive) economic inequality – the typical by-products of free (or lightly regulated) markets – is, in Rawls's view, incompatible with the demands of justice. Again, the "catallaxy as morality" paradigm sees these inequalities but has no qualms about them. Rawls *does*, and his objection (to a maximally pure catallaxy) gets us to the heart of his endeavor in *Theory*.

At the core of that objection is Rawls's (idiosyncratic and demanding) conception of equality. Now, *we* know that treating people equally requires ignoring certain things about them – race, gender, religion, sexual orientation, and so on. These traits are wholly outside the domain of human will – no one chooses to be male or female, black or white, gay or straight – and so ought not be the basis of special (or disadvantageous) treatment; they are, so to speak, morally irrelevant in the design of our social and political institutions. But Rawls pushes this compelling intuition further, and by doing so, forces us to contemplate (and then try to overcome) the overwhelming power of luck in human life. Rawls's basic idea is this: that *nothing* in human life is earned, *nothing is deserved*. No one chooses race, gender, sexual orientation – that is easy to see. But why, Rawls asks, should we stop *there*? Think, after all, of the extremely long list of extremely consequential advantages (and disadvantages) attributable exclusively to good (and bad) luck: whether we are born to spectacularly rich parents or spectacularly poor ones, a genius or a dolt, healthy and hale or sickly and weak. The list goes on and on and on.

Life, in short, is deeply unfair: nature distributes her advantages in a wholly arbitrary way, and there is really nothing we can do about that; we cannot, say, *re*distribute health or intelligence evenly across the whole human race. But there *is* something we *can* do: we can change the way that these advantages interact with the social world! We can (to use a Rawlsian idiom) redesign the basic structure of society – *including* its important economic institutions – to overcome the morally arbitrary distribution of nature's advantages. "There is no necessity," says Rawls, "for men to resign themselves to these contingencies" (*TJ* 88).[7] In fact, if we care about equality, we *have* to overcome contingency – we have to diminish the effect of nature by focusing on those to whom she is (arbitrarily) blind.

*Most* societies *fail* to do this: in a caste or aristocratic society, for example, birth is the most important (and obviously unchangeable) political fact; it confers exclusive right to wealth and power (*TJ* 88). But, according to the logic of Rawls's argument, a society in which the rich, connected, and talented possess most of the wealth and power is, at bottom, no different from a (plainly unjust) caste society; it too builds its institutions on a foundation of pure chance. Of course, the wealthy and powerful always try to obscure their own luck by crafting doctrines of, say, divinely ordained nobility (in aristocratic societies) and personal responsibility (in capitalist societies). By contrast, the mantra of a Rawlsian society is: *no merit, no desert.* If no one deserves the advantages that each possesses, then no one has exclusive access to the benefits those advantages produce. Instead, those advantages – wealth and talent chief among them – are treated as a resource held in common, to be used for the restoration of the equality absent in nature (*TJ* 87).

As we have seen, Buchanan (and his ilk) will see this as an attack on the rich and talented, who are forced to subsidize their less successful peers. But the Rawlsian rejoinder is that no one really deserves anything – success *or* failure! Mistakenly treating our luck as earned, and permitting the unlucky to languish, contravenes the fact of our equality: we are all equally vulnerable to nature's arbitrariness, that is, and so we should all be equally protected from it. Of course, the difference principle is the bridge between this moral philosophical intuition and political and economic practice: it requires that "economic inequalities ... are to be to the greatest benefit of the least advantaged members of society" (*R* 42–3). Already, this is a quite radical critique of familiar economic arrangements (and philosophies) in the West. In Rawls's view, the criterion by which we should judge our economic arrangements is *not* efficiency, utility, or even liberty – the standard arguments (*TJ* 59–65). No, our economic systems are to be judged by how well society's least advantaged members fare under it (*TJ* 229).[8] In other words, the poor and powerless are not an afterthought in justice as fairness, as many have wrongly assumed.[9] Quite the opposite: their interests are *the* fundamental consideration when evaluating (the justice of) possible economic arrangements – a reflection of their having lost the natural lottery of birth.

What does this look like in (institutionalized) practice? What does it mean to maximize the advantages of the least advantaged?[10] First, it is important to note that the difference principle does *not* entail *total* economic equality; in fact, Rawls regards economic inequality as "presumably inevitable" (*TJ* 7). "Those who have been favored [*sic*] by nature," says Rawls, "whoever they are, may gain from their good fortune" (*TJ* 87). But, Rawls continues, the fortunate may gain "only on terms that improve the situation of those who have lost out" (*TJ* 87). How, in other words, can we make society's "presumably inevitable" inequalities *just* (*TJ* 7)? When we put the question this way, the Rawlsian enterprise sounds essentially conservative: the problem is not to banish inequality, but to legitimize it (and to thus bolster the stability of inegalitarian societies threatened by class conflict). And, indeed, there *is* a long, well-established tradition of interpreting Rawls this way – as a defender of a perhaps slightly more compassionate but still radically inegalitarian (welfare-state) capitalism.[11] This interpretation is not without (occasional) grounding in Rawls's work: in *A Theory of Justice*, for example, in the context of a (brief) discussion of civil disobedience, Rawls intimates that the United States (in 1971) was a "reasonably just" regime (*TJ* 308).

But this essentially conservative image of Rawls cannot stand up to scrutiny: the world of the difference principle is a world *radically different* from the one we live in. Its purpose is not (merely) to lift people out of poverty; *that* is the aim of the welfare state – noble, yes, but insufficient from the perspective of justice (as fairness). Indeed, the aim of the difference principle is much more ambitious than that: its purpose is to create universal access to (Rawls's image of) the human good. *This* is the *real* test that a just society must pass: do all its members have stable access to meaningful autonomy – in Rawls's view, the ultimate human good – and, with it, a feeling of genuine flourishing? Do all members feel themselves capable of satisfying their desires?

Here, we encounter Rawls's notion of "goodness as rationality": his belief that human beings are rational, autonomous, ends-setting creatures, and that the human good – *happiness* – is "successfully carrying out" whatever "long-term plan of life" they have adopted (*TJ* 79; see also *TJ* §§63–4).[12] This requires *much* more than money in the bank (though that is essential too); rational autonomy, in Rawls's sense, requires a sizable index of "primary goods"; income and wealth, certainly, but also appealing and realizable opportunities for self-development – including access to positions of meaningful power (as a citizen and worker) – and a secure sense of one's value – the self-respect – necessary to pursue those opportunities.[13] The more of these (primary) goods we have, says Rawls, the more we can be "assured of greater success in carrying out [our] intentions and in advancing [our] ends, whatever these ends may be"; and that is why the difference principle is designed to maximize this index for society's "most disfavored members" – to ensure access to the human good for all, regardless of their place in society (*TJ* 79).

Rawls acknowledges the difficulty of maximizing (something ephemeral like) self-respect (or even quantifying it with any meaningful precision); neither is it possible to say in advance exactly how much income is necessary to realize the good of all, given the radical multiplicity (and different levels of demandingness) of human ends (*TJ* 80). It is therefore a mistake – as Rawls emphasizes, early and often in *Theory*[14] – to think of the difference principles as a detailed, specific, universally realizable blueprint for economic institutions; we must always work within the (highly variable) constraints of the possible, including society's level of economic development and its unique political culture.[15] Instead, its purpose (and chief merit) is to refocus our attention on society's most vulnerable members: do *they* live autonomous, rewarding, meaningful lives? Do *they* have access to economic security, rewarding work, a feeling of inclusion and secure social standing, leisure time conducive to the development of their abilities and the pursuit of knowledge? As we shall see, Rawls believes that laissez-faire capitalism, welfare state capitalism, and state socialism all fail this test: they fail to ensure meaningful autonomy for all, and so are unjust and unstable. The only regime that passes this test is property-owning democracy, a system defined by its broad dispersion of private productive assets – which is to say, an economic system that tries to overcome the concentration of capital characteristic of laissez-faire and welfare state capitalism, on the one hand, and the concentration of state power characteristic of socialism on the other.[16]

## 2

In the preface to the revised edition of *Theory*, Rawls draws our attention to an important problem – one of many, he candidly admits – with the original version of the work: that it does not "sharply" distinguish between "the idea of a property-owning democracy [and] the idea of the welfare state"; as a result, many readers were given the (*false*) impression that justice as fairness is compatible with the latter (*TJ* xiv; see also *R* §41.1). In fact, it is not: the welfare state, says Rawls, allows "large and inheritable inequalities of wealth," which in turn leads to "a small part of society ... controlling the economy and indirectly political life itself" (*TJ* xiv). This is made possible by the noble but (still relatively) unambitious aim of welfare state politics: "that none should fall below a decent standard of life, and that all should receive certain protections against accident and misfortune – for example, unemployment compensation and medical care" (*TJ* xv; see also *R* 139). In Rawls's view, a fully just society must aim *higher* than that; it must do *more* than (merely) redistribute "income to those with less at the end of each period" (*TJ* xv). A fully just society must instead "put all citizens in a position to manage their own affairs and to take part in social cooperation on a footing of mutual respect" (*TJ* xv). As we shall see, a property-owning democracy has the best chance of realizing *that* higher aim.

This is a thorough indictment of welfare state capitalism, to be sure. In Rawls's view, that economic system – which is to say, *the prevailing form of capitalism in most economies in the West* – is plagued by three fundamental *and insuperable* problems: first, its tendency to let "control of the economy and of much political life" fall into a "few hands" (*R* 138). In Rawls's view, this is a violation of the "fair value" of the political liberties: meaningful democracy requires not *only* the equal possession of the familiar (formal) bundle of civil liberties – thought and speech, association and assembly (*R* 45). For a democracy to be free *and* fair, citizens' civil liberties must be (universally) *effective* – the source of effective *influence* upon the government – and this they cannot be when the instruments of the state have been co-opted by the wealthy.[17] Second, welfare state capitalism fails to achieve meaningful equality of opportunity: "those who have the same level of talent and ability and the same willingness to use these gifts" tend not to have "a fair chance to attain ... public offices and positions" (*R* 43–4). And, third, welfare state capitalism does not adequately institutionalize the "principle of reciprocity," which is the fundamental aim of Rawlsian distributive justice: once the chosen social minimum is achieved, those at the top of the income ladder can float infinitely upward, without any corresponding duty to compensate (in primary social goods) their least advantaged co-citizens.[18] Welfare state capitalism, in short, leads to political disenfranchisement, to the narrowing of the range of (self-developing) opportunities (for the majority of society) and to destabilizing inequality and class conflict.

Now, it is important to emphasize that Rawls does *not* reject the institution of private property (in capital, the means of production or labor).[19] Quite the opposite: a property-owning democracy is built upon that institution (*R* 139). But this regime's principal commitment is to the *wide dispersal* of private property to prevent "large disparities of income" and (with it) political power (*TJ* xv). For a society to be (and remain) just, that is, the broadest possible swath of citizens must own (relatively) equal shares of productive capital, including both human and real assets. As with the difference principle, it is difficult to say *exactly* what this entails in practice (*TJ* 246–7). Rawls's discussion is tentative and brief; he often implies that these things can never be fully set out in theory in advance – that the institutional and legal workings will take different forms in different contexts, depending on a vast constellation of factors, including a given society's prevailing levels of productivity, its distinctive political culture, its history, and so on.[20]

And yet, in the *Restatement*, Rawls *does* provide *some* (albeit general) policy guidance; each of the measures he suggests is clearly designed to overcome the (three aforementioned) limitations of welfare state capitalism. First, to prevent the *entrenchment* of economic inequality, the basic structure must carefully regulate the "laws of bequest and inheritance"; the state must levy burdensome inheritance and gift taxes (on recipients) to prevent the passing down of (economic and political) advantages between succeeding generations (*R* §49.4).[21] Second, the basic structure of a property-owning democracy must secure "fair equality of opportunity" through "education and training" for society's least advantaged members (*R* 63). And, third, Rawls highlights the need for "institutions that support the fair value of the political liberties," such as limits on private donations to candidates, public funding for political parties and for debates, and regulations guaranteeing equal access to (public) media (*R* 63; see also *TJ* 198–9; and *PL* 328 and 362).[22]

## 3

According to Rawls, the overarching purpose of property-owning democracy is to "put all citizens in a position to manage their own affairs on a footing of a suitable degree of social and economic equality" (*R* 139).

*This* is what (the theory of) justice (as fairness) requires: "political justice," says Rawls, requires "mutually advantageous" social cooperation "*consistent with everyone's self-respect*" (*R* 139; italics added). Self-respect, after all, is "perhaps the most important primary good," essential for autonomy (*TJ* 386). As we have seen, welfare state capitalism does not fulfill that aim: it produces stark economic inequality and, with it, "a discouraged and depressed underclass … [that] feels left out and does not participate in the public political culture" (*R* 140). This exclusion – this "subordinate ranking public life" (*TJ* 477) – leads to widespread feelings of shame and envy, resentment and alienation (*TJ* 469; see also *TJ* 67 and 80). When, conversely, wealth is evenly dispersed – and when every individual has an effective voice and a meaningful share of power (as a worker *and* a citizen) – "an underclass will not exist" (*TJ* 469).

The secure standing *as equal* is perhaps *the* master idea of Rawls's political philosophy. Without it – when, say, the political liberties are formal, not fairly valued, when democracy is merely a disingenuous veil for plutocracy, when a few have everything and the rest have nothing – self-respect is elusive; and without self-esteem, "nothing may seem like worth doing…. All desire and activity becomes empty and vain, and we sink into apathy and cynicism" (*TJ* 386; see also *PL* viii.6). But when we are *seen* – when the basic structure recognizes and guarantees our standing as equal – we develop "a confidence in [our] abilities," the feeling that our "plan of life is worth carrying out" (*TJ* 386). And this solid psychological foundation – this "secure sense of [self-] worth" – in turn "forms the basis of the love of humankind" (*TJ* 478; see also 403). "One who is confident in himself," says Rawls, "is not grudging in the appreciation of others" (*TJ* 387). In fact, self-confidence makes us especially fit for community: when we are secure in the pursuit of *our* good, we appreciate and esteem others seeking *their* good – developing their talents, expanding their knowledge, refining their ends (*TJ* 386–7). *This* is the basis of a just, happy, *and stable* community of equals.[23] As we have seen, it is Rawls's view that this desirable sort of community cannot exist when it is riven into the domineering rich and disenfranchised poor.

# 14

# "An Endless Spiral": Piketty on the Dynamics of Wealth and Income Inequality in the Twenty-First Century

After *A Theory of Justice*, Rawls was plagued with doubt: there was, he conceded, "a serious problem internal to justice as fairness" (*PL* xv). The problem was this: that the political society described in *Theory* was not, in the end, *stable.* And its stability was compromised by Rawls's early inattention to the fact of pluralism: the conception of justice (as fairness) defended in *Theory* presumed the existence of an *ethically* homogeneous society, a society populated *exclusively* by liberals (along Kantian lines) whose fundamental, guiding aim is to secure the conditions for their rational autonomy.[1] Hence, their desire for property-owning democracy, the economic regime that recognizes the need for self-respect, enlarges the horizon of opportunities for self-development, and preserves meaningful access to power – all essential to fully realized (not formal) autonomy.

But – and here is the problem – a free society is a plural society; this means that not *everyone* in it will aspire to rational autonomy (as Rawls understands it). And this *dis*agreement (about ends) is expected, reasonable, and in fact desirable – a sign of genuine liberty and of the vitality (and diversity of ends) it produces. For example, for some, a virtuous and meaningful life must be lived in accordance with the imperatives of divine revelation and under the (potentially very strict) guidance of the religious hierarchy tasked with interpreting those commands – well and good. For others, a well-lived life requires the complete and total subsumption of individual identity in traditional familial bonds – also well and good. But, in Rawls's mind, this creates a legitimacy (and with it, a stability) problem: *those* citizens do not accept, and so cannot give their consent to, principles designed to secure *rational* autonomy; for them, a well-lived life requires devotion to authority, total self-sacrifice. And so neither can they be coerced on the basis of those liberal principles, for doing so would fail to respect their status as free and equal.[2] Hence the need for a new justificatory strategy, one that does not rely on the ideal at *Theory*'s heart – the ideal of *autonomy*, the liberal (not human) good of a *rational* life. We must find a new way to convince citizens of the desirability of justice as fairness (as the regulative conception of justice for institutions), a way that does not rely on a thick (and therefore sectarian) conception of human flourishing.

*This* is the task of *Political Liberalism*: to detach the conception of justice (as fairness) defended in *Theory* from its demanding and controversial philosophical baggage.[3] To make society legitimate and stable, that is, Rawls must show that his principles of justice can stand freely, so to speak – that they can elicit the free consent of all citizens, even those who do not regard liberal autonomy as the quintessential and fullest expression of human flourishing.[4] In fact, Rawls believes that there is already an "overlapping consensus" of political values and principles – a consensus on the desirability of justice as fairness (*or something like it*[5]) – *despite* the radical multiplicity of belief systems (what Rawls calls comprehensive doctrines) present in any free society.[6] This consensus *must* exist, he adds, for without it, no plural society can be fully, indefinitely stable; without this "overlapping consensus," citizens will simply be waiting for the right moment to co-opt the instruments of political power in the service of their sectarian ends.

To show this – to trace this history of increasing stability in the face of (seemingly disastrous) pluralism – Rawls takes us back (a long, long way) to the Wars of Religion – to a time when fidelity to one's comprehensive (religious) beliefs required that we convert others, to save their souls, by force if necessary (*PL* 37). Now, notwithstanding those (increasingly rare) fringe fundamentalisms, liberalism has tamed this converting zeal: in a well-ordered liberal society, that is, most comprehensive doctrines are (to use Rawls's phrase) *reasonable*; the adherents of these doctrines (now) recognize (after the psychologically painful and socially disastrous experience of failing to do so) the fact of pluralism – that *their* truth is not *the* truth for all – and so they can live as equals with those they disagree with, with those they think are (literally) damned to hell (*PL* 58–61). In other words, belief no longer undermines the possibility of good citizenship – as it did in the aftermath of the Reformation. In fact, in Rawls's telling, belief now (often) leads directly *to* good citizenship: our commitment to (liberal) justice, he says, is (often) an outgrowth of our deeper commitment to the tenets of our comprehensive doctrine (*PL* 254).[7]

All of this helps to explain why, despite Rawls's dissatisfaction with *Theory*, the first principle of justice, which protects the equal basic liberties, is unchanged and remains at the forefront of *Political Liberalism*. Indeed, Rawls never wavers on the correctness and persuasiveness of the first principle of justice. *This* is the sort of principle that most citizens want to live under – a principle the recognizes their equality, their need for self-respect, and their right to pursue their chosen ends – regardless of whatever else they believe. For our purposes, though, it is conspicuous and important that the same cannot be said about the difference principle: Rawls *does* waver on *its* persuasiveness; he lets it drift to the distant background of *Political Liberalism* – a reflection of his worry that it stands too far outside the overlapping consensus (which *must* exist for political liberalism to work).

Now, this move is not made explicit: there is no open renunciation of *Theory*'s account of economic justice. But in *Political Liberalism*, in the preface, Rawls starts to speak of justice as fairness *or something like it* functioning as the (freestanding) political conception of justice: "I [still] believe [justice as fairness] to be the most reasonable conception of justice" for a plural society (*PL* xlvi). But, Rawls continues, "I shouldn't deny that other conceptions also satisfy the definition of a liberal conception.... I would be simply unreasonable" to do so (*PL* xlviii). And what, exactly, do these alternative conceptions look like? They have a much less demanding account of economic justice, one that "substitutes for the difference principle" a guarantee of "a sufficient level adequate all-purpose means" – a return, in other words, to the social minimum ethos of welfare state capitalism and, by extension, a *serious* walking back of the earlier (quite radical) claims in *Theory* (*PL* xlviii). Rawls says much the same thing in lecture 6 of

*Political Liberalism,* "The Idea of Public Reason": that in an equally reasonable conception of justice – which is to say, in a conception of justice that *can* act as the central locus of an overlapping consensus – the application of the "demanding" difference principle is no longer "essential"; instead, a "social minimum providing for the basic needs of all citizens" is adequate (*PL* 228–9; see also 157). Why *did* Rawls step back? Why *is* property-owning democracy *wholly* absent from *Political Liberalism?* Because he did not believe (perhaps unconsciously) that a similar consensus exists on the second (economic redistributive) principle: we may all be egalitarians now, but this *moral* principle did not require the radical overhaul of the *economic* system.

It is important to be clear here: the claim that moral equality is compatible with (sometimes stunning) economic inequality is *not* true at the level of theory – rather, at the level of *Theory.* It is, instead, an assessment of the public culture of contemporary democracies (and of the United States in particular).[8] But this is a dangerous thing for Rawls to acknowledge: the existence of a disconnect between the demands of justice and citizens' prevailing values. After all, the central aim of *Political Liberalism* is precisely to show the synchronicity between Rawls's principles of justice and the things that citizens – real people in the real world – believe about justice. Again, if these two things do not match up – if the demands of Rawls's principles exceed what citizens are willing to do for one another – then that calls the entire theoretical enterprise of *Political Liberalism* into question. In this light, it is not terribly surprising that questions of economic organization (and justice) recede into the background of that text. Neither is it surprising that Rawls is willing to consider a less demanding regime of economic redistribution as a part of the foundational (freestanding) political conception of justice; if this less (economically) demanding theory of justice provides a more stable footing for an overlapping consensus, then perhaps that is a worthwhile trade-off – less justice in exchange for more stability.

But, as we have seen, Rawls's own economic convictions did not *stay* in the background for long. Property-owning democracy is an important – no, *essential* – element of the *Restatement;* it is treated by Rawls there as the economic system most likely to fulfill and maintain the requirements of justice (*R* 41.1). So why *did* economic concerns – and with them, property-owning democracy – return to the forefront? Of course, it is difficult to say. But if we look closely – at *Political Liberalism,* at *The*

*Law of Peoples,* and at his private correspondences too – there *are* hints that Rawls thought that things were going off the rails, so to speak. For example, we have already come across Rawls's worry that American democracy was being undermined by "the curse of money": "Politics," he laments, "is dominated by corporate and other organized interests who through large contributions to campaigns distort if not preclude public discussion and deliberation" (*PL* 449).[9] And in a (little known but fascinating) letter, written in 1998, Rawls worries about the corrupting influence of plutocracy on individual citizens' (psychic) well-being: the United States, he says, is "awash in ... meaningless consumerism," a by-product of the widespread conviction that the common project of democracy has been extinguished by "the banks and the business class."[10] Indeed, in Rawls's mind, the co-opting of social and political life by "the capitalist business class whose main goal is simply larger profit" leads to the dissolution of the bonds of community and the sapping of vitality from public life.[11] *This* is why, in *The Law of Peoples,* in the context of a realistic utopia, Rawls contemplates, and ultimately endorses, Mill's notion of an economically stationary state: it is perfectly compatible with the demands of justice, says Rawls, for a state to *simply stop growing* (*LP* §15; see also *R* 63–4).

## 1

Thomas Piketty's *Capital in the Twenty-First Century* is the most ambitious, comprehensive, and celebrated attempt to understand the class dynamics of present-day capitalism, dynamics that so deeply disturbed Rawls – *with good reason,* as we shall now see.[12] In the introduction to *Capital,* Piketty states his purpose: to arbitrate the "dialogue of the deaf," between those, like Marx, who believe that, under capitalism, "inequality is always increasing" and those, like Hayek, who believe that "inequality is naturally decreasing ... [and] that harmony comes about automatically" (*C* 3). Where, exactly, does the truth lie? Does capitalism "lead to the concentration of wealth in ever fewer hands," or "do the balancing forces of growth, competition, and technological progress lead ... to reduced inequality" (*C* 1)? To answer these questions, what is needed most are data, however "tentative and imperfect" they may be: only "by patiently searching for facts and patterns and [then] calmly analyzing the economic, social and political mechanisms that might explain them," can we (reasonably accurately) determine whether or not (massive) inequality is a temporary and eliminable aspect of capitalism (*C* 3).

In many ways, then, Piketty is inspired by Marx's example. This is not a matter of their shared title alone: Marx too sought to understand the "dynamics of industrial capitalism" – its productivity and processes of accumulation, its contradictions, crises, and (in Marx's mind inevitable) collapse – from an explicitly "scientific," data-driven perspective (*C* 7). This is exactly the right approach – an "inspiration [to] economists today" (*C* 10). And yet, Piketty also expresses strong reservations here: not only were the data available to Marx limited and incomplete; there is also the *highly* problematic (and equally undeniable) fact that Marx had already "decided on his conclusions in 1848, *before* embarking on the research needed to justify them" (*C* 10; italics added). This is bad social science, of course, and a warning bell for all researchers; open-minded inquiry must always precede the conclusions produced by it. There is also the rather pesky fact that Marx was, well, *wrong*: his dark prophecy of the violent abolition of capitalism by the proletariat never came to fruition – the peculiar, surprising, and exceptional Russian case aside – and this surely colors our approach to him.

For those social scientists coming after Marx, the explanation was obvious: despite its nineteenth-century growing pains – this is putting it *extremely* mildly, of course[13] – twentieth-century capitalism eventually produced, and *will continue to produce*, a more evenly distributed prosperity. For example, in his monumental 1953 study, *Shares of Upper Income Groups in Income and Savings*, Simon Kuznets found that, since 1913, the United States has seen a significant reduction in income inequality: the middle and lower classes of the American population saw their share of national income increase from 50–55 per cent in the 1910s and 1920s to 65–70 per cent by the late 1940s.[14] In other words, inequality *was* shrinking, and there was little reason to believe that this trend would lose momentum or reverse course. One year later, in "Economic Growth and Income Inequality," his annual address, as president, to the influential American Economic Association, Kuznets reiterates these findings: "Since the 1920s," he says, "the relative distribution of income has been moving toward equality" (4). Now, Kuznets does not deny the persistence of some (reasonable) income inequality; his point, rather, is that even those at the bottom earn generous wages, possess high purchasing power, and thus enjoy a historically unprecedented standard of good living – a standard certain to rise inexorably and (eventually even) exponentially. This is an image of a stable and cohesive society, one in which "a rising tide lifts all boats" (24).

Once again, Piketty is deeply skeptical: the Marxist penchant for "apocalyptic predictions" has here given way to "a similarly excessive fondness for fairy tales, or at any rate happy endings" (*C* 11).[15] No such optimistic reading of the facts is sustainable: Kuznets certainly had access to more and better data than Marx, including government statistics tracking total annual income taxation – an impossibly valuable public policy innovation for the social scientists of the early and middle years of the twentieth century. But, not unlike Marx, the postwar economists were still interpreting those data through an ideological – and in this case, pro-capitalist – lens. This was, after all, the height of the Cold War: the revelation that capitalism (eventually) works to the benefit of all – backed up by reliable data, and verifiable by sturdy scientific inquiry – was a major cause for celebration in the West.[16]

Unfortunately, though, this buoyant mood obscured an undeniable fact: that the flattening of income inequality was the by-product of a wholly unpredictable, and therefore impossible to replicate, exogenous shock. Here, Piketty is referring to the calamity of two world wars: "The sharp reduction in income inequality that we observe in almost all the rich countries between 1914 and 1945," he says, "was due above all to the world wars and the violent economic and political shocks they entailed" (*C* 15). War, after all, is bad for people with large fortunes: to finance the always-expensive war effort, states implement extremely burdensome progressive taxation, as well as the not uncommon appropriation of the (once privately held) instruments of production; such measures disproportionately affect the wealthy, and thus narrow the income gap between the classes. War also creates buoyant job prospects for the middle and lower classes – they build (and then rebuild) at home, and fight abroad.[17] In other words, the decline in inequality documented by Kuznets – and adopted as gospel by his massive legion of followers – was a temporary aberration – the by-product of emergency measures adopted during wartime, and thus not likely to be repeated.

Indeed, according to Piketty, the rising *divergence* of income has been the characteristic feature of capitalism in West: "Since the 1970s," he says, "inequality has *increased significantly* in rich countries, *especially* the United States" (*C* 15; italics added). Why, exactly, has inequality increased *so* dramatically? Piketty begins to answer by emphasizing that this radical divergence is by no means inevitable: there is no such thing as "economic determinism" in "inequalities of wealth and income" under capitalism (or any other economic system for that matter) (*C* 20). Neither is convergence – or shrinking inequality – predetermined. What matters most, according to Piketty, is the activity of the state: when, say, the state is committed to provide accessible, inexpensive education, inequality shrinks; when, conversely, the state decides to not regulate the remuneration of top managers and lets their wage increases conspicuously outpace both productivity and profitability, inequality *explodes*.[18] In other words, the distribution of wealth is *always* the by-product of political decisions.

Here, Piketty declares war against the doctrine of the invisible hand: the much-celebrated automaticity of the market – its apparent sole dependence on the uncoordinated actions of individuals – is totally illusory. After all, economic outcomes are inextricably linked to – and indeed can never be insulated from – public policy; hence, Buchanan's depiction of the economic domain of life as wholly apolitical is misleading and inaccurate.[19] As another example of political and economic interdependence, Piketty discusses Western governments' recent general inattention to the intergenerational transmission of wealth: when private capital – typically in the form of real estate and financial assets – is freely passed between generations, without taxation and ensuing redistribution, inequality skyrockets. And this is especially true during times of slow economic growth – times like ours, and particularly so since the 1970s – when the rate of return on capital significantly outpaces the rate of growth for the economy as a whole. After all, in stagnant economies, when it is difficult to amass wealth in the span of a single lifetime, past wealth confers a significant advantage to those (relative few) with access to it: "it takes only a small flow of net savings," says Piketty, "to increase the stock of wealth steadily and substantially" vis-à-vis those with a comparatively negligible share of capital to save, invest, and reinvest (*C* 178). Thus, inequalities get passed on, and then greatly magnified, as time passes – *here* lies the main root of sustained inequality.

Inheritance is indeed the subject of considerable scrutiny in *Capital*: inequalities of income (from labor) are pressing and acute, to be sure; but, in Piketty's mind, the future of inequality is rooted in the income generated by dynastic wealth: "almost inevitably," he says, the insular family transmission of financial and real estate assets "gives lasting, disproportionate importance to the inequalities created in the past" (*C* 378). This is hardly historically unprecedented: the nineteenth century was characterized by a kind of rentier capitalism, wherein the main source of wealth was (inherited) land, as well as the (rent) proceeds obtained from its ownership. And Piketty sees a return to such a condition in the works, a phenomenon he dubs the "new patrimonial capitalism" (*C* 173). This modern variety of capitalism is "flourishing in these early years of the twenty-first century" – years of slow economic growth and comparatively soaring real estate and stock market prices – "when capital reproduces itself faster than output increases" (*C* 237 and 571). In such a condition, income from capital gradually surpasses income from labor: today's high-income earners accumulate, and save, greater stocks of wealth, which are then passed on – relatively untaxed – to their heirs, heirs whose job and earning prospects are likely to be slimmer as the result of continued sluggish growth. *This* is the heart of *Capital*: "The entrepreneur inevitably tends to become a rentier," says Piketty, in his conclusion, "more and more dominant over those who own nothing but their labor.... *The past devours the future*" (*C* 571; italics added).

Again, Piketty's purpose is to show that this situation is the by-product of (in this case) state *in*activity – the unwillingness of governments to appropriately tax and redistribute inherited capital. And this, in turn, is the by-product of the state's ideological capture by the twentieth-century wave of classical liberals. This is a subtle yet recurring theme of *Capital*: beginning in the 1970s, says Piketty, there was a "gradual [and then greatly accelerated] transfer of public wealth into private hands" – a reflection of the ideological sea change described in chapter 13 (*C* 173). It is no coincidence that the resurgence of inequality – in both income and wealth – can be traced to this period.

Unfortunately, Piketty's philosophy of government is mostly implicit, not explicit: *Capital* is not the outspoken political treatise that many – many on the left, at least – hoped it would be. Indeed, political judgments are few and far between. For example, it is clear that Piketty thinks that stark (and growing) inequality is bad for democracies: it "undermine[s] the meritocratic values on which democratic societies are based" (*C* 1). But there is little detail on why class mobility is a constitutive democratic value or, conversely, why economic inequality is so devastatingly bad for democracy, as Piketty tantalizingly implies. How, that is, do the rich translate their wealth into control over political decision-making? How can such processes be arrested, and egalitarian democracy be restored? For answers to these sorts of questions, we must look elsewhere.[20]

And yet, there *are* telling hints, here and there, for those looking to reconstruct the political philosophy of *Capital.* And that philosophy is conspicuously Keynesian: there is a deep, thoroughgoing suspicion of capitalism, of course, particularly in its current minimally regulated[21] and minimally taxed form; and this distrust is accompanied by the belief that state intervention is the best way to tame its excesses. Like Keynes, though, Piketty stops well short of total state control: "New instruments are needed to regain control over a financial capitalism that has run amok," he says, but this does not imply a foundational reassessment – and then expansion – of the state's role in the economy. Indeed, Piketty is quite adamant that prevailing levels of income taxation are adequate – government tax collections have remained stable since 1980, despite becoming regressive at the very top (*C* 509) – and that the *significant* growth of the welfare state is neither "realistic nor desirable" (*C* 481).[22] What *is* essential, though, is an increase of state intervention in the distribution of wealth (from capital as opposed to income). Here we encounter *the* central public policy recommendation of *Capital*: the introduction of a "progressive global tax on capital" (*C* 471).

Piketty's purpose, here, is not to design an extremely burdensome, disincentivizing mechanism of redistribution or to finance an ambitious program of social spending; his intention is to regulate capitalism – to avoid "an endless inegalitarian spiral" and to regain "control over the dynamics of accumulation" (*C* 471). Hence, the main plank of his proposal is a modest 1 per cent tax on the value of assets in excess of €1 million (*C* 528).[23] The more demanding condition of Piketty's proposal, however, is that such a tax must also be global: twenty-first-century capital is highly mobile, after all, and so no national political jurisdiction can be immune from reporting the wealth lodged in its banks; universal adoption is therefore an essential feature of Piketty's proposal, and also the requirement that negates its very possibility. Indeed, in the end, Piketty has serious, ultimately immovable reservations about the requisite degree of "international cooperation" needed to implement such a policy; it *may* be possible on a "regional or continental scale" – Europe being the most promising and likely possibility, given its already existing political, economic, banking and accounting infrastructure – but a "truly global tax on capital is no doubt a utopian ideal" (*C* 37, 471, and 516). "It is hard to imagine," adds Piketty, in the final chapter, that "the nations of the world [would agree] to any such thing any time soon" (*C* 515). Thus ends *Capital* on a note of despondency: the problem of global inequality, it turns out, is equal measures grave and intractable.

## 2

Throughout *Capital*, Piketty's gaze is fixed squarely on the political economy of the world's richest, most developed countries – the United States, Great Britain, and France; he wants to understand the class dynamics of capitalism over time – centuries, ideally – and so the deeply rooted capitalism of the West is the obvious and appropriate place to focus. There is one provocative mention of the poorer developing world, though, which comes in the final section of chapter 13. There, Piketty asks, "Does the kind of social state that emerged in the developed countries in the twentieth century have a universal vocation" (*C* 490)? By "social state," Piketty means a state capable of effectively regulating "the production and distribution of wealth" within its borders – a state well-endowed and organized enough to smooth out the booms and busts of capitalist competition, issue and properly value currency, administer international trade regimes, collect revenue through taxation, and then redistribute (in various forms) the considerable resources at its disposal (*C* 472). As an example, here, Piketty mentions the financial crisis of 2008: unlike 1929, this crisis "did not trigger a crash as serious as the Great Depression," because the pragmatic "governments and central banks of the wealthy countries did not allow the financial system to collapse" (*C* 472). These states were positioned to act as a "lender of last resort," and in fact were the "*only* public institution[s] capable of averting a total collapse of the economy in an emergency" (*C* 473; italics added).

Of course, these states are essential and omnipresent in noncrises too; they are responsible not only for "central 'regalian' functions" – the maintenance of order, the enforcement of property rights, the outfitting and deployment of the military and police – but for everyday well-being, including the provision of health care, education, pensions, employment insurance, as well as a variety of transfer payments, such as family allowances, guaranteed incomes, and the like (*C* 475 and 477–9). How likely is it that the weak and poor states of sub-Saharan and North Africa, South Asia, and Latin America will eventually come to resemble the strong and rich "social states" of Western Europe, North America, and East Asia?

"Nothing could be less certain," laments Piketty (*C* 490). The main issue facing states in these regions is the underdevelopment of the state apparatus itself, and the concomitant absence of routinized, uncontested bureaucratic mechanisms of income, corporate, and wealth tax collection: whereas states in the rich world collect 30–50 per cent of national income, developing states collect only 10–20 per cent – a gap that continues to widen (*C* 490–1). Obviously, this strains the ability to perform the basic tasks of government; and, in many cases, the possibility of the state provision of more expensive social welfare is negated altogether. "After paying for a proper police force and judicial system," says Piketty, "there is not much left to pay for education and health" (*C* 491).

What is the root cause of this chronic shortage of financial resources? In Piketty's mind, the present disorder is in large part the by-product of the history – and economics – of imperialism: colonization is, by definition, exploitive – the typically violent appropriation and extraction of property, commodities, and labor without compensation, in the form of either revenue or committed institution building.[24] And the often-chaotic process of *de*colonization – in some cases, outright war; in others, the unpredictable withering of colonial largesse – has been equally, though perhaps more subtly, damaging. For example, in order to finance the basic functions of state, the majority of postcolonial regimes were forced to borrow from banks abroad. And, since the 1980s, the leading "international [lending] organizations" – primarily, the International Monetary Fund and the World Bank – have been governed by the values and assumptions of an "ultraliberal" ideology "emanating from the developed world" (*C* 491–2). What are the basic tenets of this "ultraliberalism," as Piketty dubs it? First and foremost, the international banks demand rapid, thorough trade liberalization: as a condition of approval, debtor governments must implement significant "decrease[s] in customs duties" and tariffs; they must open domestic markets to the import of (typically conspicuously cheaper) goods from abroad (*C* 492).

Now, breaking down barriers to trade is "not *necessarily* a bad thing," says Piketty (*C* 492; italics added). In fact, liberalization was spectacularly beneficial for today's wealthy countries.[25] But these states reduced their tariffs at a gradual, sensible, autonomous pace – *literally* over the course of *centuries* – always sure that replacement sources of revenue were available (*C* 492). In today's developing world, by contrast, trade liberalization is imposed "peremptorily ... from without" and (in light of the postcolonial context) in the absence of a "strong tax authority capable of collecting new taxes and other substitute sources of revenue" (*C* 492).[26] In other words, today's powerful lending institutions fail to heed "the lessons of their own historical experience"; they force poor countries to submit to the sort of practices from which their own governments were exempt, practices that contravene the most rudimentary fundamentals of public accounting (*C* 492). In Piketty's mind, this is counterproductive and unsustainable: without the ability to compensate for lost revenue, debtor states are forced into an endless cycle of debt, debt service, and underdevelopment – a new kind of financial colonialism, perhaps harder to see than the violent adventurism of the past, but no less exploitive and perhaps even more destructive.[27]

# Afterword

*Capital* can lead to despair. As Piketty ably demonstrates, the forces of convergence, once strong, have withered: there is stunning, massive economic inequality within, and even more so between, countries. And given the prevailing ideological climate in the developed world, where decisions of far-reaching global consequence are made, such inequality is likely to persist and become increasingly severe into the foreseeable future. Why? What is the (relevant) animating principle of this dominant ideology – this "new ultraliberal wave," as Piketty derisively calls it (*C* 491) – and of the governmental actors that endorse and put it into practice? That nonincome capital – capital accumulated via the ownership of financial instruments and real estate, not the expenditure of energy through (wage) labor – ought to be maximally private, which is to say, minimally taxed, now *and* in the future, when those assets get passed on to heirs; otherwise, we risk disincentivizing economic activity and accumulation, extinguishing the entrepreneurial spirit among those most likely to facilitate real growth. *This*, according to Piketty, is the root of inequality, especially so during times of low growth – *times like ours* – when returns on the ownership of labor lag far behind returns on the ownership of capital. As these advantages get passed down over time – through under- or even untaxed estates, continuously reinvested then passed down again – we fall into an "endless inegalitarian spiral" (*C* 439). Thus, the "past devour[s] the future" (*C* 571).

As we have seen, Piketty advances two main proposals to arrest this vicious downward spiral: first, a stronger commitment to public education and to specialized training – more generally, to the "diffusion of knowledge," which Piketty calls "the principal force for convergence" (*C* 22). And second, a progressive global tax on capital income, increasingly steep, all the way up to "10% for fortunes of several hundred million or several billion euros" (*C* 571). Of course, his advocacy, on this second front especially, is lukewarm (at best): Piketty concedes that such a tax is not likely to be feasible, that the level of international political cooperation needed to implement such a measure simply does not exist – not even in relatively institutionally integrated Europe – *especially* in the face of the powerful opposition it is sure to elicit from the world's wealthiest, most organized, and well-connected individuals. Hence, Piketty ends *Capital* with an ominous warning: "The long-term dynamics of the distribution of wealth," he says, "are ... terrifying" (*C* 571).

This is not the appropriate place to arbitrate *Capital*'s political institutional prescriptions, or to examine (feasible) alternatives; our aim in this book is *not* to advance a public policy agenda for global economic redistribution. Instead, let us conclude by thinking about a different, more appropriate, and infinitely worthwhile question raised by *Capital*, the last question that we will consider in this book: Why, exactly, is inequality *so bad?* As we have seen, Piketty does not have much to offer us here: he *does* say that the economic inequality characteristic of capitalism in the twenty-first century "radically undermine[s] the meritocratic values on which democratic societies are based" (*C* 1). But Piketty has little interest in defining meritocracy or democracy precisely; neither does he explain the (apparently constitutive) relationship between them. Fair enough. Piketty is, by his own admission, an economist, not a political theorist. Fortunately, *we are* – with a whole history of profound ideas about market society at our disposal – and so much better placed to answer that key question: why *does* inequality matter? Our answer to this question proceeds along the three related – no, more than that, *inextricable* – tracks outlined in the introduction: the individual, the social, and the political.

Why does inequality matter *to individuals?* An easy question, really. It matters because the deprivations that come with economic insecurity – precarious, low-paid work, poor health without access to affordable and effective care, the single-minded focus on bare survival – are antitheti-cal to the free and full development of the human personality. Indeed, much of this book has been concerned with autonomy – with competing conceptions of the good life. And while there has been deep and wide disagreement about what that life actually looks like – philosophic con-templation, civic engagement, beatitude, tranquility, service, aesthetic pleasure, the list goes on – as well as (equally) intense disagreement about whether or not the market leads us toward, or away from, that good life, all the thinkers covered in these pages agree that we have to live for *something* – the pursuit of some ideal, a way of life, a state of being.

It follows, of course, that the failure to achieve what we strive for constitutes a profound loss: talents undeveloped, growth stunted, pro-jects abandoned – tragic, all of it; the squandering of our unique inher-itance. And so, if we have an image of the sorts of activities that make life valuable and worthwhile – what, to reiterate, *is* the endeavor of philosophy, if not *that?* – then it naturally follows that we must secure the resources necessary for the full and stable realization of that ideal *for all.* If the right to be free exists and is universal, which no one can sanely deny, then it is intimately bound up with the right to not be poor; this sets up important limits to the sorts of outcomes permissible in a market society (or any society for that matter) and a large circle of agreement among the diverse thinkers covered in these pages (with the sole exception of the twentieth-century classical liberals who stand outside of this consensus).

How can we be sure that these rights – to meaningful autonomy and, with it, economic security – are respected? As with all political questions, this is partly a matter of social values – what we, as a commu-nity, think about entitlement and responsibility – and partly a matter of political institutions – how the state uses punitive power to pursue its chosen ends. In a well-ordered society, there is a *meaningful* degree of synchronicity between these two domains of life, the social and the political: our (reasonably widely) shared ideas and principles – about justice, equality, reciprocity, desert, and so on – guide, and will be re-flected in, the legal and political institutions that coerce us. When that is the case, citizens are likely to regard those institutions as legitimate and will abide by the demands placed upon them; such a society is sta-ble, politically speaking, a place where the coerced regard the power exercised over them as unobjectionable and perhaps even just. If, conversely, there is (too) little overlap between prevailing values and institutions, then citizens will possess only a shaky adherence to the laws and to the state that makes and enforces them; such a society is unstable and therefore in need of legal institutional reform. Of course, the causal arrow runs in both directions: institutions do not merely passively reflect values; *they shape them too*: institutions can innovate in the domain of values, just as values can produce institutional innovations. In other words, every society is characterized by a kind of dialectic between its ideas and its institutional practices: these two domains evolve together, modify each other, and, in a stable society, they coexist (reasonably) harmoniously. The absence of such harmony, to reiterate, is pregnant with revolution.

Notice that this discussion says nothing about the actual *content* of our values or institutions: a racist society – populated by racist citizens living under racist, discriminatory institutions – can be stable, just as a compassionate and egalitarian society can be stable. And the transformation of the former sort of society into the latter sort can be effected from below – by citizens demanding the radical overhaul of morally unacceptable laws – or from above – by political actors on the moral vanguard (and by the coercive laws they enact). Of course, it is much more realistic to assume that historical change – *progress*, in this case – will be the result of the *interaction* – the spontaneous, partly unconscious collaboration – of the ideational and institutional domains of life: the social world is an organic whole, after all, despite the (very real) possibility of (very deep) dissonance between its constituent parts; such is the nature of dialectics and, by extension, of social and political life.

We need not take this (admittedly abstract) discussion too much further: its purpose was simply to highlight the fact that the realization of specific political outcomes – in this case, relative economic equality – requires a kind of dual attention – to our ideas about social life and to the coercive institutions that give it (legal) structure. We are now very well equipped to deal with the former category: *ideas.* So, given our own area of expertise, let us return to our earlier question: What sort of society is likely to respect and institutionalize the right to meaningful economic security (as a constitutive dimension of the right to be free)? What sorts of *ideas* must circulate – and come to predominate – in such a society?

It does not take a magnifying glass to see that this book is full of them – that it can be used as a resource for the (re)design and (re)construction of a more just and humane society, certainly more just and humane than the (atomized, inegalitarian, unstable) societies described so vividly by Piketty in *Capital*. That is my hope, anyway. Consider, in this vein, a prominent theme running throughout these pages: our fundamentally social nature – the fact that, for many of the thinkers discussed in the preceding chapters, our well-being is *always* bound up with that of others, with the proper ordering of our relations to others. For creatures like us, the good life does not and cannot exist in a vacuum, that is, in total isolation from our fellows; it requires attendance to others, because we are, by nature, other-oriented beings.

Now, this can be true in two distinct senses: first, in a strong sense, according to which our own flourishing is dependent on our total immersion and dedicated participation in dense, complex networks of cooperation with the like-minded. Aristotle and Hegel (among others) fall into this category, both of whom regard patriotism as the summit of virtue *and* happiness. Of course, our essential sociability can also be understood in a second, weaker, less demanding sense, according to which our flourishing requires the genuine (not half-hearted) recognition of our projects by others. Without such recognition – when we feel ignored, unseen, powerless – we are liable to fall into despair and to lose interest in the exercise of our autonomy; when, conversely, such recognition is secure – when, for example, society's redistributive arrangements guarantee the resources necessary for the pursuits of our projects, and all regard those arrangements as just and worthwhile – we are confident in ourselves and so better placed to recognize the endeavors of others (however different they may be from our own) by happily contributing to those shared (autonomy-securing) institutions. Rousseau and Rawls (among others) fall into this latter category.

Once again, the afterword is not the appropriate place to arbitrate this debate. Luckily, though, it does not matter which paradigm we find more persuasive, at least not in the context of our current discussion – the Aristotelian-Hegelian, which employs a monist conception of worthwhile human ends, or the more modern Rawlsian version, which allows for a much wider variety of ends, but still emphasizes the need to associate, be seen, and recognized, by others as an essential precondition of lasting self-confidence and, with it, civic virtue. It does not matter, here, anyway, because both paradigms, even the less demanding one, treat *reciprocity* as the foundation and core of well-ordered, stable, happy communities: citizens in such societies regard their community as a *mutually beneficial* cooperative venture and do not want to benefit at the expense of their compatriots.

Of course, this is obvious in the context of the Aristotelian-Hegelian view: citizens (in the absolute fullest sense of that word) regard their own flourishing as inextricable from the flourishing of others; prosperity (again, in the absolute fullest sense of that word) must therefore extend to every member of the enterprise. But this is no less true of the Rousseauvian-Rawlsian view: the desire to live together, *as equals*, means that the terms of our cooperation must be fair, which is to say conducive to the advancement of the interests of all; *that* is simply what equality demands. It follows, then, *in both cases*, that we cannot be happy if others live on the edge of destitution; neither can we be happy if others experience life in their community as the source of alienation and humiliation.

The list of things this rules out is very long indeed, and demanding too: anything below a generous level of universal economic security, the indignity of low social status, total reliance on the arbitrary, unchecked will of others, the concentration of political power in the hands of a small faction. To be sure, a world very different and much better than the one described in *Capital* – our world *today* – a world without reciprocity, a world in which the political energy of the rich is employed in the service of evading public responsibilities, and the political energy of the poor is sapped by decades of disenfranchisement. This book is, in the end, a testament to the fact that a better world is articulable and deeply desirable; the key political task for the twenty-first century, then, is to replenish the frayed but not irrevocably lost bonds of reciprocity and to thus show that that different and better social world is not only necessary and desirable but also, because reconcilable with our nature, *possible*.

# Notes

**Introduction**

1 See, e.g., Ronald Beiner, *Political Philosophy: What It Is and Why It Matters* (Cambridge: Cambridge University Press, 2014), xvi: "One can define the [political] theory tradition from Plato onward as a dialogue between rival conceptions of the good. One can only participate in this tradition in a meaningful way if one is committed to some particular determined view of the ends of life."

2 In each chapter, I have tried to provide an account of the relevant historical context; some cases (e.g., Lenin and Hayek) require more attention to context than others. But, again, this is a history of *ideas*, not events, as befits my own interests and expertise. Those looking for more historical detail should pay close attention to the endnotes, which highlight the essential sources that I have used in the writing of this book.

3 In fact, the (increasing) complexity – the *otherworldliness* – of these models may have (inadvertently) blocked (interest in) the sort of reflection we undertake here.

4 See, e.g., Henri Pirenne, *Economic and Social History of Medieval Europe* (New York: Harcourt, 1956), 63; and R.H. Tawney, *Religion and the Rise of Capitalism* (London: Verso, 2015), chap. 1, esp. §2.

5 For economic society in the Middle Ages, see, e.g., H.S. Bennett, *Life on the English Manor: A Study of Peasant Conditions, 1150–1400* (Cambridge: Cambridge University Press, 1960); Marc Bloch, *French Rural History: An Essay on Its Basic Characteristics*, trans. Janet Sondheimer (Berkeley: University of California Press, 1994); Georges Duby, *The Three Orders:*

*Feudal Society Reimagined*, trans. Arthur Goldhammer (Chicago: University of Chicago Press, 1980); and Johan Huizinga, *The Waning of the Middle Ages* (Mineola, NY: Dover Publications, 1999), esp. chap. 3.

6 See, e.g., Tawney, *Religion and the Rise of Capitalism*, chap. 4, esp. §3. See also Karl Polanyi, *The Great Transformation: The Political and Economic Origins of Our Time* (Boston: Beacon, 2001), part 2; and Robert Heilbroner and William Milberg, *The Making of Economic Society* (Upper Saddle River, NJ: Prentice-Hall, 2002), chap. 3.

7 See, e.g., Walter Scheidel, *The Great Leveler: Violence and the History of Inequality from the Stone Age to the Twenty-First Century* (Princeton: Princeton University Press, 2017), part 1.

8 See, e.g., Brink Lindsay and Steven Teles, *The Captured Economy: How the Powerful Enrich Themselves, Slow Down Growth, and Increase Inequality* (Oxford: Oxford University Press, 2017), 1–15.

9 See, e.g., Jürgen Habermas, *Theory of Communicative Action*, vol. 2: *Lifeworld and System* (Boston: Beacon Press, 1984), §6.

10 See, e.g., Daniel Bell, *The Cultural Contradictions of Capitalism* (New York: Basic Books, 1996), part 1.

## 1 Plato, Aristotle, and Aquinas on Moneymaking

1 For the rise and fall of the Athenian empire, see, e.g., Victor Ehrenberg, *From Solon to Socrates: Greek History and Civilization during the 6th and 5th Centuries B.C.* (New York: Routledge, 2011), part 8; Simon Hornblower, *The Greek World, 479–323 BC* (London: Methuen, 1983), chaps. 12–13; Josiah Ober, *The Rise and Fall of Classical Greece* (Princeton, NJ: Princeton University Press, 2015), esp. chap. 8; Robin Osbourne, *Classical Greece, 500–323 BC* (Oxford: Oxford University Press, 2000), esp. 111–38 and 185–94; and P.J. Rhodes, *A History of the Classical Greek World, 478–323 BC* (Malden, UK: Blackwell, 2006), chaps. 14–15.

2 For the rise and workings of the ancient Greek economy, see, e.g., Douglas A. Irwin, *Against the Tide: An Intellectual History of Free Trade* (Princeton, NJ: Princeton University Press, 1996), chap. 1, esp. 11–15; Paul Millet, *Lending and Borrowing in Ancient Athens* (Cambridge: Cambridge University Press, 1991), chaps. 4 and 5; Karl Polanyi, *Trade and Market in Early Empires: Economies in History and Theory* (Glencoe, IL: Free Press, 1957), chap. 5; Paul Rahe, *Republics Ancient and Modern: Classical Republicanism and the American Revolution* (Chapel Hill: University of North Carolina Press, 1992), vol. 1, chap. 3; and Joseph Schumpeter, *History of Economic Analysis* (Oxford: Oxford University Press, 1954), part 2, chap. 1, esp. 50–62.

3 For the rise of the medieval economy, see, e.g., Lester K. Little, *Religious Poverty and the Profit Economy in Medieval Europe* (Ithaca, NY: Cornell

University Press, 1978), part 1, esp. 3–41; and Pirenne, *Economic and Social History of Medieval Europe*, part 4, chap. 1.

4  See, e.g., John W. Baldwin, *Medieval Theories of the Just Price: Romanists, Canonists and Theologians in the Twelfth and Thirteenth Centuries* (Philadelphia: American Philosophical Society, 1959), esp. 10–15 and 68–81; Little, *Religious Poverty and the Profit Economy in Medieval Europe*, part 4, esp. 173–83; Schumpeter, *History of Economic Analysis*, part 2, chap. 2, esp. 71–90; and Jacob Viner, *Essays on the Intellectual History of Economics* (Princeton, NJ: Princeton University Press , 1991), esp. 42–4.

5  Quoted in Jerry Z. Muller, *The Mind and the Market: Capitalism in Modern European Thought* (New York: Alfred A. Knopf, 2002), 3.

6  Muller, *The Mind and the Market*, 3.

## 2  Machiavelli and Hobbes on Delightful Living

1  Page references are to the 1995 Hackett edition of *The Prince* (Indianapolis, IN: Hackett, 1995).

2  For the history of the Italian Peninsula before and during Machiavelli's life, see, e.g., Felix Gilbert, *Machiavelli and Guicciardini: Politics and History in Sixteenth-Century Florence* (New York: W.W. Norton, 1981), chap. 6, esp. part 3; and Garrett Mattingly, *Renaissance Diplomacy* (Boston: Houghton Mifflin, 1955), part 2, esp. chap. 9.

3  The hardening of Machiavelli's political worldview can be traced to his career as a Florentine diplomat. See, e.g., Gisela Bock, Quentin Skinner, and Maurizio Viroli, *Machiavelli and Republicanism* (Cambridge: Cambridge University Press, 2011), esp. part 1; and Roberto Ridolfi, *The Life of Niccoló Machiavelli* (Chicago: University of Chicago Press, 1963), esp. 15–22. For the history of Florence before and during Machiavelli's political career, see, e.g., H.C. Butters, *Governors and Government in Early Sixteenth-Century Florence, 1502–1519* (Oxford: Clarendon, 1985); Nicolai Rubinstein, *The Government of Florence under the Medici, 1434–1494* (Oxford: Clarendon, 1997); and Donald Weinstein, *Savonarola: The Rise and Fall of a Renaissance Prophet* (New Haven, CT: Yale University Press, 2011).

4  For a notable exception, see chap. 5 of *The Prince.*

5  In his *Discourses*, Machiavelli contemplates a wholly different path to glory – a path for citizens, not princes: republican self-government. See, e.g., Bock, Skinner, and Viroli, *Machiavelli and Republicanism*, part 2; J.G.A. Pocock, *The Machiavellian Moment: Florentine Political Thought and the Atlantic Republican Tradition* (Princeton, NJ: Princeton University Press, 2003), part 2, chap. 7; Russell Price, "The Theme of Gloria in Machiavelli," *Renaissance Quarterly* 30, no. 4 (1977), esp. 594–9; and Maurizio Viroli, *From Politics to Reason of State: The Acquisition and Transformation of the Language of Politics, 1250–1600* (Cambridge:

Cambridge University Press, 1992), chap. 3, esp. 130–2. For an examination of the puzzle surrounding Machiavelli's authorship of both *The Prince* and the *Discourses* – two seemingly incompatible works – see, e.g., Hans Baron, "Machiavelli the Republican Citizen and Author of *The Prince*," in *In Search of Florentine Civic Humanism: Essays on the Transition from Medieval to Modern Thought*, ed. Hans Baron (Princeton, NJ: Princeton, University Press, 1988), 101–51; Felix Gilbert, *History: Choice and Commitment* (Cambridge, MA: Harvard University Press, 1977), esp. 115–33; and Leo Strauss, *Thoughts on Machiavelli* (Glencoe, IL: Free Press, 1958), chap. 1.

6  See, e.g., John Aubrey, *Brief Lives*, ed. John Buchanan-Brown (London: Penguin Classics, 2000), 132–60; Thomas Hobbes, *Behemoth* (Chicago: University of Chicago Press, 1990), esp. dialogue 1; Quentin Skinner, "The Ideological Context of Hobbes's Political Thought," *Historical Journal* 9, no. 3 (1966): 286–317, esp. 288–9; and Johan P. Somerville, *Thomas Hobbes: Political Ideas in Historical Context* (London: Macmillan, 1992).

7  Hobbes does not deny God's existence – an obvious implication of his scientific worldview – and in fact speaks about him often. But he does say that, much like the natural forces operating in the world, God is characterized by the fact that he is "incomprehensible, and above [our] understanding" (1.12.53). And so, by extension, all those who claim to have insight into his will are ambitious deceivers.

8  Hobbes would therefore surely agree with Christopher Hitchens's *God Is Not Great: How Religion Poisons Everything* (New York: Twelve, 2009), 17: "[Religion] may speak about the bliss of the next world, but it wants power in this one." Indeed, this is precisely the spirit in which Hobbes criticizes the Roman papacy: "For who is there that does not see, to whose benefit it conduceth, to have it believed, that a King hath not his authority from Christ, unlesse a Bishop crown him? Or who does not see, to whose profit redound the Fees of private Masses, and Vales of Purgatory; with other signes of private interest, enough to mortifie the most lively Faith" (1.12.60).

9  See also C.B. Macpherson, *The Political Theory of Possessive Individualism: Hobbes to Locke* (Oxford: Clarendon, 1962), esp. chap. 2, §3. Indeed, the discussion of *Leviathan* in this chapter is deeply indebted to that text. See also Macpherson's illuminating introduction to the 1968 Penguin edition of *Leviathan*.

10  John Rawls, *Lectures on the History of Political Philosophy*, ed. Samuel Freeman (Cambridge, MA: Harvard University Press, 2007), 78.

11  In some ways, this departs from the standard interpretation of Hobbes, which emphasizes – strongly so – the fear of violent death as the fundamental source of human motivation. See, e.g., 1.13.63, where Hobbes says that we are "enclined to Peace" by the "Feare of death." And yet, *in the very same sentence*, Hobbes adds to the list of "Passions" that drive us into civil

society: "Desire of such things as are necessary to commodious living; and a Hope by their Industry to obtain them."

12  But, again, only those who take their politically radical views out into the public sphere – who call for others to join them in their disobedience – will be subject to punishment by the state.

13  According to Hobbes, sovereign authority can be invested in either a single person – his preference (2.19.96) – or an administrative council.

## 3 Locke on Labor and the Right to Accumulate

1  See, e.g., John Bowle, *Hobbes and His Critics* (London: Routledge, 2013), chap. 1; and Macpherson, *Political Theory of Possessive Individualism*, 90–5.

2  For the historical context of Locke's *Second Treatise*, as well as arguments regarding the precise date of its composition, see, e.g., John Dunn, *The Political Thought of John Locke: An Historical Account of the Argument of the "Two Treatises of Government"* (Cambridge: Cambridge University Press, 1969), esp. chap. 5; Peter Laslett, "Introduction," in *Locke's Two Treatises of Government*, ed. Peter Laslett, 3–126 (Cambridge: Cambridge University Press, 2012), esp. 45–67; J.R. Jones, *The First Whigs: The Politics of the Exclusion Crisis, 1678–1683* (Oxford: Oxford University Press, 1966); and Rawls, *Lectures on the History of Political Philosophy*, esp. 103–9.

3  The familiarity of Locke's worldview ought not obscure the fact that, in his own day, there was a vibrant intellectual movement that directly opposed it. This movement included the Levellers, whose series of manifestos, "An Agreement of the People," argued for a radically egalitarian form of democracy, in opposition to the property qualifications for the franchise endorsed by Locke (see below). And there was also the comparatively small proto-communist Diggers movement, which was dedicated to the abolition of the institution of private property altogether. For a representative example, see Gerrard Winstanley, *A Declaration from the Poor Oppressed People of England* (1649): "The earth was not made purposely for you, to be Lords of it, and we to be your Slaves, Servants, and Beggars; but it was made to a common Livelihood to all, without respect of persons: And that the buying and selling of Land, and Fruits of it, one to another, is *The cursed thing....* Therefore we are resolved to be cheated no longer, nor to be held under the slavish fear of you no longer, see the Earth was made for us, as well as for you: And if the Common Land belongs to us who are the poor oppressed, surely the woods that grow upon the Commons belong to us likewise" (from the *The Works of Gerrard Winstanley*, ed. G.H. Sabine [New York: Russell & Russell, 1965], 269 and 273). See also Macpherson, *Political Theory of Possessive Individualism*, esp. chap. 3; *Winstanley and the Diggers, 1649–1999*, ed. A. Bradstock (Portland, OR: Frank Cass, 2000); and John Gurney, *Gerrard Winstanley: The Digger's Life and Legacy* (London: Pluto, 2013).

4 Hobbes too operates under the assumption that individuals own their labor, along with its output, and that this necessarily entails the institution of market-directed wage labor: "A mans Labour," he says, "is a commodity exchangeable for benefit, as well as any other thing" (2.24.127). But Hobbes mentions this only briefly, in the context of a discussion of the state's conspicuously expansive economic powers. In Locke's thought, by contrast, the institution of wage labor is front and center from the very beginning – a direct outgrowth of our natural freedom. See below.

5 See, e.g., Bennett, *Life on the English Manor*; Bloch, *French Rural History*; G.G. Coulton, *Medieval Village, Manor and Monastery* (New York: Dover, 1989); Duby, *Three Orders*; and Pirenne, *Economic and Social History of Medieval Europe*.

6 See, e.g., "Documents Illustrative of Feudalism," in *Translations and Reprints from the Original Sources of European History*, ed. Edward P. Cheyney (New York: Longman's, Green, 1902), vol. 4, no. 3.

7 See, e.g., Tawney, *Religion and the Rise of Capitalism*, esp. chap. 1.

8 In chapter 10, Locke says that the legislative branch of government can take many different "*form*[s]" – it can be a democracy or an oligarchy, an elective or hereditary monarchy, or even some mixture of these different elements – and that the decision on how to formally constitute the legislature belongs to "the community, ... as they think good" (§132).

9 For some important exceptions, see chap.14, esp. §159–61.

10 Recall that Hobbes teaches the opposite: the state, for him, is the *solution* to the fear and anxiety of being exposed to the inevitable covetousness and unpredictable violence of *other people* (1.13.62), and this is why it must be designed for single-minded action.

**4 Smith and Kant on the Benefits of Commerce**

1 See chapter 3, note 2.

2 See, e.g., Milton Myers, *The Soul of Modern Economic Man: Ideas of Self-Interest, Hobbes to Smith* (Chicago: University of Chicago Press, 1983).

3 For the history of British political economy before and during Smith's life, see, e.g., Paul Langford, *A Polite and Commercial People: England, 1727–1783* (Oxford: Oxford University Press, 1989); and Keith Wrightson, *Earthly Necessities: Economic Lives in Early Modern Britain* (New Haven, CT: Yale University Press, 2000).

4 Such *widespread* prosperity *was* becoming a reality in Smith's day. We return to this theme in the concluding section below. See, e.g., Stephen Baxter, *England's Rise to Greatness, 1660–1763* (Berkeley: University of California Press, 1983), esp. 81–90; and John Brewer, Neil McKendrick, and J.H. Plumb, *The Birth of a Consumer Society: The Commercialization of Eighteenth-Century England* (Bloomington: University of Indiana Press, 1982).

5 See, e.g., *WN* 3.4, where Smith discusses the emergence of "good government" out of the "continual state of war" and "servile dependency"

characteristic of feudalism. In the early phase of feudal Europe, he says, lords spent the entirety of the capital surplus generated by their land on armed retainers, and the result was that "the open country ... was a scene of violence, rapine, and disorder" (*WN* 3.4.9). But, with the rise of foreign commerce and trade, local markets were flooded with "diamonds [and] buckles, ... trinkets and baubles" (*WN* 3.4.15); rich lords coveted these luxuries and were willing to disband their retainers in order to afford them. And thus, "for the gratification of the most childish, the meanest, and the most sordid of all vanities, they gradually bartered their whole power and authority ... [and] became as insignificant as any substantial burgher or tradesman in [the] city" (*WN* 3.4.10 and 3.4.15). Indeed, the eventual result of this desire for "frivolous and useless" (*WN* 3.4.10) things – a desire keenly satisfied by merchants – was that "the great proprietors were no longer capable of interrupting the regular execution of justice or of disturbing the peace of the country" (*WN* 3.4.15). Domestic peace, in other words, was unwittingly achieved through the operation of the profit motive, a theme to which we return below.

6  The essays by Kant referred to in this chapter can be found in the Cambridge edition of *Kant: Political Writings,* ed. H.S. Reiss (Cambridge: Cambridge University Press, 1991). Page numbers correspond to the second edition of that work.

7  According to Smith, the state is also responsible to provide welfare and well-being for wage-laborers disadvantaged by the market's inexorable advance. See the concluding section below.

8  In *Theory and Practice,* Kant acknowledges that civil liberty thus understood "may over a series of generations create considerable inequalities in wealth among the members of the commonwealth" (*TP* 76). This is, in his opinion, permissible and even good. But economic inequalities cannot generate "hereditary privilege": the wealthy man "may not prevent his subordinates from raising themselves to his own level if they are able and entitled to do so by their talent, industry and good fortune" (76). And, even more importantly, regardless of income or occupation, "all are equal as subjects *before the law*" (75). In the *Metaphysics of Morals,* Kant even gestures towards the necessity of some form of economic redistribution: "It makes it much easier for the government to perform its business of governing the people by laws if the public sense of propriety is not dulled by affronts to the moral sense such as begging, uproar in the streets, offensive smells and public prostitution.... The nature of the state thus justifies the government in compelling prosperous citizens to provide the means of preserving those who are unable to provide for themselves ... by lawful taxation" (*MM* 149–50).

9  Kant is equally critical of the colonial policy of Europe's "commercial states": "The injustice which they display in *visiting* foreign countries and peoples (which in their case is the same as *conquering* them) seems appallingly great.... In East India, foreign troops were brought in under

the pretext of merely setting up trading posts. This led to oppression of the natives, incitement of the various Indian states to widespread wars, famine, insurrection, treachery and the whole litany of evils which can afflict the human race" (*PP* 106).

10  Consider, here, the contrast to *WN* 1.1 (especially part 1), where Smith defends the absolute necessity of a strong, disciplined, well-equipped standing army, especially as states become more economically developed. And in this section, Smith also raises concerns about the mental stultification suffered by workers, and their resultant unsuitability for military participation and the unlikelihood of military valor: for "the man whose life is spent in performing a few simple operations ... the uniformity of his stationary life naturally corrupts the courage of his mind, and makes him regard with abhorrence the irregular, uncertain, and adventurous life of a soldier" (*WN* 1.1.178; see also the afterword below). By comparison, Kant's recommendation (less than twenty years later) that states abolish standing *altogether* is quite striking; and so too is his belief that conscription itself is antithetical to the moral personhood of the drafted: "The hiring of men to kill or to be killed," he says, "seems to mean using them as mere machines and instruments in the hands of someone else (the state), which cannot easily be reconciled with the rights of man in one's own person" (*PP* 95).

11  There are certain limits to citizenship – limits that reflect Kant's eighteenth-century heritage: A citizen, he says, "must be his *own master* [and must] have some *property* to support himself" (*TP* 78).

12  In *Theory and Practice*, Kant acknowledges that republics need not be democratic in the modern sense of ballot box participation; republicanism is, counterintuitively, compatible with the rule of one person. See, e.g., *TP* 79: the "legislator" must "frame his laws in such a way that they *could have been* produced by the united will of a whole nation.... If the law is such that a whole people could not *possibly* agree to it (for example, if it stated that a certain class of *subjects* must be privileged as a hereditary *ruling class*), it is unjust; but if it at least *possible* that a people could agree to it, it is our duty to consider the law as just."

13  See n. 4 above.

14  See, e.g., Margaret Fay, Johannes Hengstenberg, and Barbara Stuckey, "The Influence of Adam Smith on Marx's Theory of Alienation," *Science & Society* 47, no. 2 (1983): 129–51, esp. 133–5.

15  Again, this is bad for the individual members of the working class, whose character, without education, is "mutilated and deformed" (*WN* 5.1.10). But it is even worse for society at large: the less educated the populace, worries Smith, the more prone they are to "the delusions of enthusiasm and superstition" and to the "complaints of faction and sedition" (*WN* 1.1.182). In other words, Smith's account of education is advanced in the ultimate service of social order and stability. Now, that said, Smith's own view is more liberal and humane than the views of his contemporaries,

many of whom were fearful of the consequences of universal literacy. See, e.g., Viner, *Essays on the Intellectual History of Economics*, esp. 283–4.

## 5 Rousseau on Modern Discontent

1 See, e.g., Allan Bloom, *Giants and Dwarfs: Essays, 1960–1990* (New York: Simon & Schuster, 1990), esp. 277–94.

2 Despite these genuine concerns, Burke *was* a stout supporter of free commerce – domestic and international – along conspicuously Smithian lines. See, e.g., his "Third Letter on a Regicide Peace": "The love of lucre, though sometimes carried to a ridiculous, sometimes to a vicious excess, is the grand cause of prosperity to all States" (*The Philosophy of Edmund Burke: A Selection from His Speeches and Writings*, edited by Louis I. Bredcold and Ralph G. Ross [Ann Arbor: University of Michigan Press, 1960], 9:347–8). See also Burke's "Letter to a Noble Lord," which makes explicit reference to Smith's influence on Burke's economic thought (*Writings and Speeches*, 9:159–60), as well as the "Letter to Harford, Cowles and Co." (*The Correspondence of Edmund Burke*, ed. Thomas W. Copeland [Chicago: University of Chicago Press, 1958], 3:442). Burke's most detailed remarks on political economy is his "Thoughts and Details on Scarcity" (*Philosophy of Edmund Burke*, vol. 9, esp. 126–37), where he criticizes the decision to set wages by the justices of the peace of Speenhamland. See also, e.g., Carl Cone, *Burke and the Nature of Politics*, vol. 1 (Louisville: University of Kentucky Press, 2014), esp. chap. 12; and C.B. Macpherson, *Burke* (Oxford: Oxford University Press, 1980), chap. 5, esp. 61ff.

3 The page references to Rousseau's First and Second Discourses correspond to the second edition of *Basic Political Writings*, trans. and ed. Donald A. Cress (Indianapolis, IN: Hackett, 2011).

4 Of course, this is Rousseau's implicit critique of Hobbes and Locke; specifically, their inaccurate portraits of the state of nature: "They spoke about savage man and it was civilized man that they depicted" (*SD* 46). Consider, for example, Locke's state of nature, where private property exists and is (for the most part) respected, contracts are made and (for the most part) fulfilled, and a general sense of reciprocity (usually) prevails. Rousseau forces us to ask, How genuinely *natural* is any of this?

5 Rousseau does not regard his history as *true*: it is, rather, a hypothetical history – and, in his mind, a reasonable conjecture based on available evidence. See, e.g., Rousseau's introduction to the *Second Discourse*: this investigation, he says, "should not be taken for historical truths, but only for hypothetical and conditional reasonings, better suited to shedding light on the nature of things than on pointing out their true origins."

6 Consider, as a contrast, Hobbes's *bellum omnium contra omnes*. See, e.g., *De Cive*, chap. 10, §1; and *Leviathan*, chap. 13.

7 For the meaning of *amour-propre*, see, e.g., Nicholas Dent, *Rousseau* (London: Routledge, 2005), chap. 2; Dent, *A Rousseau Dictionary* (London:

Wiley-Blackwell, 1992), 33–6; and Frederick Neuhouser, "Freedom, Dependence, and the General Will," *Philosophical Review* 102, no. 3 (1993): 363–95, esp. 376–80.

8   See also *SC* 1.1.1: "He who believes himself the master of others does not escape being more of a slave than they."

9   Here Rousseau quotes Ovid's *Metamorphoses* (bk. 11, line 127): "Horrified by the newness of the ill, both the poor man and the rich man hope to flee from wealth, hating what they once had prayed for."

10   See also *SC* 1.1.1: "Man is born free, and everywhere he is in chains."

11   See *SD* 86, where Rousseau discusses the "various forms" that governments can take. Whatever form a regime ultimately takes – a monarchy, an aristocracy, or a democracy – is a direct reflection of the distribution of wealth (and power) at "the moment of institution." See also *SC* 3.3–7.

12   See also Jean-Jacques Rousseau, *Letter to Beaumont, Letters Written from the Mountain, and Related Writings*, ed. Christopher Kelly and Eve Grace, trans. Christopher Kelly and Judith R. Bush (Hanover, NH: University Press of New England, 2001), fragment 1019: "I hate servitude as the source of all evils of the human race."

13   *SC* is a work of immense complexity, profound depth, and at times frustrating obscurity. And so the short discussion that follows is only a brief introduction to it. See also, e.g., Roger D. Masters, *The Political Philosophy of Rousseau* (Princeton, NJ: Princeton University Press, 2015), esp. part 2; Arthur Melzer, *The Natural Goodness of Man: On the System of Rousseau's Thought* (Chicago: University of Chicago Press, 1990), esp. chaps. 7–12; James Miller, *Rousseau: Dreamer of Democracy* (New Haven, CT: Yale University Press, 1996), 59–75; and Patrick Riley, *Will and Political Legitimacy* (Cambridge, MA: Harvard University Press, 2014), chap. 4.

14   See also "Discourse on Political Economy," in *The Social Contract and Other Late Political Writings*, ed. and trans. Victor Gourevitch (Cambridge: Cambridge University Press, 1997), 22: "[Education is] certainly the State's most important business." For a general survey of the influence of the ancients on Rousseau's thought, see, e.g., Allan Bloom's introduction to *Letter to D'Alembert*, ed. and trans. Bloom (Hanover, NH: University Press of New England, 2004), xiv; R.A. Leigh, "Jean-Jacques Rousseau and the Myth of Antiquity," in *Classical Influences on Western Thought, 1650–1870*, ed. R.R. Bolgar, 155–68 (Cambridge: Cambridge University Press, 1979); Fergus Millar, *The Roman Republic in Political Thought* (Hanover, NH: University Press of New England, 2002), 113–20; and Judith Shklar, *Men and Citizens: A Study of Rousseau's Social Theory* (Cambridge: Cambridge University Press, 1969), chap. 1, esp. 12–32.

15   See also *SC* 2.10.

16   See also *SC* 3.4, esp. para. 5.

17   See also "Considerations on the Government of Poland," in *The Social Contract and Other Late Political Writings*, 209–16.

18  See also "Discourse on Political Economy," 9: "It is to law alone that men
    owe [their] freedom.... [Law is] the most sublime of all human institutions."

19  See *SC* 1.8 for the benefits that accompany such participation: the citizen's
    "faculties are exercised and developed, his ideas are broadened, his feel-
    ings are ennobled, his entire soul is elevated."

20  The *execution* of the law is a different matter altogether. See *SC* 3.1 and 3.4:
    "It is not good for the one who makes the laws to execute the laws."

21  See *SC* 2.4: "Equality of right and the notion of justice it produces are
    derived from the preference each person gives to himself, and thus from
    the nature of man."

22  The founding of the political community described in *SC* is the subject
    of 2.7, a most mysterious chapter. See, e.g., Isaiah Berlin, *Freedom and Its
    Betrayal: Six Enemies of Human Liberty* (Princeton, NJ: Princeton Univer-
    sity Press, 2014), 49–50; J.L. Talmon, *The Origins of Totalitarian Democracy*
    (Boulder, CO: Westview, 1985), chap. 3; and Robert Wokler, *Rousseau and
    Liberty* (New York: St. Martin's, 1995), 189–212.

23  See, e.g., Terrence Ball, *Reappraising Political Theory: Revisionist Studies in the
    History of Political Thought* (Oxford: Clarendon, 1995), chap. 5, esp. 125–8;
    and Ronald Beiner, *Civil Religion: A Dialogue in the History of Political Philoso-
    phy* (Cambridge: Cambridge University Press, 2011), chap. 1, esp. 12–16.

24  See also "Poland," 179: "To put law over man is a problem in politics
    which I compare to that of squaring the circle in geometry."

25  See also *d'Alembert*, 67 and 300, *Beaumont*, 292, and "Political Economy," 22.

26  See, e.g., Jean-Jacques Rousseau, *The Confessions*, trans. Christopher Kelly
    (Hanover, NH: University Press of New England, 1995), 539.

27  See, e.g., *Beaumont*, 293.

28  See, e.g., Jean-Jacques Rousseau, *The Reveries of the Solitary Walker,* ed.
    Christopher Kelly, trans. Charles E. Butterworth, Alexandra Cook, and Ter-
    rence E. Marshall (Hanover, NH: University Press of New England, 1990), 46.

29  See, e.g., Jean-Jacques Rousseau, *Rousseau, Judge of Jean-Jacques: Dialogues,*
    ed. Christopher Kelly and Roger D. Masters (Hanover, NH: University
    Press of New England, 1990), 144; and *Reveries*, 41–7.

## 6  Hegel on the Ethical Dimensions of the Market

1  Here, Kant candidly admits that, when it comes to the design of our
   constitutional and legal arrangements, "a perfect solution is impossible.
   Nothing straight can be constructed from such warped wood as that which
   man is made of" (*IUH* 46).

2  The Rousseauvian echoes here are undeniable. See *SC* 1.8. See also, e.g.,
   Ernst Cassirer, *The Question of Jean-Jacques Rousseau*, trans. Peter Gay (New
   Haven, CT: Yale University Press, 1989); and Cassirer, *Rousseau, Kant, Goethe:
   Two Essays*, trans. James Guttman, Paul Oskar Kristeller, and John Herman
   Randall, Jr. (Princeton, NJ: Princeton University Press, 1945), esp. 25–35.

3  See, e.g., Michael Hardimon's *Hegel's Social Philosophy: The Project of Reconciliation* (Cambridge: Cambridge University Press, 1994); and John Rawls, *Lectures on the History of Moral Philosophy*, ed. Barbara Herman (Cambridge, MA: Harvard University Press, 2000), 331–6.

4  It is no surprise, as we shall see, that Hegel was a close reader and avid admirer of Smith. See, e.g., Laurence Dickey, *Hegel: Religion, Economics and the Politics of Spirit, 1770–1807* (Cambridge: Cambridge University Press, 1987), 194; Georg Lukács, *The Young Hegel: Studies in the Relations between Dialectics and Economics*, trans. Rodney Livingstone (Cambridge, MA: MIT Press, 1976), 172; and Ernst Mandel, *The Formation of the Economic Thought of Karl Marx: 1843 to Capital* (London: NLB, 1975), 11–12.

5  Another representative example of this critical line of thinking can be found in the work of Hegel's friend Friedrich Hölderlein. In his poem "The Archipelago," Hölderlein writes that, in modernity, "each man is forged to his labour." Of course, Hegel would also have been familiar with this line of critique, given his familiarity with Smith's *Wealth of Nations*.

6  For Hegel's analysis of the Protestant Reformation, see the introduction to the *Philosophy of History*.

7  For Hegel's analysis of the French Revolution, see *PR* §5 and §258. See also Rebecca Comay, *Mourning Sickness: Hegel and the French Revolution* (Stanford, CA: Stanford University Press, 2011).

8  See, e.g., Isaiah Berlin, *Roots of Romanticism*, ed. Henry Hardy (Princeton, NJ: Princeton University Press, 2013), esp. chap. 5; and Charles Taylor, *Hegel and Modern Society* (Cambridge: Cambridge University Press, 1979), esp. 7–11.

9  See, e.g., Gerald Izenberg, *Impossible Individuality: Romanticism, Revolution, and the Origins of Modern Selfhood, 1787–1802* (Princeton, NJ: Princeton University Press 1992), esp. chaps. 1–2.

10  This, says Hegel, is the source of patriotic pride and of our commitment to stability and vitality of our political institutions. See, e.g., §260: "The state is the actuality of concrete freedom. But *concrete freedom* requires that personal individuality and its particular interests reach their *full development* and gain *recognition of their right* for itself.... The principle of modern states has enormous strength and depth because it allows the principle of subjectivity to attain fulfillment in the *self-sufficient extreme* of personal particularity." See also §268 and §289A, where Hegel discusses patriotism – a "political disposition" rooted in citizens' recognition that their "substantial and personal interest[s] [are] preserved" by "the institutions within the state."

11  See, e.g., Jeffrey Bercuson, *John Rawls and the History of Political Thought: The Rousseauvian and Hegelian Heritage of Justice as Fairness* (New York: Routledge, 2014), esp. chap. 2.

12  Throughout his discussion of the family (§§158–80), Hegel is deeply critical of arranged marriages: marriage, he says, ought not to be the result of the "initiative of parents" in pursuit of the accumulation of wealth (§162).

Instead, marriage should be the expression of "love [and] trust" between the "destined *partners*" (§162R; italics added).

13  Modern readers are rightly troubled by Hegel's conspicuously patriarchal depiction of family life and the division of familial responsibilities: "Woman," says Hegel, "has her substantial vocation in the family" (§166R), though "the family ... must be represented by the husband as its head. In addition, he is primarily responsible for external acquisition, as well as for the control and administration of the family's resources" (§171). See also, e.g., Seyla Benhabib, "On Hegel, Women and Irony," in *Feminism and History of Philosophy*, ed. G. Lloyd, 281–98 (Oxford: Oxford University Press, 2002); and Kelly Oliver, "Antigone's Ghost: Undoing Hegel's *Phenomenology of Spirit*," *Hypatia* 11, no. 1 (1996): 69–70, esp. 70–84.

14  See, e.g., Rawls, *Lectures on the History of Moral Philosophy*, 332.

15  See note 13.

16  Here, at §124R, Hegel draws a contrast between "modern" states and the states of "antiquity." Only the former permit the complete flourishing of free individuality. See also §185R/A, where Hegel criticizes the political proposals of Plato's *Republic*: the ideal city outlined there is nothing more than "a dream of abstract thought," Hegel says, precisely because of its total denial of "the development of self-sufficient particularity," i.e., because of its endorsement of communism and concomitant denial of the institution of private property (at least for the political class).

17  See note 4.

18  For Smith, the division of labor is important because of its contribution to "the productive power of labour" (*WN* 1.1.1). This is important for Hegel too, of course (see, e.g., §198), but the division of labor *also* makes an essential contribution to human freedom by investing abstract agency with concrete moral content. See below.

19  See, e.g., Norbert Waszek, *The Scottish Enlightenment and Hegel's Account of "Civil Society"* (Dordrecht, Netherlands: Kluwer, 1988), esp. 56–83.

20  See, e.g., James J. Sheehan, *German History, 1770–1866* (Oxford: Clarendon, 1989), esp. chaps. 1 and 3 (part 4).

21  One more possible solution canvassed by Hegel is colonization, i.e., the opening of new "market[s] and sphere[s] of industrial activity" (§248). But, again, Hegel does not seem fully convinced: navigation by sea, he says, is the sphere of "danger and destruction" (§247).

## 7  Marx on Alienation and Emancipation

1  Sheehan, *German History*, 72–105. See also Allen W. Wood, "Introduction," *Philosophy of Right*, by G.W.F. Hagel, trans. Wood (Cambridge: Cambridge University Press, 1991), ix–x; and Mack Walker, *German Home Towns: Community, State, and General Estate, 1648–1871* (Ithaca, NY: Cornell University Press), esp. 18–26 and 73–93.

2  Waszek, *Scottish Enlightenment and Hegel's Account of "Civil Society,"* 75; and David Lindenfeld, *The Practical Imagination: The German Sciences of State in the Nineteenth Century* (Chicago: University of Chicago Press, 1997), 59–67.

3  Lindenfeld, *Practical Imagination*, esp. 90–4 and 111–31. See also Sheehan, *German History*, 426–8; and Walker, *German Home Towns*, 283–87.

4  Cited in Sheehan, *German History*, 305.

5  Cited in Sheehan, *German History*, 425.

6  For an account of Marx's intellectual life before his discovery of Hegel, see David McClellan, *Karl Marx: His Life and Thought* (New York: Harper & Row, 1974), esp. 13–31. All page references in this chapter are to the second edition of the *Marx-Engels Reader* (ed. Robert C. Tucker).

7  According to Marx, this obsession with money is particularly acute among Jews – "not the [real] *Sabbath Jew,*" mind you, "but the *everyday Jew,*" for whom "*huckstering*" is a way of life and "money" the only "worldly god" (48). In other words, "On the Jewish Question" is, at times, deeply offensive, reiterating the common anti-Semitic tropes of Marx's day. See, e.g., Jacob Katz, *From Prejudice to Destruction: Anti-Semitism, 1700–1933* (Cambridge, MA: Harvard University Press, 1980), chap. 13. The essay is also fertile grounds for psychological analysis, given Marx's own Jewish heritage. See, e.g., Frank E. Manuel, *A Requiem for Karl Marx* (Cambridge, MA: Harvard University Press, 1995), esp. chap. 1. In any case, it *is* an important early statement of Marx's views and so ought not be dismissed altogether despite its open, troubling anti-Semitism.

8  Of course, this argument bears a strong resemblance to Rousseau's notion of perfectibility, as outlined in the *Second Discourse*. See chapter 5 above, esp. section 1.

9  This is the original germ of a doctrine that came to be known as "historical materialism," which (in 1859) Marx calls "the guiding thread for my studies." For the clearest, most pithy statement of this view, see "Preface to A Contribution to the Critique of Political Economy." See also Marx's letter of December 28, 1846, to P.V. Annenkov (esp. 136–7) and *The German Ideology* (esp. 149–50 and 154–5).

10  Of course, we have already encountered this argument – surprisingly, for many – in the work of Adam Smith. See chapter 4 above, esp. section 4 and note 13.

11  Marx's account of communist society is the subject of a short discussion below.

12  See, e.g., Rawls, *Lectures on the History of Political Philosophy*, 319.

13  See, e.g., Leszek Kołakowski, *Main Currents of Marxism: Its Rise, Growth, and Dissolution* (Oxford: Clarendon, 1978), esp. vol. 1, chaps. 11–12.

14  In the preface to the 1872 German edition of the *Manifesto*, Marx and Engels refer to the Paris Commune, "where the proletariat for the first time held political power for two whole months" (470). This, in other words, was history's first example of the dictatorship of the proletariat. See

Marx's political pamphlet, "The Civil War in France," esp. 629–36, where Marx celebrates the Commune – its egalitarian character, its democratic institutions, and its smashing of the army, police, and bureaucracy.

## 8 Lenin on the Revolutionary Vanguard

1  See, e.g., Robert C. Allen, *Farm to Factory: A Reinterpretation of the Russian Industrial Revolution* (Princeton, NJ: Princeton University Press, 2003), chap. 1, esp. 11–13; and Geoffrey Hosking, *Russia: People and Empire, 1552–1917* (Cambridge, MA: Harvard University Press, 1997), part 4, esp. 315–45.

2  Of course, Russia was not *wholly lacking* in industry: far from it. See, e.g., Bertram D. Wolfe, *Three Who Made a Revolution: A Biographical History* (New York: Cooper Square, 2001), 21–3, which details the energetic industrial development of Peter the Great, for whom "industrialization was an aspect of militarization. It came from the top downward" (21). In fact, when the Bolsheviks came to power in 1917, they inherited "the largest state economic machine in the world" (23). See also Robert K. Massie, *Peter the Great: His Life and World* (New York: Modern Library, 2012), part 5.

3  For Lenin's life and career, see, e.g. Robert Service, *Lenin: A Biography* (Cambridge, MA: Harvard University Press, 2000); and Beryl Williams, *Lenin* (New York: Longman, 2000).

4  References in this chapter are to the Progress Publishers edition of Lenin's *Collected Works* (volume, followed by page number).

5  This emphasis on secrecy is a recurring theme in Lenin's early polemical work, and a key part of his argument for the need for a well-trained revolutionary vanguard. This is particularly true in Russia, he adds – a paranoid police state. See, e.g., 5.376–8, 5.442, and 5.484, where Lenin laments the failures of earlier revolutionaries who were insufficiently sensitive to the forces of state censorship – always anxious and ready to seize inflammatory material and to arrest agitators. See also Wolfe, *Three Who Made a Revolution*, 125, for a catalogue of the techniques employed by Lenin to evade the watchful tsarist police: secret codes, ciphers, invisible ink, and hollow bottom trunks.

6  As an example, here, Lenin cites the wave of factory strikes that washed over Russia in the middle years of the 1890s. See, e.g., 5.376–7. In Lenin's mind, though, these strikes, while salutary, were insufficiently well organized: their spontaneity undermines their effectiveness and furnishes proof of the need for the careful guidance of a full-time revolutionary intelligentsia. See also Orlando Figes, *A People's Tragedy: The Russian Revolution, 1891–1924* (New York: Penguin, 1998), chap. 4, esp. part 2.

7  This is a reference to the German socialist and politician Eduard Bernstein, whose *Principles of Socialism* was published in Russia in 1901. See also, e.g., Peter Gay, *The Dilemma of Democratic Socialism: Eduard Bernstein's Challenge to Marx* (New York: Octagon Books, 1979), esp. 131–56 and 213–48.

8  See note 5.

9  See, e.g., Yemelyan Yaroslavsky, *History of the Communist Party* (Moscow: Novosti Press Agency, 1975), vol. 5, chap. 10, p. 15: "Those members of the Party who gave their entire time to the Party got very small remuneration, sometimes as low as 3, 5, or 10 rubles."

10  See, e.g., Figes, *People's Tragedy*, chap. 5, esp. 164–92.

11  Figes, *People's Tragedy*, part 3. See also, e.g., Richard Pipes, *The Russian Revolution* (New York: Vintage Books, 1991), part 2; Robert Service, *The Russian Revolution, 1900–1927* (London: Red Globe, 2009), chap. 2; and James D. White, *The Russian Revolution, 1917–1921: A Short History* (New York: Edward Arnold, 1994), chap. 5.

12  Service, *Lenin: A Biography*, part 3.

13  See note 7.

14  Service, *Lenin*, chaps. 25–6.

15  See, e.g., Pipes, *Russian Revolution*, chap. 18; and White, *Russian Revolution*, chap. 12.

## 9  Tawney on Equality and Democracy

1  See, e.g., Figes, *People's Tragedy*, chap. 11; China Miéville, *October: The Story of the Russian Revolution* (New York: Verso, 2017), chap. 10 and epilogue; Service, *Russian Revolution*, chap. 3; and White, *Russian Revolution*, 13.

2  See, e.g., Robert Conquest, *Stalin: Breaker of Nations* (New York: Viking, 1991); Robert Conquest, *The Great Terror: A Reassessment* (Oxford: Oxford University Press, 2008); Robert Service, *A History of Modern Russia from Nicholas II to Vladimir Putin* (Cambridge, MA: Harvard University Press, 2003); Lewis Siegelbaum and Andrei Sokolov, eds., *Stalinism as a Way of Life: A Narrative in Documents* (New Haven, CT: Yale University Press, 2000); Ronald Suny, *The Soviet Experiment: Russia, the USSR, and the Successor States*, 2nd ed. (Oxford: Oxford University Press, 1998); and Suny, *The Structure of Soviet History: Essays and Documents*, 2nd ed. (Oxford: Oxford University Press, 2003).

3  See, e.g., Gad Horowitz, *Canadian Labour in Politics* (Toronto: University of Toronto Press, 1968); and Norman Penner, *The Canadian Left: A Critical Analysis* (Englewood Cliffs, NJ: Prentice-Hall, 1977), esp. chap. 3.

4  See, e.g. Lawrence Goldman, *The Life of R.H. Tawney: Socialism and History* (London: Bloomsbury Academic, 2013), chap. 1; Tim Rogan, *The Moral Economists: R.H. Tawney, Karl Polanyi, E.P. Thompson, and the Critique of Capitalism* (Princeton, NJ: Princeton University Press, 2018), 18–22; and Ross Terrill, *R.H. Tawney and His Times: Socialism as Fellowship* (Cambridge, MA: Harvard University Press, 1973), esp. chap. 1.

5  See, e.g., L.T. Hobhouse, *Liberalism and Other Writings* (Cambridge: Cambridge University Press, 1994), 70 and 84–7; J.A. Hobson, *Work and Wealth: A Human Valuation* (London: Allen & Unwin, 1933), 226–7; and

A.W. Wright, *R.H. Tawney* (Manchester: University of Manchester Press, 1987), 58–60.

6  See also Tawney's *Religion and the Rise of Capitalism*, 25–6, for his discussion of the essential malleability of human nature.

7  In *The Acquisitive Society* (London: Collins, 1961), Tawney discusses six ways by which the private control of industry can be terminated. See 96–111 (esp. 100–1). There is, he says, "no single formula," and the path taken is necessarily a "matter of expediency to be decided in each particular case." For a critical view of Tawney's politics, see Alasdair Macintyre, "The Socialism of R.H. Tawney," in *Alasdair Macintyre's Engagement with Marxism*, ed. Paul Blackledge and Neil Douglas Davidson, 299–303 (London: Brill, 2008).

8  For the political and intellectual history of pre- and postwar English (guild) socialism, see, e.g., Ivor Brown, "Aspects of the Guild Idea" *New Age* 17, no. 1 (1915): 150–1; G.D.H. Cole, *Labour in the Commonwealth: A Book for the Younger Generation* (London: Headley Brothers, 1919), chap. 3; Cole, *Social Theory* (London: Methuen, 1920), chaps. 6 and 9; Michael Freeden, *Liberalism Divided: A Study in British Political Thought, 1914–1930* (Oxford: Oxford University Press, 1986), chap. 3, esp. 66–77; W.H. Greenleaf, *The British Political Tradition*, vol. 2: *The Ideological Heritage* (London: Methuen, 1983), 417–39; Ben Jackson, "Equality or Nothing? Social Justice on the British Left, c. 1911–31," *Journal of Political Ideologies* 8, no. 1 (2003): 83–110; Cécile Laborde, *Pluralist Thought and the State in Britain and France, 1900–25* (New York: St. Martin's, 2000), 69–100; and Marc Stears, "Guild Socialism and Ideological Diversity on the British Left, 1914–1926" *Journal of Political Ideologies* 3, no. 3 (1998): 289–306.

9  Locke, *Second Treatise*, chap. 9, §124. Tawney quotes Locke at *RRC*, 20.

10  See the discussion of Aquinas in chap. 1, esp. §5.

11  See also *RRC*, 105, where Tawney discusses the "medieval conception of the social order." See also, e.g., Sandra M. Den Otter, *British Idealism and Social Explanation: A Study in Late Victorian Thought* (Oxford: Oxford University Press, 1996), part 5; and Arthur O. Lovejoy, *The Great Chain of Being: A Study of the History of an Idea* (Cambridge, MA: Harvard University Press, 1936), 67–98.

12  Is it a coincidence that this shattering of the medieval cosmos coincides with the massive "expansion of finance and international trade in the sixteenth century" (*RRC*, 10)? In any case, Tawney describes how illequipped was medieval theology to deal with these transnational and impersonal modes of economic activity; after all, the conventional religious teaching emphasized the deeply personal nature of our economic interactions and the strict limits on our behavior generated by such intimacy. When I no longer know my "neighbour ... how exactly am I to make my love for him effective in practice" (*RRC* 187–8)?

13  See also Max Weber, *The Protestant Ethic and the Spirit of Capitalism*, trans. Stephen Kalberg (London: Routledge, 2010), 18.

14  See, e.g., Stefan Collini, *English Pasts: Essays in Culture and History* (Oxford: Oxford University Press, 1999), 182.

15  See, e.g., Goldman, *Life*, 182: "The spirit of a social Christianity ... was perhaps the most powerful of all the external influences on Tawney."

## 10  Nietzsche on a Higher Concept of Culture

1  See, e.g., Henry Scott Holland, *Our Neighbours* (London: A.R. Mowbray, 1911), 145: "That is just what our faith [in the Incarnation] means. It is, itself, the assertion that God and man cannot be kept in separate compartments. God must be concerned with every scrap and detail that is human.... The Incarnation itself, then, is the decisive reason why Jesus Christ has a social and economic significance." Scott Holland was one of the founders of the Christian Social Union, which Tawney joined as an undergraduate at Oxford. The mandate of the CSU was to adapt Christianity to the modern age by drawing out the social, political, and economic implications of Christian theology. See, e.g., Rogan, *Moral Economists*, 40–3; and Goldman, *Life*, 21. For an account of the relationship between Christianity and socialism, see, e.g., Gregory Claeys, *Citizens and Saints: Politics and Anti-Politics in Early British Socialism* (Cambridge: Cambridge University Press, 1989), esp. part 3; Peter D'Alroy Jones, *The Christian Socialist Revival, 1877–1914: Religion, Class and Social Conscience in Late Victorian England* (Princeton, NJ: Princeton University Press, 1968), chap. 6; and E.R. Norman, *The Victorian Christian Socialists* (Cambridge: Cambridge University Press, 1987), esp. chap. 9.

2  R.H. Tawney, "A Note on Christianity and the Social Order," in *The Attack, and Other Papers* (London: Allen & Unwin, 1953), 176. See also Rogan, *Moral Economists*, 41–2.

3  Tawney, *Attack*, 182–3. See also *R.H. Tawney's Common Place Book*, ed. J.M. Winter and D.M. Joslin (Cambridge: Cambridge University Press, 2006), 78–9.

4  R.H. Tawney, *The Radical Tradition: Twelve Essays on Politics, Education, and Literature* (New York: Pantheon Books, 1964), 70–81.

5  See *Religion and the Rise of Capitalism*, 19–20 and 187–8, where Tawney laments the privatization of religious belief in the aftermath of the Reformation, as well as the church's inability to reformulate its economic doctrines "in new and living terms." For Tawney's own attempt to articulate a modern vision of Christian social justice, see the 1918 Church of England report, *Christianity and Industrial Problems*, which emphasized the need for (among other things) ethical consumption, a living wage for all workers, "more complete equality," the "abolition of privilege and social authority on the part of individuals or classes," and industrial "government or management by all." For an account of Tawney's (large, leading) contribution to the report, see J.E. Kirby, "R.H. Tawney and Christian

Social Teaching: Religion and the Rise of Capitalism Reconsidered," *English Historical Review* 131, no. 551 (2016): 793–822.

6  See also Nietzsche, *Ecce Homo: How One Becomes What One Is*, trans. R.J. Hollingdale (New York: Penguin, 1979), part 3: "The truth of the *first* inquiry [of *GM*] is the birth of Christianity." Of course, Nietzsche does not give us the familiar history of early Christianity; he has no interest in events, in dates and details. Instead, he traces the *psychological origins* of Christian ideas about morality.

7  The more fundamental aim of *On the Genealogy of Morals* is to locate the "origin of our moral prejudices ... where our ideas of good and evil really *originated*" (§1 and §3). "Under what conditions," asks Nietzsche, "did man devise these value judgments good and evil" (§3)? And this inquiry necessitates, in turn, an account of the founding, and spread, of Christianity – *the* fundamental source of moral judgments in modern life. Of course, Nietzsche *also* wants to know – sacrilegiously, no doubt – whether (or not) the process of Christianization has been *good* for humankind: have Christianity's moral values – its definition of goodness and evil – "hindered or furthered human prosperity" (§3)? What, in other words, is "the *value* of morality" (§5)? *What if* our ideas about goodness and evil were, in fact, "a symptom of regression" (§6)? *What if* "morality was the danger of dangers" (§6)?

8  For a discussion of this concept, see, e.g., Rüdiger Bittner, "Ressentiment" in *Nietzsche, Genealogy, Morality*, ed. Richard Schacht (Berkeley: University of California Press, 1994), 128; Gilles Deleuze, *Nietzsche and Philosophy*, trans. Hugh Tomlinson (New York: Columbia University Press, 1983), chap. 4; Walter Kaufmann's introduction to the *Genealogy* in the Modern Library's *Basic Writings of Nietzsche* (New York: Modern Library, 2000), esp. §3; Simon May, *Nietzsche's Ethics and His War on "Morality"* (Oxford: Oxford University Press, 1999), 42–50; Peter Poellner, *Nietzsche and Metaphysics* (Oxford: Oxford University Press, 1995), 130–1 and 253–4; and John Richardson, *Nietzsche's System* (Oxford: Oxford University Press, 1996), chap. 3.

9  See also, e.g., *GM* §11, where Nietzsche discusses the portrayal of the Athenians in Thucydides's *History*; he focuses, in particular, on Pericles's Funeral Oration, which celebrates the Athenians' "shocking cheerfulness, and depth of delight in all destruction, in all the debauches of victory and cruelty."

10  In fact, Nietzsche makes no distinction between Judaism and Christianity; to him, they are the same despite their (again to him, superficial) theological and ritualistic differences: both are, at bottom, the life-denying expression of weakness. See, e.g., *GM* §9: "Everything is being made appreciably Jewish, Christian or plebian (never mind the words!)."

11  See, e.g., *GM* §14, where Nietzsche calls men of *ressentiment* "cellar rats full of revenge and hatred," and *GM* §11, where he says that the idea of (masters as) evil comes from "the cauldron of unassuaged hatred." And yet, in Nietzsche's telling, *ressentiment* is not *entirely* negative: the priestly revolt in

morality, he says, makes man "*an interesting animal*" for the first time; it is only *after* this revolt that the "human soul ... [acquired] *depth* ... [became] brooding and emotionally explosive" (*GM* §6). Hence Nietzsche's belief that *ressentiment*, despite its association with hatred and vengefulness, *is* "the actual instrument of culture" (*GM* §11). Without it – without an injection of the "intellect of the powerful" – "the history of mankind would be far too stupid a thing" (*GM* §7). See also *BGE*, preface and §188.

12  Why *do* the strong submit (to the weak, no less)? Because the priests are patient and cunning, and the nobility is (somewhat counterintuitively) an easy target: imprudent, forgetful, not inclined to worry about their enemies (*GM* §10). In other words, they fail to recognize the danger that priests pose to their rule and, over time, allow themselves to be made to feel guilty about their mastery. For Nietzsche's discussion of how slaves insinuate themselves into the company of masters, see, e.g., *TI* §5 and §§8–9. See also, e.g., Mark Migotti, "Slave Morality, Socrates, and the Bushmen: A Reading of the First Essay of On the Genealogy of Morals," *Philosophy and Phenomenological Research* 58, no. 4 (1998): 745–79, esp. 755–60.

13  See also *BGE* §202: Judeo-Christian "morality says stubbornly and inexorably, 'I am morality itself, and nothing besides is morality.'"

14  Of course, this is another way of speaking about the will to power, a key concept that runs throughout Nietzsche's oeuvre. See, e.g., *BGE* §§13, 43, 56, 201–3, 211–12, 257–60, 268, and 287; *D* §201; *GS*, §§55 and 290; *EH* 1:2; *WP* §§400, 876, 897, 944, 957, 962, and 999. See also, e.g., Raymond Geuss, "Nietzsche and Morality," *European Journal of Philosophy* 5, no. 1 (1997): 1–20, esp. 11–15; Alexander Nehamas, *Nietzsche: Life as Literature* (Cambridge, MA: Harvard University Press, 1985), chap. 7, esp. 227–34; and Richard Schacht, *Nietzsche: Life as Literature* (Cambridge, MA: Harvard University Press, 1985), chap. 6.

15  See also *WP* §1017, where Nietzsche calls "the socialist ideal ... the residue of Christianity," and *WP* §765, where he describes the way that socialists shrewdly "appeal to Christian instincts." There is another important similarity between the Christian and socialist revolts: both originate in the feeling that the (so-called) masters are not worthy of their high social standing. See, e.g., *WP*, §874, where Nietzsche blames the decadent "Roman Caesars" for the triumph of "the insanity of Christianity," and *GS* §40, where he describes workers' unsatisfying "submission to unknown and uninteresting persons, which is what all the luminaries of industry are." See section 3 below for Nietzsche's critical discussion of the capitalist system of values.

16  Of course, there is one *crucial* difference between Christianity and socialism: the former – at least in its original teaching, before its conscientious politicization (*WP* §211) – "condemns, disparages, [and] curses the world," while the latter transfers "the arrival of the 'kingdom of God' into the future, on earth, in human form" (*WP* §§373 and 339), See also *WP*, §390, where Nietzsche claims that, despite its debt, socialism is

"nothing but a clumsy misunderstanding of [the] Christian moral ideal."
Interestingly, at *WP* §§95 and 755, Nietzsche identifies the novel (*this*)
worldliness of socialism with Rousseau: in the *Social Contract*, for example,
Rousseau describes the reorganization of political institutions necessary
to restore, and effectively harness, our natural goodness. Of course,
Nietzsche's reading is incommensurable with the account of Rousseau
offered in chapter 5, section 4 above.

17  See also *BGE* §61, where Nietzsche argues that "ordinary human beings –
the vast majority [i.e., workers] ... exist for service and the general
advantage and ... *may* exist only for that," and *AC* §57, where Nietzsche
describes "high culture" as a "pyramid: it can stand only on a broad base."
Hence, Nietzsche's disdain for all those socialist agitators who undermine
"the worker's sense of satisfaction with his small existence," who make
the (unthinking) majority desirous of equal standing with the (creative)
minority; hence his belief that "injustice ... lies in the demand for 'equal'
rights" (*AC* §57). And yet, Nietzsche *does* have a (not inconsiderable)
number of interpreters who (somehow) discern in his philosophy an egal-
itarian streak and who extract from it egalitarian political implications.
See, e.g., Romand Coles, "Liberty, Equality and Receptive Generosity:
Neo-Nietzschean Reflections on Ethics and Politics of Coalition," *American
Political Science Review* 90, no. 2 (1996): 375–88, esp. 381–6; Lawrence
Hatab, *A Nietzschean Defense of Democracy: An Experiment in Postmodern Politics*
(Chicago: Open Court, 1995), chaps. 4 and 5; and Bonnie Honig, *Political
Theory and the Displacement of Politics* (Ithaca, NY: Cornell University Press,
1993), chap. 3. It goes without saying, of course, that such an interpretation
requires considerable bracketing out of fundamental, recurring features of
Nietzsche's political philosophy (see, e.g., *WP* §§861, 872, and 936).

18  See, e.g., Francis Fukuyama, *The End of History and the Last Man* (New York:
Free Press, 2006), 316; and Ayn Rand, *Capitalism: The Unknown Ideal* (New
York: New American Library, 1966), 45. See also Michael Kilivris, "Beyond
Goods and Services: Toward a Nietzschean Critique of Capitalism," *Kritike*
5, no. 2 (2011): 26–40, esp. 35–9.

19  See also Nietzsche's 1865 letter to his sister, written over twenty years before
*Ecce Homo*: there, he describes how it is "so difficult to accept everything
that [he] has been brought up on – what is considered truth in the circle
of relatives and of many good men" and his resultant desire "to strike new
paths, [fight] the habitual, [experience] the insecurity of independence."
*The Portable Nietzsche*, ed. Walter Kaufmann (New York: Viking, 1954), 29.

20  See *UM* 168: "Certainly, he who has lived among Germans suffers greatly
from the notorious greyness of their life and thought, from their form-
lessness, their stupidity and dull-mindedness, their coarseness in more
delicate affairs.... He is pained and offended by their rooted joy in what
is false and un-genuine, ... their search for success and profit." See also
*EH* 775–7, "The Case of Wagner," §2, where Nietzsche accuses his fellow

Germans of "indecency," "idiotic judgment[s]," "untruthfulness," and perhaps worst of all, "cowardice before the truth." "Nationalism," he adds, is a form of "*anti-cultural* sickness."

21  See, e.g., Kauffman, *Nietzsche: Philosopher, Psychologist, Antichrist* (Princeton, NJ: Princeton University Press, 1968), esp. part 3, chap. 10.

22  For a much less generous interpretation, see Ronald Beiner, *Dangerous Minds: Nietzsche, Heidegger, and the Return of the Far Right* (Philadelphia: University of Pennsylvania Press, 2018), chap. 1. We return (briefly) to the question of Nietzsche's culpability for the fascistic interpretations of his philosophy in the introductory section of chapter 11 below.

23  The use of the term *fascism* is complex and contested: in its narrowest sense – the sense employed in the present chapter – it refers to the Italian ideology and (later) political party headed by Mussolini between 1919 and 1945. For a detailed discussion of fascism as a general, "generic" concept, see Roger Griffin, *The Nature of Fascism* (New York: St. Martin's, 1991), chap. 1, esp. 12–13; and Griffin, *Fascism: A Reader* (Oxford: Oxford University Press, 1995), 15. For Nietzsche's connection to European fascism, see, e.g., Robert C. Holub, *Nietzsche's Jewish Problem: Between Anti-Semitism and Anti-Judaism* (Princeton, NJ: Princeton University Press, 2016), 10–11; S.J. Woolf, "Mussolini as Revolutionary," *Journal of Contemporary History* 1, no. 2 (1966): 187–96, esp. 190; Zeev Sternhell (with Mario Sznajder and Maia Asheri), *The Birth of Fascist Ideology: From Cultural Rebellion to Political Revolution*, trans. David Maisel (Princeton, NJ: Princeton University Press, 1994), chap. 5, esp. 200; Jacob Golomb and R.S. Wistrich, "Introduction," *Nietzsche, Godfather of Fascism? On the Uses and Abuses of History* (Princeton, NJ: Princeton University Press, 2002), 1–18, esp. 2; and Mario Sznajder, "Nietzsche, Mussolini, and Italian Fascism," in *Nietzsche, Godfather of Fascism? On the Uses and Abuses of History*, ed. Jacob Golomb and Robert Wistrich (Princeton, NJ: Princeton University Press, 2002), 235–62.

24  For Italian politics and culture in the first half of the twentieth century, see, e.g., Sheri Berman, *The Primacy of Politics: Social Democracy and the Making of Europe's Twentieth Century* (Cambridge: Cambridge University Press, 2006), 127–31; Anthony Cardoza, *Agrarian Elites and Italian Fascism: The Province of Bologna, 1901–1926* (Princeton, NJ: Princeton University Press, 1982), esp. chaps. 6–7; Paul Corner, *The Fascist Party and Popular Opinion in Mussolini's Italy* (Oxford: Oxford University Press, 2012), esp. chap. 2; Felix Gilbert, *The End of the European Era: 1890 to the Present* (New York: Norton, 1970), 185–6; Walter Laqueur, ed., *Fascism: A Reader's Guide* (Berkeley: University of California Press, 1976), 129–35; and Edward Tannenbaum, *The Fascist Experience: Italian Society and Culture, 1922–1945* (New York: Basic Books, 1972), esp. chap. 2.

25  "The Futurist Manifesto" can be found in its entirety in *Readings in Political Ideologies since the Rise of Modern Science*, ed. H.B. McCullough and Wolfgang Depner (Oxford: Oxford University Press 2013), 155–7.

26  See also, e.g., Benito Mussolini, "The Political and Social Doctrine
of Fascism," *Political Quarterly* 4, no. 3 (1933): 341–56. Fascism, says
Mussolini, "repudiates the doctrine of Pacifism – born of a renunciation
of the struggle and an act of cowardice in the face of sacrifice. War alone
ups to its highest tension all human energy and puts the stamp of nobility
upon the peoples who have the courage to meet it. All other trials are substitutes." See also the introductory section of chapter 11.
27  See, e.g., James Joll, *Three Intellectuals in Politics* (New York: Pantheon
Books, 1961), part 3.

**11 Keynes on the Art of Enjoyment**

 1  See also, e.g., *AC* §33; *GM* 2, §24; and *UM* 3, §§3–4.
 2  In his December 15, 1880, letter to his friend Erwin Rohde, Nietzsche says
that his philosophy is "fishhooks for catching" the philosophers of the
future. See Nietzsche, *Selected Letters*, ed. and trans. Christopher Middleton
(Indianapolis: Hackett, 1996), 72–3. See also, e.g., Daniel Breazeale's
introduction to *Philosophy and Truth: Selections from Nietzsche's Notebooks of
the Early 1870s*, ed. Breazeale (Atlantic Highlands, NJ: Humanities, 1979),
xxiii–xxviii; and Steven V. Hicks and Alan Rosenberg, "Nietzsche and
Untimeliness: The 'Philosopher of the Future' as the Figure of Disruptive
Wisdom," *Journal of Nietzsche Studies* 25, no. 1 (2003): 1–34, esp. 4–10.
 3  See, e.g., *BGE* §208; and *EH*, "Why I Am a Destiny," §1. See also
chapter 10, section 4 above.
 4  Of course, we know what sorts of political arrangements Nietzsche
cannot accept – egalitarian democracy chief among them. After all,
the leveling ethos of democracy extinguishes the aristocratic pathos of
distance. See, e.g., *BGE* §257: "Every enhancement of the type 'man' has
so far been the work of an aristocratic society – and it will be so again
and again – a society that believes in the long ladder of an order of rank
and differences in value between man and man, and that needs slavery
in some sense or other." See also *BGE* §262, where Nietzsche celebrates
the "aristocratic commonwealth – say, an ancient Greek *polis*, or Venice."
"Every aristocratic morality," he adds, "is intolerant – in the education of
youth, in their arrangements for women, in their marriage customs, in the
relations of old and young, in their penal laws." These sentiments also gel
with the passages highlighted in chapter 10, note 17, where Nietzsche emphasizes the necessarily passive role of the (vast) majority in processes of
cultural creation. And yet, it is also true that there is no *constructive* political philosophy anywhere in Nietzsche's oeuvre: he has absolutely *no* interest in the institutional workings – the quotidian dimensions – of political
life; his thought, as a result, is a kind of blank canvas for those with
aristocratic, antidemocratic, reactionary leanings. Given his inflammatory, provocative, and (at times) irresponsible rhetoric – in passages like

*BGE* §§257 and 262, and many, many, *many* others – Nietzsche is hardly blameless for the fascist (and now neofascist/alt-right) appropriation of his thought. See note 6 below. See also, e.g., Beiner, *Dangerous Minds*, chap. 1; and Geoff Waite, *Nietzsche's Corps/e: Aesthetics, Politics, Prophecy, or, the Spectacular Technoculture of Everyday Life* (Durham, NC: Duke University Press, 1996), chap. 3.

5  Nietzsche, *Selected Letters*, 227.

6  In fact, Nietzsche should *still* be concerned! As Ronald Beiner points out in his introduction to *Dangerous Minds*, the intellectual leaders of today's far-right (*alt*-right) ideological movements – Richard B. Spencer, Aleksandr Dugin, and Julius Evola, to name the most prominent – all draw intellectual sustenance from Nietzsche, just as their twentieth-century fascist forebears did. See also, e.g., Charles Clover, *Black Wind, White Snow: The Rise of Russia's New Nationalism* (New Haven, CT: Yale University Press, 2016), part 3; Mark Sedgwick, *Against the Modern World: Traditionalism and the Secret Intellectual History of the Twentieth Century* (Oxford: Oxford University Press, 2004), chaps. 5 and 9; and Nicholas Goodrick-Clarke, *Black Sun: Aryan Cults, Esoteric Nazism, and the Politics of Identity* (New York: New York University Press, 2002), chap. 3.

7  Joll, *Three Intellectuals in Politics*, 135–6.

8  See, e.g., Anne Bowler, "Politics as Art: Italian Futurism and Fascism," *Theory & Society* 20, no. 6 (1991): 763–94, esp. 766–71; and Ernest Ialongo, "Filippo Tomasso Marinetti: The Futurist as Fascist, 1929–37," *Journal of Modern Italian Studies* 18, no. 4 (2013): 393–418, esp. 401–7.

9  Gilbert, *End of the European Era*, 186. See also, e.g., Alexander J. De Grand, *Italian Fascism: Its Origins and Development* (Lincoln: University of Nebraska Press, 1982), 106; A. James Gregor, *Italian Fascism and Developmental Dictatorship* (Princeton, NJ: Princeton University Press, 1979), 158; Gregor, *Young Mussolini and the Intellectual Origins of Fascism* (Berkeley: University of California Press, 1979), esp. 191–2; Gaetano Salvemini, *Under the Axe of Fascism* (New York: H. Fertig, 1969), 418; and Salvemini, "Platform of the Fasci di Combattimento," in *A Primer of Italian Fascism*, ed. Jeffrey Schnapp (Lincoln: University of Nebraska Press, 2000), 3–5.

10  For context (and for a reprint of Hoffman's photo), see Hans Sluga, *Heidegger's Crisis: Philosophy and Politics in Nazi Germany* (Cambridge, MA: Harvard University Press, 1993), chap. 8, esp. 179–86. See also, e.g., Max Whyte, "The Uses and Abuses of Nietzsche in the Third Reich: Alfred Baeumler's 'Heroic Realism,'" *Journal of Contemporary History* 43, no. 2 (2008): 171–94, esp. 191–3.

11  See chapter 10, note 23.

12  See, e.g., Shelly D. Kasper, "The Legacy of Keynes as Public Intellectual," in *Keynes's General Theory after Seventy Years*, ed. R.W. Dimand, R.A. Mundell, and A. Vercelli (London: Palgrave Macmillan, 2011), 44–52; and Robert Skidelsky, *John Maynard Keynes* (New York: Viking, 1986), 1:377–8.

For Keynes's leadership at Bretton Woods, see, e.g., Armand Van Dormael, *Bretton Woods: Birth of a Monetary System* (London: Macmillan, 1978), esp. chaps. 1 and 4; and Richard Gardner, *Sterling-Dollar Diplomacy in Current Perspective: The Origins and the Prospects of Our International Economic Order* (New York: Columbia University Press, 1980), esp. chap. 1.

13 For a notable exception, see Craufurd D. Goodwin, "The Art of an Ethical Life: Keynes and Bloomsbury," in *The Cambridge Companion to Keynes*, ed. R.E. Backhouse and B.W. Bateman (Cambridge: Cambridge University Press, 2006), esp. 218–23. See also Skidelsky, *John Maynard Keynes*, 3:168.

14 "The Political Doctrines of Edmund Burke" can be found in the John Maynard Keynes Papers in King's College, Cambridge. The unpublished essay is filed at KP: UA.20.3.13. The essay is also reprinted in part 1 of *The Essential Keynes*, ed. Robert Skidelsky (Penguin, 2016).

15 See, Burke, *Reflections on the Revolution in France*, ed. J.G.A. Pocock (Indianapolis: Hackett, 1987), esp. 50–2.

16 See, e.g., Simon Schama, *Citizens: A Chronicle of the Revolution* (New York: Knopf, 1989), esp. part 4.

17 Page references in the remaining sections of this chapter refer to the Cambridge edition of Keynes's *Collected Writings*, ed. Elizabeth Johnson and Donald Moggridge (Cambridge: Royal Economic Society, 1978).

18 See, e.g., Daniel Yergen and Joseph Stanislaw, *The Commanding Heights: The Battle between Government and the Marketplace That Is Remaking the Modern World* (New York: Simon & Schuster, 1998), 3–4: in Britain, there was the widespread feeling that the capitalist class "had surely failed [the nation]; they had underinvested and demonstrated no entrepreneurial drive. Instead, flinty and mean-spirited businessmen had hoarded profits, eschewing new technologies, avoiding innovation and depriving their workers."

19 Keynes says much the same thing about the rate of interest: it too must be carefully managed by the state and be set low enough to stimulate investment, employment, and consumption. After all, low rates of interest are much more likely to unleash the "intelligence and determination and executive skill of the financier, the entrepreneur" (7.376). When, conversely, the rate of interest is too high, the hoarding of capital is encouraged, and the economic health of society compromised (7.374–6). This measure would also have the positive effect of making capital much less scarce and could even eventually lead, Keynes fantasizes, to "the euthanasia of the rentier, and, consequently, the euthanasia of the oppressive power of the capitalist to exploit the scarcity-value of capital" (7.375).

20 See, e.g., F. Bastiat, *Economic Harmonies*, trans. W. Hayden Boyers, ed. George B. de Huszar (Irvington-on-Hudson, NY: Foundation for Economic Education, 1996), which Keynes cites as a typical example of the quasi-religious disposition of the adherents of laissez-faire: "All principles, all motives, all springs of action, all interests, cooperate towards a grand final result ... the indefinite approximation of all classes towards a level,

which is always rising…. He who has arranged the material universe has not withheld His regard from the arrangements of the social world" (9.280).

21  See, e.g., Robert Skidelsky, *Keynes: The Return of the Master* (New York: Public Affairs, 2009), esp. chaps. 4 and 5; and Peter Clarke, *The Keynesian Revolution in the Making, 1924–1936* (Oxford: Clarendon, 1988), esp. part 4.

22  See also Keynes, "A Short View from Russia," in which the author – despite serious reservations about Leninism in particular, and state socialism in general – praises the Soviet attempt to extirpate the "pecuniary motives" through statecraft (e.g., stiff progressive taxation): "Everyone should work for the community – the new creed runs – and, if he does his duty, the community will uphold him," and money-making will thus become "disgraceful" (9.259–60). "A society in of which this is even partially true," adds Keynes, "is a tremendous innovation" (9.259–60). See below.

23  See, e.g., John T. Flynn, *The Road Ahead: America's Creeping Revolution* (New York: Devin-Adair, 1949), 149; and William Foster, *Outline Political History of the Americas* (New York: International Publishers, 1951), 597. See also Schumpeter, *History of Economic Analysis*, part 5, chap. 5, esp. 1171–4.

24  See, e.g., 9.266: "I do not think that [Russian communism] contains, or is likely to contain, any piece of useful economic technique which we could apply."

25  Of course, Keynes is in familiar company here: he recalls – consciously or not, likely the former – another English (liberal) philosopher: John Stuart Mill. Indeed, the argument of the concluding chapter of Keynes's *General Theory* is, in many ways, a restatement of Mill's canonical *On Liberty*, the essential thesis of which is that cultural and intellectual diversity is the inevitable outcome of liberty, and that such diversity is an intrinsic good that every society ought to value and work toward through its public policy. See, e.g., *On Liberty* in *The Basic Writings of John Stuart Mill*, ed. Dale E. Miller (New York: Modern Library, 2002), 14–15 and 58–66.

## 12  Hayek on the Limits of Knowledge

1  Eric Hobsbawm, *The Age of Extremes: A History of the World, 1914–1991* (New York: Vintage, 1996), 258–61. See also Stephen Marglin and Juliet Schor, eds., *The Golden Age of Capitalism: Reinterpreting the Postwar Experience* (Oxford: Oxford University Press, 1990), esp. chaps. 1–2.

2  Marglin and Schor, *Golden Age of Capitalism*, 259.

3  Marglin and Schor, *Golden Age of Capitalism*, 282.

4  Marglin and Schor, *Golden Age of Capitalism*, 269 and 273. See also Yergen and Stanislaw, *Commanding Heights*, 3–9.

5  See, e.g., Nicholas Timmins, *The Five Giants: A Biography of the Welfare State* (London: HarperCollins, 1995), esp. 12–15, 25, and 34.

6  Hobsbawm, *Age of Extremes*, 285. See also Mark Mazower, *Dark Continent: Europe's Twentieth Century* (New York: A.A. Knopf, 1999), 333–6.

7  See, e.g., Yergen and Stanislaw, *Commanding Heights*, 44.

8  See, e.g., Hobsbawn, *Age of Extremes*, 285–6.

9  See, e.g., Yergen and Stanislaw, *Commanding Heights*, 47.

10  Charles A. Gulick, *Austria from Habsburg to Hitler* (Berkeley: University of California Press, 1948), 1:439–45.

11  Gulick, *Austria from Habsburg to Hitler*, 1:448.

12  Gulick, *Austria from Habsburg to Hitler*, 1:492–3. See also Barbara Jelavich, *Modern Austria: Empire and Republic, 1815–1956* (Cambridge: Cambridge University Press, 1987), 177–85.

13  See, e.g., Bruce Caldwell's introduction to *The Road to Serfdom* (Chicago: University of Chicago Press, 2007), 8–14. See also Arthur Marwick, "Middle Opinion in the Thirties: Planning Progress and Political 'Agreement,'" *English Historical Review* 79, no. 311 (1964): 285–98.

14  National Executive Committee of the Labour Party, *The Old World and the New Society: A Report on the Problems of the War and Peace Reconstruction* (London: Transport House, 1942), 3–4, cited in Caldwell's introduction to *The Road to Serfdom*, 12.

15  See, e.g., Heilbroner and Milberg, *Making of Economic Society*, 108–9.

16  In fact, Friedrich Hayek goes further than that: in *The Constitution of Liberty*, ed. Bruce Caldwell (Chicago: University of Chicago Press, 1960), esp. 374–7, he provides a spirited defense of (something along the lines of) welfare state redistribution – within limits, of course. See the introductory section of chapter 13.

17  See chapter 11, §3.

18  This sets up yet another deeply fascinating contrast between Hayek and Keynes: whereas the former thinks of work as a – if not *the* – quintessential expression of human freedom, the latter believes that freedom *begins* only when works *ends* – with those nobler human pursuits that require *leisure*.

19  For an intellectual history of this period, see, e.g., R.M. Hartwell, *A History of the Mont Pelerin Society* (Indianapolis, IN: Liberty Fund, 1995), esp. part 2; and Yergin and Stanislaw, *Commanding Heights*, esp. 87–93.

### 13  Rawls on Plutocracy and Economic Justice

1  See, e.g., Hartwell, *History of the Mont Pelerin Society*, esp. part 1.

2  See also, e.g., Tony Judt and Timothy Snyder, *Thinking the Twentieth Century* (New York: Penguin, 2012), chap. 9: According to Hayek, says Judt, "If you begin with welfare policies of any sort – directing individuals, taxing for social ends, engineering the outcomes of market relationships – you will end up with Hitler. Not merely with social democratic housing projects or right-wing subsidies for 'honest' winegrowers, but Hitler." As it turns out, this view is a deeply misled caricature. And yet, many of Hayek's *followers* (not *just* his critics) have adopted it earnestly.

3  See, e.g., Friedrich Hayek, *Law, Legislation, and Liberty: A New Statement of the Liberal Principles of Justice and Political Economy* (London: Routledge, 2013), 3:395: "The assurance of a certain minimum income for everyone,

or a sort of floor below which nobody need fall even when he is unable to provide for himself, appears not only to be a wholly legitimate protection against a risk common to all, but a necessary part of the Great Society."

4  The members of the Mont Pelerin Society knew of, and engaged with, Rawls's work. See, e.g., Hayek's "'Social' or Distributive Justice Appendix: Justice and Individual Rights," in *Law, Legislation and Liberty*, 2:113, where he says that *A Theory of Justice* cannot be properly interpreted "as lending support to socialist demands." As it turns out, Hayek was wrong about that! See sections 2 and 3 below.

5  See *TJ* §12 (esp. 57–8); and *R* §41.1 for Rawls's discussion of "the system of natural liberty," in which "the economy is roughly a free market system" animated by "the principle of efficiency." In such a system, the distribution of "wealth and income, authority and responsibility" is "fair ... whatever this allocation turns out to be," even if a small minority possesses everything and the majority nothing. In other words, the system of natural liberty "includes an element of pure procedural justice." See also, e.g., Robert Nozick, *Anarchy, State, and Utopia* (New York: Basic Books, 1974), chap. 7, part 2.

6  It is important to note that Rawls employs the (classical liberal) conception of persons as utility-maximizers. The difference principle does not apply to the actions and decisions of individuals; it applies to the design and regulation of the basic structure, i.e., to the decisions made by legislators. See, e.g., *TJ* 242 (italics added): "The main problem of distributive justice is the choice of a social *system.*"

7  In other words, the starting assumption of *Theory* is that the basic structure is not fixed: its institutions are malleable; the illegitimate inequalities they produce (and reproduce) are therefore subject to revision *on the basis of our convictions about justice*. Now, the claim that our institutions are malleable and so amenable to principles (of justice) may strike *us* as patently obvious: what *is* political philosophy if not (at least in part) the articulation of justice principles for institutions? And yet, Rawls *did* feel the need to emphasize this fact: that (economic) outcomes – and the institutions that produce and legitimate them over time – are mutable and can be bent back towards justice (whatever that turns out to be). Perhaps he was concerned about the creeping dominance of laissez-faire's constitutive anti-political philosophical attitude? In any case, Rawls wants to fight the Hayekian principle that spontaneity is the only path to justice. See, e.g., Hayek's discussion of "social justice" in *Law, Legislation and Liberty*, 2:96: social justice, he says, "is wholly devoid of meaning or content" in a market society, a society in which the distribution of income is the *exclusive* by-product of impersonal processes of economic exchanges. There is, in other words, no space, or need, for the intentional (re)distribution of income by the state. By extension, neither is there any need for action-guiding (justice) principles – the death of political philosophy!

Again, Rawls disagrees: political philosophy is a noble and worthwhile enterprise, and its essential purpose (in part) is to articulate practical, action-guiding principles of justice for the basic structure of society. For Rawls's conception of the proper role of political philosophy, see, e.g., *Justice as Fairness: A Restatement* (Cambridge, MA: Harvard University Press, 2001), §§1.2 and 1.3; and the introduction to the *Lectures on the History of Political Philosophy*, 10–11. For a typical statement of Rawls's preferred principles of justice, see, e.g., *R*, part 2, esp. §13. These are the principles that would be chosen in the original position, Rawls's thought experiment, in which the representatives of free and equal citizens are placed behind a "veil of ignorance." This (veil) obscures all knowledge of the participants and their place in society, which forces them to consider things from an impartial perspective. They are then asked to decide upon a regulative conception of justice and, in Rawls's view, adopt the two principles of justice as fairness. See *TJ*, chap. 3, esp. §26; and *R* 14–17. See also, e.g., Ronald Dworkin, *Taking Rights Seriously* (Cambridge, MA: Harvard University Press, 1977), chap. 6, §1; and Nozick, *Anarchy, State, and Utopia*, chap. 7, §2.

8 For Rawls's conception of the "least advantaged" members of society, see *TJ* §15. A very illuminating and detailed discussion of Rawlsian distributive justice can be found in Samuel Freeman, *Rawls* (London: Routledge, 2007), chap. 3, esp. 99–115, where (according to Freeman's learned and persuasive interpretation of Rawls's theory) the "least advantaged are, in effect, people who earn the least and whose skills are least in demand – in effect, the class of minimum-wage workers." See also, e.g., Ronald Dworkin, *Sovereign Virtue: The Theory and Practice of Equality* (Cambridge, MA: Harvard University Press, 2000), 112–19; and Will Kymlicka, *Contemporary Political Philosophy: An Introduction* (Oxford: Clarendon, 1990), 70–3.

9 For a thorough list of scholars who interpreted Rawls along these lines, see Richard Krouse and Michael Macpherson, "Capitalism, 'Property-Owning Democracy,' and the Welfare State," in *Democracy and the Welfare State*, ed. Amy Gutmann (Princeton, NJ: Princeton University Press, 1988), 79n1. See also Rodney Peffer, *Marxism, Morality and Social Justice* (Princeton, NJ: Princeton University Press, 1990), 378; Hilary Putnam, "A Half-Century of Philosophy, Viewed from Within," *Daedalus* 126, no. 1 (1997): 311–32; and Michael Sandel, *Liberalism and the Limits of Justice* (Cambridge: Cambridge University Press, 1982), chap. 2. For an early exception to this scholarly consensus, see Arthur DiQuattro, "Rawls and Left Criticism," *Political Theory* 11, no. 1 (1983): 53–78, 54: "Rawls's theory is not wedded to a defense of capitalist market society ... and, indeed, dismisses it as inherently unjust."

10 As we shall see, this is a difficult question to answer. See note 15 below. For Rawls's abstract illustration of the difference principle – specifically, how the difference principle helps us to arbitrate between different economic

systems (and the distributive outcomes they produce) – see *R* §13, esp. 62–3. The basic idea here is that an increase in economic inequality is permissible only if it benefits the less advantaged *optimally*. In other words, at some point an increase in inequality is to the detriment of the worse-off – a violation of the difference principle and grounds for reverting to the optimal distribution.

11  See note 9 above.

12  See also *TJ* 372: "From the definition [of goodness as rationality] alone very little can be said about the content of a rational plan, or the particular activities that comprise it." Hence, Rawls's frequent reference to rational autonomy as a *thin* (or purely *formal*) theory of the good. See, e.g., *TJ* 348. But Rawls's ideal of autonomy is also connected to (what he calls) the Aristotelian Principle, which entails a much more substantial claim about human nature and (in turn) human flourishing. See *TJ* §65, esp. 374: "The intuitive idea here is that human beings take more pleasure in doing something as they become more proficient at it, and of two activities they do equally well, they prefer the one calling on a larger repertoire of more intricate and subtle discriminations."

13  See, e.g., *TJ* 54–5, 78–81, and 386–91. See also *CP*, chap. 17, esp. 362–4.

14  See, e.g., *TJ* xv–xvi.

15  See, e.g., *TJ* 248: "The theory of justice [as fairness] does not by itself favor either form of [capitalist or socialist] regime.... The decision as to which system is best for a given people depends upon their circumstances, institutions and historical traditions." For example, it is possible to imagine the least advantaged forsaking income and wealth for decision-making power (and, in turn, self-respect). Such decisions always need to be made democratically and can never be fixed in theory in advance.

16  Rawls takes the idea of property-owning democracy from James E. Meade's *Efficiency, Equality and the Ownership of Property* (London: Allen & Unwin, 1964), chap. 5. For a history of the concept, see, e.g., Ben Jackson, "Revisionism Reconsidered: 'Property-Owning Democracy' and Egalitarian Strategy in Post-war Britain," in *Twentieth-Century British History* 16, no. 4 (2005): 416–40; and Amit Ron, "Visions of Democracy in 'Property-Owning Democracy': Skelton to Rawls and Beyond," *History of Political Thought* 29, no. 1 (2008): 168–87.

17  See, e.g., *TJ* §36, esp. 197–9; *PL* §§8.7 and 8.12; and "The Idea of Public Reason Revisited," *PL* 449, where Rawls says that (American) politics must be "set free from the curse of money." See also, e.g., Jeffrey Bercuson, "Democracy," in *The Cambridge Rawls Lexicon*, ed. Jon Mandle and David Reidy (Cambridge: Cambridge University Press, 2015), 191–2.

18  See note 10 above. See also Joshua Cohen, "Democratic Equality," *Ethics* 99, no. 4 (1989): 727–51, esp. 745–7. Rawls's argument against this idea of a social minimum is also connected to *the* fundamental *philosophical* aim of *Theory*: to provide an alternative to utilitarianism (*TJ* xvii; see also *PL*

xiv–xv). After all, in Rawls's view, the distributive aim of the welfare state is utility, not reciprocity – to find that social minimum for the poor that maximizes the utility of society, i.e., to alleviate poverty without creating disincentives to work (and thus distorting labor markets and undermining general economic output more generally). See also Freeman, *Rawls*, 224–5.

19 Rawls spends very little time on command-economy state socialism. This system is unacceptable to him because its emphasis on the need for society-wide economic planning makes it incompatible with "the important liberty of free choice of occupation" (*TJ* 242; see also *R* 138).

20 For example, in some cases, property-owning democracy will entail private ownership of the means of production by corporations with high levels of internal democracy; in others, the means of production will be owned and managed directly by unions or cooperatives of workers. In some cases, a high level of society's output will be directed towards generous transfer payments to individuals; in others, there will be a stronger emphasis on saving for future generations. For a catalog of possible arrangements along these lines, see, e.g., Branko Horvat, "Labour-Managed Economies," in *The New Palgrave Dictionary of Economics*, ed. Matias Vernengo, Esteban Perez Caldentey, and Barkley J. Rosser, Jr., 79–84 (London: Palgrave Macmillan, 1987); and John Roemer, *A Future for Socialism* (Cambridge, MA: Harvard University Press, 1994), §9.

21 The intergenerational transmission of wealth is a prominent theme of chap. 14 below.

22 See also *PL* 359–60, where Rawls expresses dismay at the Supreme Court's refusal (in *Buckley* and *First National*) to place limits on election campaign donations (and expenditures). This is incompatible with the fair value of the political liberties, which requires preventing "those with greater property and wealth, and the greater skills of organization which accompany them, from controlling the electoral process to their advantage." This is doubly disappointing, says Rawls, because the "fair value" thesis is implicit in the Constitution (Article 1, §2), and in many of the Supreme Court's past interpretations of it (*Wesberry* and *Reynolds*).

23 For a general account of the idea of stability in Rawls's philosophy, see Edward F. McClennan, "Justice and the Problem of Stability," *Philosophy & Public Affairs* 18, no. 1 (1989): 3–30. See also the introductory section of chapter 14 below.

## 14 Piketty on Wealth and Inequality

1 See, e.g., *TJ* §40 (esp. 222) and §77 (esp. 442). See also, e.g., Thomas E. Hill, Jr, "The Problem of Stability in Political Liberalism," *Pacific Philosophical Quarterly* 75 (1994): 332–52.

2  See, e.g., *PL* 37, where Rawls acknowledges the "paradoxical" quality of *liberal* oppression. And yet he holds steadfast to the belief that a society "united ... on the reasonable liberalisms of Kant or Mill ... would require the sanctions of state power to remain so." See also Burton Dreben, "On Rawls and Political Liberalism," in *The Cambridge Companion to Rawls*, ed. Samuel Freeman (Cambridge: Cambridge University Press, 2006), 319: "This, I claim, has never been said before in the history of philosophy. It is a totally radical view."

3  Some interpreters regard this project as worthwhile and successful; others find it incoherent and unappealing. For the former group, see, e.g., Samuel Scheffler, "The Appeal of Political Liberalism," *Ethics* 105, no. 1 (1994): 4–22; and Paul Weithman, *Why Political Liberalism? On John Rawls's Political Turn* (Oxford: Oxford University Press, 2010), esp. chaps. 9–10. For the latter group, see, e.g., Beiner, *Political Philosophy*, chap. 13, esp. 205–11; and Jeremy Waldron, *God, Locke and Equality: Christian Foundations of John Locke's Political Thought* (Cambridge: Cambridge University Press, 2002), chap. 8, esp. §6.

4  For Rawls's concept of a "freestanding political conception" of justice, see *PL* 10–13 and 140–5. For the (related) distinction between political and comprehensive liberalism, see *PL* xxvi–xviii and xlii–xliii.

5  See, e.g., *PL* xlvi–xlviii. We return to this important point – concession, really – below.

6  For Rawls's concept of the "overlapping consensus," see *PL* 144–6 and 168–72. For the concept of comprehensive doctrines, see *PL* 13 and 59.

7  Rawls acknowledges that this is not always the case: that some comprehensive doctrines do not gel easily with liberal principles and institutions. But even the adherents of these doctrines are reasonable enough to see the value of liberal institutions, without which they would not be able to pursue their chosen way of life. Being reasonable, they accept that state power cannot be used to convert nonbelievers, for this power could be used against them. See, e.g., *PL* 169, where Rawls discusses the relationship between the freestanding political conception of justice and the various comprehensive doctrines that exist in society. This relationship varies: some comprehensive doctrines are "congruent with" the (freestanding) political conception, others are "supportive of" it, others are (at least) "not in conflict with ... the political conception of justice for a democratic regime."

8  See Simone Chambers, "Justice or Legitimacy, Barricades or Public Reason? The Politics of Property-Owning Democracy," in *Property-Owning Democracy: Rawls and Beyond*, ed. Martin O'Neill and Thad Williamson (London: Blackwell, 2012), 17–32, esp. 24–7. There, Chambers examines the lingering hold that ideas of desert and personal responsibility still exercise over the public cultures of Western democracies (especially the United States). See also, e.g., Kymlicka, *Contemporary Political Philosophy*, chap. 3, esp. 58; and Samuel Scheffler, "Responsibility, Reactive Attitudes,

and Liberalism in Philosophy and Politics," *Philosophy & Public Affairs* 21, no. 4 (1992): 299–323, esp. 305–10.

9 See chapter 13, note 22 above.

10 The letter to Phillipe Van Parijs, dated June 23, 1998, can be found in a special issue of *Revue de philosophie économique* 7, no. 1 (2003): 7–20.

11 For Rawls's account of political institutional maintenance as a common project (indeed, a common *good*), see, e.g., *TJ* §79; *PL* §8.6; and *LP* §15. See also, e.g., Bercuson, *John Rawls and the History of Political Thought*, chap. 2, esp. 52–4.

12 See, e.g., Heather Boushey, J. Bradford DeLong, and Marshall Steinbaum, eds., *After Piketty: The Agenda for Economics and Inequality* (Cambridge, MA: Harvard University Press, 2017), esp. part 1.

13 See, e.g., Friedrich Engels, *The Condition of the Working Class in England*, ed. David McLellan (Oxford: Oxford University Press, 1993), esp. chap. 2.

14 Simon Kuznets, "Shares of Upper Income Groups in Income and Savings," National Bureau of Economic Research #55, no. 1 (1953), 1–67. See also Kuznets, "Economic Growth and Income Inequality," *American Economic Review* 45, no. 1 (1955): 1–28, esp. 3–6.

15 For an equally skeptical account of Kuznets's theory, see Scheidel, *Great Leveler*, chap. 13.

16 Kuznets, "Economic Growth and Income Inequality," 28. In the concluding remarks of his presidential address, Kuznets acknowledges the political ideological implications of his conclusions: if capitalism is in fact conducive to widely shared, evenly spread prosperity, then there is a powerful and compelling argument to keep the "underdeveloped countries within the orbit of the free [i.e., noncommunist] world."

17 See, e.g., Claudia Goldin and Robert A. Margo, "The Great Compression: The Wage Structure in the United States at Mid-Century," *Quarterly Journal of Economics* 107, no. 1 (1992): 1–34.

18 See, e.g., *C* 24, figure 1.1: "The top decile share in US national income dropped from 45–50 per cent in the 1910s–1920s to less than 35 per cent in the 1950s (this is the fall documented by Kuznets); it then rose from less than 35 per cent in the 1970s to 45–50 per cent in the 2000s–2010s." This is in large part a by-product of the emergence of what Piketty (264–5) calls "supermanagers" – top executives who possess the freedom to set their own level of (unsurprisingly spectacular) remuneration. This phenomenon is particularly pronounced in the United States (291–6), where such incomes have been subject to plummeting rates of marginal income taxation.

19 See, e.g., Buchanan's discussion of the "political role of markets": markets, he says, "reduce or even eliminate the need for hands-on intrusions" by the state in the economic domain (*NAC* 66).

20 We turn to this issue in the afterword below. See also, e.g., Lindsey and Teles, *Captured Economy*, esp. chap. 7; and Joseph Stiglitz, *The Price of Inequality: How*

*Today's Divided Society Endangers Our Future* (New York: W.W. Norton, 2012), esp. chap. 4.

21  See, e.g., *C* 476: "The financial markets were much less tightly regulated after 1980 than before."

22  See, e.g., *C* 477: "The state's great leap forward has already taken place: there will be no second leap – not like the first one, in any event." There is one notable exception here: Piketty criticizes today's states for "spend[ing] far more in interest on the debt" than they do "invest[ing] in higher education" (567; for Piketty's own proposal for reform in higher education, see 486–7). This is a recurring theme of *Capital*: that an essential front in the fight against income inequality is "the diffusion of knowledge [wrought by] investment in training and skills" (30). After all, education is "the public good par excellence"; without widespread, easy access to it, the economic structure ossifies (30). As an example, here, Piketty discusses the case of China, where the state-sponsored democratization of education has produced a flattening of income inequality. Of course, not everyone is convinced by this correlation: Scheidel, *Great Leveler* (793–5), for example, suggests that this convergence is the by-product of a decline in income for marginally better-educated workers, not a substantial convergence across classes.

23  The 1 per cent tax applies to net assets worth less than €5 million. For those with net assets above €5 million, Piketty suggests a 2 per cent tax; and for those whose assets exceed €1 billion, a 5–10 per cent tax. See 517–18 and 529–30.

24  See, e.g., Daron Acemoglu and James A. Robinson, *Why Nations Fail: The Origins of Power, Prosperity, and Poverty* (New York: Crown Publishers, 2012), chap. 3, esp. 73–6, 79–83, and 87–95, and chap. 9.

25  See, e.g., Kevin O'Rourke and Jeffrey Williamson, *Globalization and History: The Evolution of a Nineteenth-Century Atlantic Economy* (Cambridge, MA: MIT Press, 1999), esp. chaps. 1–3.

26  See also Julia Cagé and Lucie Gadenne, "The Fiscal Cost of Trade Liberalization," *Explorations in Economic History* 70, no. 1 (2018): 1–24, esp. §§1 and 2; and Thomas Piketty and Nancy Qian, "Income Inequality and Progressive Income Taxation in China and India, 1986–2015," *American Economic Journal: Applied Economics* 1, no. 2 (2009): 53–63, esp. 60–1.

27  Piketty's verdict is grim: it is undeniably true, he says, that a not insignificant "part of the blame [for chronic economic and political underdevelopment in debtor states] lies with the rich countries and international organizations" (*C* 491).

# Bibliography


Acemoglu, Daron, and James A. Robinson. *Why Nations Fail: The Origins of Power, Prosperity, and Poverty.* New York: Crown Publishers, 2012.

Allen, Robert C. *Farm to Factory: A Reinterpretation of the Soviet Industrial Revolution.* Princeton, NJ: Princeton University Press, 2003.

Aubrey, John. *Brief Lives.* Edited by John Buchanan-Brown. London: Penguin Classics, 2000.

Baldwin, John W. *The Medieval Theories of the Just Price: Romanists, Canonists and Theologians in the Twelfth and Thirteenth Centuries.* Philadelphia: American Philosophical Society, 1959.

Ball, Terrence. *Reappraising Political Theory: Revisionist Studies in the History of Political Thought.* Oxford: Clarendon, 1995.

Baron, Hans. "Machiavelli the Republican Citizen and Author of The Prince." In *In Search of Florentine Humanism: Essays on the Transition from Medieval to Modern Thought,* edited by Hans Baron, 101–51. Princeton, NJ: Princeton University Press, 1988.

Bastiat, Frédéric. *Economic Harmonies.* Translated by W. Hayden Boyers. Edited by George B. de Huszar. Irvington-on-Hudson, NY: Foundation for Economic Education, 1996.

Baxter, Stephen. *England's Rise to Greatness, 1660–1763.* Berkeley: University of California Press, 1983.

Beiner, Ronald. *Civil Religion: A Dialogue in the History of Political Philosophy.* Cambridge: Cambridge University Press, 2011.

– *Dangerous Minds: Nietzsche, Heidegger, and the Return of the Far Right.* Philadelphia: University of Pennsylvania Press, 2018.

– *Political Philosophy: What It Is and Why It Matters.* Cambridge: Cambridge University Press, 2014.

Bell, Daniel. *The Cultural Contradictions of Capitalism.* New York: Basic Books, 1996.

Benhabib, Seyla. "On Hegel, Women and Irony." In *Feminism and History of Philosophy*, edited by Genevieve Lloyd, 281–98. Oxford: Oxford University Press, 2002.

Bennett, H.S. *Life on the English Manor: A Study of Peasant Conditions, 1150–1400*. Cambridge: Cambridge University Press, 1960.

Bercuson, Jeffrey. "Democracy." In *The Cambridge Rawls Lexicon*, edited by Jon Mandle and David Reidy, 190–4. Cambridge: Cambridge University Press, 2015.

– *John Rawls and the History of Political Thought: The Rousseauvian and Hegelian Heritage of Justice as Fairness*. New York: Routledge, 2014.

Berlin, Isaiah. *Freedom and Its Betrayal: Six Enemies of Human Liberty*. Edited by Henry Hardy. Princeton, NJ: Princeton University Press, 2014.

– *The Roots of Romanticism*. Edited by Henry Hardy. Princeton, NJ: Princeton University Press, 2013.

Berman, Shari. *The Primacy of Politics: Social Democracy and the Making of Europe's Twentieth Century*. Cambridge: Cambridge University Press, 2006.

Bittner, Rüdiger. "Ressentiment." In *Nietzsche, Genealogy, Morality*, edited by Richard Schacht, 127–38. Berkeley: University of California Press, 1994.

Bloch, Marc. *French Rural History: An Essay on Its Basic Characteristics*. Translated by Janet Sondheimer. Berkeley: University of California Press, 1970.

Bloom, Allan. *Giants and Dwarfs: Essays, 1960–1990*. New York: Simon & Schuster, 1990.

Bock, Gisela, Quentin Skinner, and Maurizio Viroli, eds. *Machiavelli and Republicanism*. Cambridge: Cambridge University Press, 2011.

Boushey, Heather, J. Bradford DeLong, and Marshall Steinbaum. *After Piketty: The Agenda for Economics and Inequality*. Cambridge, MA: Harvard University Press, 2017.

Bowle, John. *Hobbes and His Critics*. London: Routledge, 2013.

Bowler, Anne. "Politics as Art: Italian Futurism and Fascism." *Theory & Society* 20, no. 6 (1991): 763–94.

Bradstock, Andrew, ed. *Winstanley and the Diggers, 1649–1999*. Portland, OR: Frank Cass, 2000.

Brewer, John, Neil McKendrick, and J.H. Plumb. *The Birth of a Consumer Society: The Commercialization of Eighteenth-Century England*. Bloomington: University of Indiana Press, 1982.

Brown, Ivor. "Aspects of the Guild Idea." *New Age* 17, no. 1 (1915): 150–1.

Burke, Edmund. *The Correspondence of Edmund Burke*. Edited by Thomas W. Copeland. Chicago: University of Chicago Press, 1958.

– *The Philosophy of Edmund Burke: A Selection from His Speeches and Writings*. Edited by Louis I. Bredcold and Ralph G. Ross. Ann Arbor: University of Michigan Press, 1960.

– *Reflections on the Revolution in France*. Edited by J.G.A. Pocock. Indianapolis, IN: Hackett, 1987.

Butters, H.C. *Governors and Government in Early Sixteenth-Century Florence, 1502–1519*. Oxford: Clarendon, 1985.

Cagé, Julia, and Lucie Gadenne. "The Fiscal Cost of Trade Liberalization." *Explorations in Economic History* 70, no. 1 (2018): 1–24.

Cardoza, Anthony L. *Agrarian Elites and Italian Fascism: The Province of Bologna, 1901–1926.* Princeton, NJ: Princeton University Press, 1982.

Cassirer, Ernst. *The Question of Jean-Jacques Rousseau.* Translated by Peter Gay. New Haven, CT: Yale University Press, 1989.

– *Rousseau, Kant, Goethe: Two Essays.* Translated by James Guttman, Paul Oskar Kristeller, and John Herman Randall, Jr. Princeton, NJ: Princeton University Press, 1945.

Chambers, Simone. "Justice or Legitimacy, Barricades or Public Reason? The Politics of Property-Owning Democracy." In *Property-Owning Democracy: Rawls and Beyond,* edited by Martin O'Neill and Thad Williamson, 17–32. London: Blackwell, 2012.

Cheyney, Edward P. *Translations and Reprints from the Original Sources of European History: Established in 1894.* New York: Longman's & Green, 1902.

Claeys, Gregory. *Citizens and Saints: Politics and Anti-Politics in Early British Socialism.* Cambridge: Cambridge University Press, 1989.

Clarke, Peter F. *The Keynesian Revolution in the Making, 1924–1936.* Oxford: Clarendon, 1988.

Clover, Charles. *Black Wind, White Snow: The Rise of Russia's New Nationalism.* New Haven, CT: Yale University Press, 2016.

Cohen, Joshua. "Democratic Equality." *Ethics* 99, no. 4 (1989): 727–51.

Cole, G.D.H. *Labour in the Commonwealth: A Book for the Younger Generation.* London: Headley Bros., 1919.

– *Social Theory.* London: Methuen, 1920.

Coles, Romand. "Liberty, Equality, and Receptive Generosity: Neo-Nietzschean Reflections on Ethics and Politics of Coalition." *American Political Science Review* 90, no. 2 (1996): 375–88.

Collini, Stefan. *English Pasts: Essays in Culture and History.* Oxford: Oxford University Press, 1999.

Comay, Rebecca. *Mourning Sickness: Hegel and the French Revolution.* Stanford, CA: Stanford University Press, 2011.

Cone, Carl. *Burke and the Nature of Politics.* Louisville: University of Kentucky Press, 2014.

Conquest, Robert. *The Great Terror: A Reassessment.* Oxford: Oxford University Press, 2008.

Corner, Paul. *The Fascist Party and Popular Opinion in Mussolini's Italy.* Oxford: Oxford University Press, 2012.

Coulton, G.G. *The Medieval Village.* New York: Dover Publications, 1989.

De Grand, Alexander J. *Italian Fascism: Its Origins and Development.* Lincoln: University of Nebraska Press, 1982.

Deleuze, Gilles. *Nietzsche and Philosophy.* Translated by Hugh Tomlinson. New York: Columbia University Press, 1983.

Den Otter, Sandra M. *British Idealism and Social Explanation: A Study in Late Victorian Thought.* Oxford: Oxford University Press, 1996.

Dent, Nicholas. *Rousseau.* London: Routledge, 2005.

– *A Rousseau Dictionary.* London: Wiley-Blackwell, 1992.

Dickey, Laurence. W. *Hegel: Religion, Economics, and the Politics of Spirit, 1770–1807.* Cambridge: Cambridge University Press, 1987.

DiQuattro, Anthony. "Rawls and Left Criticism." *Political Theory* 11, no. 1 (1983): 53–78.

Dreben, Burton. "On Rawls and Political Liberalism." In *The Cambridge Companion to Rawls,* edited by Samuel Freeman, 316–46. Cambridge: Cambridge University Press, 2006.

Duby, Georges. *The Three Orders: Feudal Society Imagined.* Translated by Arthur Goldhammer. Chicago: University of Chicago Press, 1980.

Dunn, John. *The Political Thought of John Locke: An Historical Account of the Argument of the "Two Treatises of Government."* Cambridge: Cambridge University Press, 1969.

Dworkin, Ronald. *Sovereign Virtue: The Theory and Practice of Equality.* Cambridge, MA: Harvard University Press, 2000.

– *Taking Rights Seriously.* Cambridge, MA: Harvard University Press, 1977.

Ehrenberg, Victor. *From Solon to Socrates: Greek History and Civilization during the 6th and 5th Centuries B.C.* New York: Routledge Classics, 2011.

Engels, Friedrich. *The Condition of the Working Class in England.* Edited by David McLellan. Oxford: Oxford University Press, 1993.

Fay, Margaret, Johannes Hengstenberg, and Barbara Stuckey. "The Influence of Adam Smith on Marx's Theory of Alienation." *Science & Society* 47, no. 2 (1983): 129–51.

Ferguson, Adam. *An Essay on the History of Civil Society.* Edited by Fania Oz-Salzberger. Cambridge: Cambridge University Press, 1995.

Figes, Orlando. *A People's Tragedy: The Russian Revolution, 1891–1924.* New York: Penguin, 1998.

Flynn, John T. *The Road Ahead: America's Creeping Revolution.* New York: Devin-Adair, 1949.

Foster, William Z. *Outline of the Political History of the Americas.* New York: International Publishers, 1951.

Freeden, Michael. *Liberalism Divided: A Study in British Political Thought, 1914–1939.* Oxford: Oxford University Press, 1986.

Freeman, Samuel. *Rawls.* London: Routledge, 2007.

Fukuyama, Francis. *The End of History and the Last Man.* New York: Free Press, 2006.

Gardner, Richard N. *Sterling-Dollar Diplomacy in Current Perspective: The Origins and the Prospects of Our International Economic Order.* New York: Columbia University Press, 1980.

Gay, Peter. *The Dilemma of Democratic Socialism: Eduard Bernstein's Challenge to Marx.* New York: Octagon Books, 1979.

Geuss, Raymond. "Nietzsche and Morality." *European Journal of Philosophy* 5, no. 1 (1997): 1–20.

Gilbert, Felix. *The End of the European Era, 1890 to the Present.* New York: Norton, 1970.

– *History: Choice and Commitment.* Cambridge, MA: Harvard University Press, 1977.

– *Machiavelli and Guicciardini: Politics and History in Sixteenth-Century Florence.* New York: W.W. Norton, 1981.

Goldin, Claudia, and Robert A. Margo. "The Great Compression: The Wage Structure in the United States at Mid-Century." *Quarterly Journal of Economics* 107, no. 1 (1992): 1–34.

Goldman, Lawrence. *The Life of R.H. Tawney: Socialism and History.* London: Bloomsbury Academic, 2013.

Golomb, Jacob, and R.S. Wistrich, eds. *Nietzsche, Godfather of Fascism?: On the Uses and Abuses of a Philosophy.* Princeton, NJ: Princeton University Press, 2002.

Goodrick-Clarke, Nicholas. *Black Sun: Aryan Cults, Esoteric Nazism, and the Politics of Identity.* New York: New York University Press, 2002.

Goodwin, Craufurd D. "The Art of an Ethical Life: Keynes and Bloomsbury." In *The Cambridge Companion to Keynes,* edited by R.E. Backhouse and B.W. Bateman, 217–36. Cambridge: Cambridge University Press, 2006.

Greenleaf, W.H. *The British Political Tradition.* London: Methuen, 1983.

Gregor, A. James. *Italian Fascism and Developmental Dictatorship.* Princeton, NJ: Princeton University Press, 1979.

– *Young Mussolini and the Intellectual Origins of Fascism.* Berkeley: University of California Press, 1979.

Griffin, Roger, ed. *Fascism: A Reader.* Oxford: Oxford University Press, 1995.

– *The Nature of Fascism.* New York: St. Martin's, 1991.

Gulick, Charles A. *Austria from Habsburg to Hitler.* Berkeley: University of California Press, 1948.

Gurney, John. *Gerrard Winstanley: The Digger's Life and Legacy.* London: Pluto, 2013.

Habermas, Jürgen. *The Theory of Communicative Action.* Vol. 2, *Lifeworld and System.* Translated by Thomas McCarthy. Boston: Beacon, 1984.

Hardimon, Michael O. *Hegel's Social Philosophy: The Project of Reconciliation.* Cambridge: Cambridge University Press, 1994.

Hartwell, Richard M. *A History of the Mont Pelerin Society.* Indianapolis, IN: Liberty Fund, 1995.

Hatab, Lawrence J. *A Nietzschean Defense of Democracy: An Experiment in Postmodern Politics.* Chicago: Open Court, 1995.

Hayek, Friedrich A, ed. *Collectivist Economic Planning: Critical Studies on the Possibilities of Socialism.* London: Routledge, 1935.

– *The Constitution of Liberty.* Edited by Bruce Caldwell. Chicago: University of Chicago Press, 1960.

– *The Essence of Hayek.* Edited by Chiaki Nishiyama and Kurt R. Leube. Stanford: Hoover Institution Press, 1984.

- *Law, Legislation and Liberty: A New Statement of the Liberal Principles of Justice and Political Economy.* London: Routledge, 2013.
- *The Road to Serfdom: Text and Documents.* Edited by Bruce Caldwell. Chicago: University of Chicago Press, 2007.
- "The Use of Knowledge in Society." *American Economic Review* 35, 4 (1945): 519–30.

Hegel. G.W.F. *Elements of the Philosophy of Right.* Translated by Allen W. Wood. Cambridge: Cambridge University Press, 1991.

Heilbroner, Ronald L., and William S. Milberg. *The Making of Economic Society.* Upper Saddle River, NJ: Prentice Hall, 2002.

Hicks, Stephen V., and Alan Rosenberg. "Nietzsche and Untimeliness: The 'Philosopher of the Future' as the Figure of Disruptive Wisdom." *Journal of Nietzsche Studies* 25, no. 1 (2003): 1–34.

Hill, Thomas E., Jr. "The Problem of Stability in Political Liberalism." *Pacific Philosophical Quarterly* 75 (1994): 333–52.

Hitchens, Christopher. *God Is Not Great: How Religion Poisons Everything.* New York: Twelve, 2007.

Hobbes, Thomas. *Behemoth.* Edited by Stephen Holmes. Chicago: University of Chicago Press, 1990.

- *Leviathan.* Edited by C.B. Macpherson. London: Penguin, 1968.

Hobhouse, L.T. *Liberalism and Other Writings.* Cambridge: Cambridge University Press, 1994.

Hobsbawm, Eric. *The Age of Extremes: A History of the World, 1914–1991.* New York: Vintage, 1996.

Hobson, J.A. (1933). *Work and Wealth: A Human Valuation.* London: G. Allen & Unwin, 1933.

Holland, Henry Scott. *Our Neighbours.* London: A.R. Mowbray, 1911.

Holub, Robert C. *Nietzsche's Jewish Problem: Between Anti-Semitism and Anti-Judaism.* Princeton, NJ: Princeton University Press, 2016.

Honig, Bonnie. *Political Theory and the Displacement of Politics.* Ithaca, NY: Cornell University Press, 1993.

Hornblower, Simon. *The Greek World, 479–323 BC.* London: Methuen, 1983.

Horowitz, Gad. *Canadian Labour in Politics.* Toronto: University of Toronto Press, 1968.

Horvat, Branko. "Labour-Managed Economies." In *The New Palgrave Dictionary of Economics,* edited by Matias Vernengo, Esteban Perez Caldentey, and Barkley J. Rosser, Jr., 79–84. London: Palgrave Macmillan, 1987.

Hosking, Geoffrey A. *Russia: People and Empire, 1552–1917.* Cambridge, MA: Harvard University Press, 1997.

Huizinga, Johan. *The Waning of the Middle Ages.* Mineola, NY: Dover Publications, 1999.

Ialongo, Ernest. "Filippo Tomasso Marinetti: The Futurist as Fascist, 1929–37." *Journal of Modern Italian Studies* 18, no. 4 (2013): 393–418.

Irwin, Douglas A. *Against the Tide: An Intellectual History of Free Trade.* Princeton, NJ: Princeton University Press, 1996.

Izenberg, Gerald N. *Impossible Individuality: Romanticism, Revolution, and the Origins of Modern Selfhood, 1787–1802*. Princeton, NJ: Princeton University Press, 1992.

Jackson, Ben. "Equality of Nothing? Social Justice on the British Left, c. 1911–31." *Journal of Political Ideologies* 8, no. 1 (2003): 83–110.

– "Revisionism Reconsidered: 'Property-Owning Democracy' and Egalitarian Strategy in Post-war Britain." *Twentieth-Century British History* 16, no. 4 (2005): 416–40.

Jelavich, Barbara. *Modern Austria: Empire and Republic, 1815–1986*. Cambridge: Cambridge University Press, 1987.

Joll, James. *Three Intellectuals in Politics*. New York: Pantheon Books, 1961.

Jones, J.R. *The First Whigs: The Politics of the Exclusion Crisis, 1678–1683*. Oxford: Oxford University Press, 1966.

Jones, Peter d'Alroy. *The Christian Socialist Revival, 1877–1914: Religion, Class, and Social Conscience in Late-Victorian England*. Princeton, NJ: Princeton University Press, 1968.

Judt, Tony, and Timothy Snyder. *Thinking the Twentieth Century*. New York: Penguin, 2012.

Kant, Immanuel. "Idea of a Universal History with a Cosmopolitan Purpose." In *Kant: Political Writings*, edited by H.S. Reiss, 41–53. Cambridge: Cambridge University Press, 1991.

– "On the Common Saying: 'This May Be True in Theory But Does Not Apply in Practice.'" In *Kant: Political Writings*, edited by H.S. Reiss, 61–92. Cambridge: Cambridge University Press, 1991.

– "The Metaphysics of Morals." In *Kant: Political Writings*, edited by H.S. Reiss, 131–75. Cambridge: Cambridge University Press, 1991.

– "Perpetual Peace: A Philosophical Sketch." In *Kant: Political Writings*, edited by H.S. Reiss, 93–130. Cambridge: Cambridge University Press, 1991.

Kasper, Shari D. "The Legacy of Keynes as Public Intellectual." In *Keynes's General Theory after Seventy Years*, edited by R.W. Dimand, R.A. Mundell, and A. Vercelli, 43–62. London: Palgrave Macmillan, 2011.

Katz, Jacob. *From Prejudice to Destruction: Anti-Semitism, 1700–1933*. Cambridge, MA: Harvard University Press, 1980.

Kaufmann, Walter A. *Nietzsche: Philosopher, Psychologist, Antichrist*. Princeton, NJ: Princeton University Press, 1968.

Keynes, John Maynard. "The Arts Council of Great Britain: Its Policies and Hopes." In *The Collected Writings of John Maynard Keynes*, edited by Elizabeth Johnson and Donald Moggridge, 28:295–372. Cambridge: Royal Economic Society, 1978.

– "Economic Consequences of the Peace." In *The Collected Writings of John Maynard Keynes*, edited by Elizabeth Johnson and Donald Moggridge, 2:1–191. Cambridge: Royal Economic Society, 1978.

– "The End of Laissez-Faire." *In The Collected Writings of John Maynard Keynes*, edited by Elizabeth Johnson and Donald Moggridge, 9:272–94. Cambridge: Royal Economic Society, 1978.

– *The General Theory of Employment, Interest and Money.* In *The Collected Writings of John Maynard Keynes,* edited by Elizabeth Johnson and Donald Moggridge, 7:1–428. Cambridge: Royal Economic Society, 1978.

– "The Political Doctrine of Edmund Burke." Collected Papers at King's College (UA/20.3), 1904.

– "A Short View from Russia." In *The Collected Writings of John Maynard Keynes,* edited by Elizabeth Johnson and Donald Moggridge, 9:255–71. Cambridge: Royal Economic Society, 1978.

Kilivris, Michael. "Beyond Goods and Services: Toward a Nietzschean Critique of Capitalism." *Kritike* 5, no. 2 (2011): 26–40.

Kirby, James E. "R.H. Tawney and Christian Social Teaching: Religion and the Rise of Capitalism Reconsidered." *English Historical Review* 131, no. 551 (2016): 793–822.

Kołakowski, Leszek. *Main Currents of Marxism: Its Rise, Growth, and Dissolution.* Translated by P.S. Falla. Oxford: Clarendon, 1978.

Krouse, Richard, and Michael Macpherson. "Capitalism, 'Property-Owning Democracy,' and the Welfare State." In *Democracy and the Welfare State,* edited by Amy Gutmann, 79–106. Princeton, NJ: Princeton University Press, 1988.

Kuznets, Simon. "Economic Growth and Income Inequality." *American Economic Review* 45, no. 1 (1955): 1–28.

– "Shares of Upper Income Groups in Income and Savings." *National Bureau of Economic Research #55* 1, no. 1 (1953): 1–67.

Kymlicka, Will. *Contemporary Political Philosophy: An Introduction.* Oxford: Clarendon, 1990.

Laborde, Cécile. *Pluralist Thought and the State in Britain and France, 1900–25.* New York: St. Martin's, 2000.

Langford, Paul. *A Polite and Commercial People: England, 1727–1783.* Oxford: Oxford University Press, 1989.

Laqueur, Walter. *Fascism: A Reader's Guide.* Berkeley: University of California Press, 1976.

Laslett, Peter. "Introduction." In *Locke's Two Treatises of Government,* edited by Peter Laslett, 3–126. Cambridge: Cambridge University Press, 2012.

Leigh, R.A. "Jean-Jacques Rousseau and the Myth of Antiquity." In *Classical Influences on Western Thought, 1650–1870,* edited by R.R. Bolgar, 155–68. Cambridge: Cambridge University Press, 1979.

Lenin, Vladimir. "The Immediate Tasks of the Soviet Government." In *Collected Works,* edited by Victor Jerome, 27:235–78. Moscow: Progress Publishers, 1960.

– "Lecture on the 1905 Revolution." In *Collected Works,* edited by Victor Jerome, 23:236–53. Moscow: Progress Publishers, 1960.

– "Left-Wing Communism: An Infantile Disorder." In *Collected Works,* edited by Victor Jerome, 31:17–118. Moscow: Progress Publishers, 1960.

– "Letter to the American Workers." In *Collected Works,* edited by Victor Jerome, 28:62–75. Moscow: Progress Publishers, 1960.

– "The Proletarian Revolution and the Renegade Kautsky." In *Collected Works*, edited by Victor Jerome, 28:105–13. Moscow: Progress Publishers, 1960.

– "State and Revolution." In *Collected Works*, edited by Victor Jerome, 25:385–540. Moscow: Progress Publishers, 1960.

– "The Tasks of the Russian Social-Democrats." In *Collected Works*, edited by Victor Jerome, 2:323–54. Moscow: Progress Publishers, 1960.

– "Two Tactics of Social Democracy in the Democratic Revolution." In *Collected Works*, edited by Victor Jerome, 9:15–140. Moscow: Progress Publishers, 1960.

– "What Is to Be Done?" In *Collected Works*, edited by Victor Jerome, 5:347–568. Moscow: Progress Publishers, 1960.

Lindenfeld, David. *The Practical Imagination: The German Sciences of State in the Nineteenth Century*. Chicago: University of Chicago Press, 1997.

Lindsey, Brink, and Steven Teles. *The Captured Economy: How the Powerful Enrich Themselves, Slow Down Growth, and Increase Inequality*. Oxford: Oxford University Press, 2017.

Little, Lester K. *Religious Poverty and the Profit Economy in Medieval Europe*. Ithaca, NY: Cornell University Press, 1978.

Locke, John. *Second Treatise of Government*. Edited by C.B. Macpherson. Indianapolis, IN: Hackett, 1980.

Lovejoy, Arthur O. *The Great Chain of Being: A Study of the History of an Idea*. Cambridge, MA: Harvard University Press, 1936.

Lukács, Georg. *The Young Hegel: Studies in the Relations between Dialectics and Economics*. Translated by Rodney Livingstone. Cambridge, MA: MIT Press, 1976.

Machiavelli, Niccolò. *The Prince*. Edited and translated by David Wootton. Indianapolis, IN: Hackett, 1995.

MacIntyre, Alasdair. "The Socialism of R.H. Tawney." In *Alasdair Macintyre's Engagement with Marxism*, edited by Paul Blackledge and Neil Douglas Davidson, 299–303. London: Brill, 2008.

Macpherson, C.B. *Burke*. Oxford: Oxford University Press, 1980.

– *The Political Theory of Possessive Individualism: Hobbes to Locke*. Oxford: Clarendon, 1962.

Mandel, Ernest. *The Formation of the Economic Thought of Karl Marx: 1843 to Capital*. London: NLB, 1975.

Manuel, Frank E. *A Requiem for Karl Marx*. Cambridge, MA: Harvard University Press, 1995.

Marglin, Stephen A., and Juliet B. Schor, eds. *The Golden Age of Capitalism: Reinterpreting the Postwar Experience*. Oxford: Oxford University Press, 1990.

Marinetti, F.T. "The Futurist Manifesto." In *Readings in Political Ideologies since the Rise of Modern Science*, edited by H.B. McCullough and Wolfgang Depner, 155–7. Oxford: Oxford University Press, 2013.

Marwick, Arthur. "Middle Opinion in the Thirties: Planning, Progress and Political 'Agreement.'" *English Historical Review* 79, no. 311 (1964): 285–98.

Marx, Karl. "The Civil War in France." In *The Marx-Engels Reader*, edited by Robert C. Tucker, 618–53. New York: Norton, 1978.

– "Contribution to the Critique of Hegel's Philosophy of Right." In *The Marx-Engels Reader*, edited by Robert C. Tucker, 16–25. New York: Norton, 1978.

– "Critique of the Gotha Program." In *The Marx-Engels Reader*, edited by Robert C. Tucker, 525–41. New York: Norton, 1978.

– "Discovering Hegel (Marx to His Father)." In *The Marx-Engels Reader*, edited by Robert C. Tucker, 7–8. New York: Norton, 1978.

– "Economic and Philosophic Manuscripts of 1844." In *The Marx-Engels Reader*, edited by Robert C. Tucker, 66–125. New York: Norton, 1978.

– "The Eighteenth Brumaire of Louis Bonaparte." In *The Marx-Engels Reader*, edited by Robert C. Tucker, 594–617. New York: Norton, 1978.

– "For a Ruthless Critique of Everything Existing (Marx to Arnold Ruge)." In *The Marx-Engels Reader*, edited by Robert C. Tucker, 12–15. New York: Norton, 1978.

– "On the Jewish Question." In *The Marx-Engels Reader*, edited by Robert C. Tucker, 26–52. New York: Norton, 1978.

– "Preface to a Contribution to the Critique of Political Economy." In *The Marx-Engels Reader*, edited by Robert C. Tucker, 3–6. New York: Norton, 1978.

– "Theses on Feuerbach." In *The Marx-Engels Reader*, edited by Robert C. Tucker, 143–5. New York: Norton, 1978.

Marx, Karl, and Friedrich Engels. *Manifesto of the Communist Party*. In *The Marx-Engels Reader*, edited by Robert C. Tucker, 469–500. New York: Norton, 1978.

Massie, Robert. K. *Peter the Great: His Life and World*. New York: Modern Library, 2012.

Masters, Roger D. *The Political Philosophy of Rousseau*. Princeton, NJ: Princeton University Press, 2015.

Mattingly, Garrett. *Renaissance Diplomacy*. Boston: Houghton Mifflin, 1955.

May, Simon. *Nietzsche's Ethics and His War on "Morality."* Oxford: Oxford University Press, 1999.

Mazower, Mark. *Dark Continent: Europe's Twentieth Century*. New York: A.A. Knopf, 1999.

McClennan, Edward F. "Justice and the Problem of Stability." *Philosophy & Public Affairs* 18, no. 1 (1989): 3–30.

McLellan, David. *Karl Marx: His Life and Thought*. New York: Harper & Row, 1974.

Meade, James E. *Efficiency, Equality and the Ownership of Property*. London: Allen & Unwin, 1964.

Melzer, Arthur M. *The Natural Goodness of Man: On the System of Rousseau's Thought*. Chicago: University of Chicago Press, 1990.

Miéville, China. *October: The Story of the Russian Revolution*. New York: Verso, 2017.

Migotti, Mark. "Slave Morality, Socrates, and the Bushmen: A Reading of the First Essay of On the Genealogy of Morals." *Philosophy and Phenomenological Research* 58, no. 4 (1998): 745–79.

Mill, John Stuart. *The Basic Writings of John Stuart Mill*. Edited by Dale E. Miller. New York: Modern Library, 2002.

Millar, Fergus. *The Roman Republic in Political Thought*. Hanover, NH: University Press of New England, 2002.

Miller, James. *Rousseau: Dreamer of Democracy*. New Haven, CT: Yale University Press, 1996.

Millett, Paul. *Lending and Borrowing in Ancient Athens*. Cambridge: Cambridge University Press, 1991.

Muller, Jerry Z. *The Mind and the Market: Capitalism in Modern European Thought*. New York: Alfred A. Knopf, 2002.

Mussolini, Benito. "The Political and Social Doctrine of Fascism." *Political Quarterly* 4, no. 3 (1933): 341–56.

Myers, Milton. *The Soul of Modern Economic Man: Ideas of Self-Interest, Hobbes to Smith*. Chicago: University of Chicago Press, 1983.

Nehamas, Alexander. *Nietzsche: Life as Literature*. Cambridge, MA: Harvard University Press, 1985.

Neuhouser, Frederick. "Freedom, Dependence, and the General Will." *Philosophical Review* 102, no. 3 (1993): 363–95.

Nietzsche, Friedrich. "The Antichrist." In *The Portable Nietzsche*, edited by Walter Kaufmann, 565–657. New York: Viking, 1954.

– "Beyond Good and Evil." In *Basic Writings of Nietzsche*. Translated and edited by Walter Kaufmann, 179–436. New York: Modern Library, 2000.

– "The Dawn." In *The Portable Nietzsche*, edited by Walter Kaufmann, 76–92. New York: Viking, 1954.

– *Ecce Homo: How One Becomes What One Is*. Translated by R.J. Hollingdale. New York: Penguin, 1979.

– "Homer's Contest." In *The Portable Nietzsche*, edited by Walter Kaufmann, 32–9. New York: Viking, 1954.

– "On the Genealogy of Morals." In *Basic Writings of Nietzsche*. Translated and edited by Walter Kaufmann, 437–600. New York: Modern Library, 2000.

– *Philosophy and Truth: Selections from Nietzsche's Notebooks of the Early 1870s*. Edited by Daniel Breazale. Atlantic Highlands, NJ: Humanities, 1979.

– *Selected Letters of Friedrich Nietzsche*. Edited and Translated by Christopher Middleton. Indianapolis, IN: Hackett, 1996.

– *Thus Spoke Zarathustra*. Translated by R.J. Hollingdale. London: Penguin, 1969.

– *Twilight of the Idols*. Translated by Richard Polt. Indianapolis, IN: Hackett, 1997.

– *Untimely Meditations*. Edited by Daniel Breazale. Translated by R.J. Hollingdale. Cambridge: Cambridge University Press, 1997.

– *The Will to Power*. Translated by R.J. Hollingdale and Walter Kaufmann. New York: Random House, 1967.

Norman, Edward R. *The Victorian Christian Socialists*. Cambridge: Cambridge University Press, 1987.

Nozick, Robert. *Anarchy, State, and Utopia*. New York: Basic Books, 1974.

Ober, Josiah. *The Rise and Fall of Classical Greece*. Princeton, NJ: Princeton University Press, 2015.

Oliver, Kelly. "Antigone's Ghost: Undoing Hegel's *Phenomenology of Spirit.*" *Hypatia* 11, no. 1 (1996): 67–90.

O'Rourke, Kevin H., and Jeffrey G. Williamson. *Globalization and History: The Evolution of a Nineteenth-Century Atlantic Economy.* Cambridge, MA: MIT Press, 1999.

Osbourne, Robin. *Classical Greece, 500–323.* Oxford: Oxford University Press, 2000.

Peffer, Rodney G. *Marxism, Morality, and Social Justice.* Princeton, NJ: Princeton University Press, 1990.

Penner, Norman. *The Canadian Left: A Critical Analysis.* Englewood Cliffs, NJ: Prentice-Hall, 1977.

Piketty, Thomas. *Capital in the Twenty-First Century.* Translated by Arthur Goldhammer. Cambridge, MA: Belknap Press of Harvard University Press, 2014.

Piketty, Thomas, and Nancy Qian. "Income Inequality and Progressive Income Taxation in China and India, 1986–2015." *American Economic Journal: Applied Economics* 1, no. 2 (2009): 53–63.

Pipes, Richard. *The Russian Revolution.* New York: Vintage Books, 1991.

Pirenne, Henri. *Economic and Social History of Medieval Europe.* New York: Harcourt, 1956.

Pocock, J.G.A. *The Machiavellian Moment: Florentine Political Thought and the Atlantic Republican Tradition.* Princeton, NJ: Princeton University Press, 2003.

Poellner, Peter. *Nietzsche and Metaphysics.* Oxford: Oxford University Press, 1995.

Polanyi, Karl. *The Great Transformation: The Political and Economic Origins of Our Time.* Boston: Beacon, 2001.

– *Trade and Market in the Early Empires: Economies in History and Theory.* Glencoe, IL: Free Press, 1957.

Price, Russell. "The Theme of Gloria in Machiavelli." *Renaissance Quarterly* 30, no. 4 (1977): 588–631.

Putnam, Hilary. "A Half-Century of Philosophy, Viewed from Within." *Daedalus* 126, no. 1 (1997): 311–32.

Rahe, Paul A. *Republics Ancient and Modern: Classical Republicanism and the American Revolution.* Chapel Hill: University of North Carolina Press, 1992.

Rand, Ayn. *Capitalism: The Unknown Ideal.* New York: New American Library, 1966.

Rawls, John. *Collected Papers.* Edited by Samuel Freeman. Cambridge, MA: Harvard University Press, 1999.

– "The Idea of Public Reason Revisited." *University of Chicago Law Review* 64, no. 3 (1997): 765–807.

– *Justice as Fairness: A Restatement.* Edited by Erin Kelly. Cambridge, MA: Harvard University Press, 2001.

– *The Law of Peoples with The Idea of Public Reason Revisited.* Cambridge, MA: Harvard University Press, 1999.

– *Lectures on the History of Moral Philosophy.* Edited by Barbara Herman. Cambridge, MA: Harvard University Press, 2000.

– *Lectures on the History of Political Philosophy.* Edited by Samuel Freeman. Cambridge, MA: Belknap Press of Harvard University Press, 2007.

– *Political Liberalism.* New York: Columbia University Press, 2005.

– *A Theory of Justice.* Cambridge, MA: Belknap Press of Harvard University Press, 1999.

– "Three Letters on The Law of Peoples and the European Union." *Revue de philosophie économique* 7, no. 1 (2003): 7–20.

Rhodes, P.J. *A History of the Classical Greek World: 478–323 B.C.* Malden, MA: Blackwell, 2006.

Richardson, John. *Nietzsche's System.* Oxford: Oxford University Press, 1996.

Ridolfi, Roberto. *The Life of Niccoló Machiavelli.* Chicago: University of Chicago Press, 1963.

Riley, Patrick. *Will and Political Legitimacy.* Cambridge, MA: Harvard University Press, 2014.

Roemer, John. *A Future for Socialism.* Cambridge, MA: Harvard University Press, 1994.

Rogan, Tim. *The Moral Economists: R.H. Tawney, Karl Polanyi, E.P. Thompson, and the Critique of Capitalism.* Princeton, NJ: Princeton University Press, 2018.

Ron, Amit. "Visions of Democracy in 'Property-Owning Democracy': Skelton to Rawls and Beyond." *History of Political Thought* 29, no. 1 (2008): 168–87.

Rousseau, Jean-Jacques. *The Confessions.* Translated by Christopher Kelly. Hanover, NH: University Press of New England, 1995.

– "Considerations on the Government of Poland." In *The Social Contract and Other Later Political Writings.* Edited and translated by Victor Gourevitch, 181–265. Cambridge: Cambridge University Press, 1997.

– "Discourse on Political Economy." In *The Social Contract and Other Later Political Writings.* Edited and translated by Victor Gourevitch, 1–38. Cambridge: Cambridge University Press, 1997.

– "Discourse on the Origin and Foundations of Inequality among Men." In *Basic Political Writings.* Translated and edited by Donald A. Cress, 27–92. Indianapolis, IN: Hackett, 2011.

– "Discourse on the Sciences and the Arts." In *Basic Political Writings.* Translated and edited by Donald. A Cress, 1–26. Indianapolis, IN: Hackett, 2011.

– *Émile: Or on Education.* Translated by Allan Bloom. New York: Basic Books, 1979.

– *Letter to Beaumont and Letters Written from the Mountain.* Edited by Christopher Kelly and Eve Grace. Translated by Christopher Kelly and Judith R. Bush. Hanover, NH: University Press of New England, 2001.

– *Letter to D'Alembert.* Edited and translated by Allan Bloom. Hanover, NH: University Press of New England, 2004.

– "On the Social Contract." In *Basic Political Writings.* Translated and edited by Donald A. Cress, 153–252. Indianapolis, IN: Hackett, 2011.

– *The Reveries of the Solitary Walker.* Edited by Christopher Kelly. Translated by Charles E. Butterworth, Alexandra Cook, and Terrence E. Marshall. Hanover, NH: University Press of New England, 2000.

– *Rousseau, Judge of Jean-Jacques: Dialogues.* Edited by Roger D. Masters and Christopher Kelly. Hanover, NH: University Press of New England, 1990.

Rubinstein, Nicolai. *The Government of Florence under the Medici, 1434–1494.* Oxford: Clarendon, 1997.

Salvemini, Gaetano. *Under the Axe of Fascism.* New York: H. Fertig, 1969.

Sandel, Michael. *Liberalism and the Limits of Justice.* Cambridge: Cambridge University Press, 1982.

Schama, Simon. *Citizens: A Chronicle of the French Revolution.* New York: Knopf, 1989.

Scheffler, Samuel. "The Appeal of Political Liberalism." *Ethics* 105, no. 1 (1994): 4–22.

– "Responsibility, Reactive Attitudes, and Liberalism in Philosophy and Politics." *Philosophy & Public Affairs* 21, no. 4 (1992): 299–323.

Scheidel, Walter. *The Great Leveler: Violence and the History of Inequality from the Stone Age to the Twenty-First Century.* Princeton, NJ: Princeton University Press, 2017.

Schiller, Friedrich. *On the Aesthetic Education of Man.* Translated by Elizabeth M. Wilkinson and L.A. Willoughby. Oxford: Clarendon, 1992.

Schnapp, Jeffrey T., ed. *A Primer of Italian Fascism.* Lincoln: University of Nebraska Press, 2000.

Schumpeter, Joseph. *History of Economic Analysis.* Oxford: Oxford University Press, 1954.

Sedgwick, Mark J. *Against the Modern World: Traditionalism and the Secret Intellectual History of the Twentieth Century.* Oxford: Oxford University Press, 2004.

Service, Robert. *A History of Modern Russia from Nicholas II to Vladimir Putin.* Cambridge, MA: Harvard University Press, 2003.

– *Lenin: A Biography.* Cambridge, MA: Harvard University Press, 2000.

– *The Russian Revolution, 1900–1927.* London: Red Globe, 2009.

Sheehan, James J. *German History, 1770–1866.* Oxford: Clarendon, 1989.

Shklar, Judith N. *Men and Citizens: A Study of Rousseau's Social Theory.* Cambridge: Cambridge University Press, 1969.

Siegelbaum, Lewis H., and Andrei K. Sokolov. *Stalinism as a Way of Life: A Narrative in Documents.* New Haven, CT: Yale University Press, 2000.

Skidelsky, Robert. *John Maynard Keynes.* New York: Viking, 1986.

– *Keynes: The Return of the Master.* New York: Public Affairs, 2009.

Skinner, Quentin. "The Ideological Context of Hobbes's Political Thought." *Historical Journal* 9, no. 3 (1966): 286–317.

Sluga, Hans D. *Heidegger's Crisis: Philosophy and Politics in Nazi Germany.* Cambridge, MA: Harvard University Press, 1993.

Smith, Adam. *An Inquiry into the Nature and Causes of the Wealth of Nations.* Edited by R.H. Campbell, A.S. Skinner, and William B. Todd. Indianapolis, IN: Liberty Fund, 1982.

– *Lectures on Jurisprudence.* Edited by R.L. Meek, D.D. Raphael, and P.G. Stein. Indianapolis, IN: Liberty Classics, 1982.

– *The Theory of Moral Sentiments.* New York: Penguin, 2010.

Somerville, Johan P. *Thomas Hobbes: Political Ideas in Historical Context.* London: Macmillan, 1992.

Stears, Marc. "Guild Socialism and Ideological Diversity on the British Left, 1914–1926." *Journal of Political Ideologies* 3, no. 3 (1998): 289–306.

Sternhell, Zeev (with Mario Sznajder and Maia Asheri). *The Birth of Fascist Ideology: From Cultural Rebellion to Political Revolution*. Translated by David Maisel. Princeton, NJ: Princeton University Press, 1994.

Stiglitz, Joseph. *The Price of Inequality: How Today's Divided Society Endangers Our Future*. New York: W.W. Norton, 2012.

Strauss, Leo. *Thoughts on Machiavelli*. Glencoe, IL: Free Press, 1958.

Suny, Ronald G. *The Soviet Experiment: Russia, the USSR, and the Successor States*. Oxford: Oxford University Press, 1998.

– *The Structure of Soviet History: Essays and Documents*. Oxford: Oxford University Press, 2003.

Sznajder, Mario. "Nietzsche, Mussolini, and Italian Fascism." In *Nietzsche, Godfather of Fascism? On the Uses and Abuses of History*, edited by Jacob Golomb and Robert Wistrich, 235–62. Princeton, NJ: Princeton University Press, 2002.

Talmon, J.L. *The Origins of Totalitarian Democracy*. Boulder, CO: Westview, 1985.

Tannenbaum, Edward R. *The Fascist Experience: Italian Society and Culture, 1922–1945*. New York: Basic Books, 1972.

Tawney, R.H. *The Acquisitive Society*. London: Collins, 1961.

– *The Attack and Other Papers*. London: Allen & Unwin, 1953.

– *Equality*. London: Unwin, 1964.

– *The Radical Tradition: Twelve Essays on Politics, Education, and Literature*. New York: Pantheon Books, 1964.

– *Religion and the Rise of Capitalism: A Historical Study*. London: Verso, 2015.

– *R.H. Tawney's Commonplace Book*. Edited by J.M. Winter and D.M. Joslin. Cambridge: Cambridge University Press, 2006.

Taylor, Charles. *Hegel and Modern Society*. Cambridge: Cambridge University Press, 1979.

Terrill, Ross. *R.H. Tawney and His Times: Socialism as Fellowship*. Cambridge, MA: Harvard University Press, 1973.

Timmins, Nicholas. *The Five Giants: The Biography of the Welfare State*. London: HarperCollins, 1995.

Van Dormael, Armand. *Bretton Woods: Birth of a Monetary System*. London: Macmillan, 1978.

Viner, Jacob. *Essays on the Intellectual History of Economics*. Princeton, NJ: Princeton University Press, 1991.

Viroli, Maurizio. *From Politics to Reason of State: The Acquisition and Transformation of the Language of Politics, 1250–1600*. Cambridge: Cambridge University Press, 1992.

Waite, Geoff. *Nietzsche's Corps/e: Aesthetics, Politics, Prophecy, or, the Spectacular Technoculture of Everyday Life*. Durham, NC: Duke University Press, 1996.

Waldron, Jeremy. *God, Locke, and Equality: Christian Foundations of John Locke's Political Thought*. Cambridge: Cambridge University Press, 2002.

Walker, Mack. *German Home Towns: Community, State, and General Estate, 1648–1871*. Ithaca, NY: Cornell University Press, 1998.

Waszek, Norbert. *The Scottish Enlightenment and Hegel's Account of "Civil Society."* Dordrecht, Netherlands: Kluwer Academic Publishers, 1988.

Weber, Max. *The Protestant Ethic and the Spirit of Capitalism.* Translated by Stephen Kalberg. Oxford: Oxford University Press, 2010.

Weinstein, Donald. *Savonarola: The Rise and Fall of a Renaissance Prophet.* New Haven, CT: Yale University Press, 2011.

Weithman, Paul J. *Why Political Liberalism? On John Rawls's Political Turn.* Oxford: Oxford University Press, 2010.

White, James D. *The Russian Revolution, 1917–1921: A Short History.* New York: Edward Arnold, 1994.

Whyte, Max. "The Uses and Abuses of Nietzsche in the Third Reich: Alfred Baeumler's 'Heroic Realism.'" *Journal of Contemporary History* 43, no. 2 (2008): 171–94.

Williams, Beryl. *Lenin.* New York: Longman, 2000.

Winstanley, Gerard. *The Works of Gerrard Winstanley.* Edited by G.H. Sabine. New York: Russell & Russell, 1965.

Wokler, Robert. *Rousseau and Liberty.* New York: St. Martin's, 1995.

Wolfe, Bertram D. *Three Who Made a Revolution: A Biographical History.* New York: Cooper Square, 2001.

Woolf, S.J. "Mussolini as Revolutionary." *Journal of Contemporary History* 1, no. 2 (1966): 187–96.

Wright, Anthony. *R.H. Tawney.* Manchester: Manchester University Press, 1987.

Wrightson, Keith. *Earthly Necessities: Economic Lives in Early Modern Britain.* New Haven, CT: Yale University Press, 2000.

Yaroslavsky, Yemelyan. *History of the Communist Party.* Moscow: Novosti Press Agency, 1975.

Yergin, Daniel, and Joseph Stanislaw. *The Commanding Heights: The Battle between Government and the Marketplace That Is Remaking the Modern World.* New York: Simon & Schuster, 1998.

# Index